THE
FABULOUS
GOURMET
FOOD
PROCESSOR
COOKBOOK

THE
FABULOUS
GOURMET
FOOD
PROCESSOR
COOKBOOK
Judy Gethers

BALLANTINE BOOKS • NEW YORK

Illustrations by Cecilia DeCastro

Cover photograph by Anthony Loew

Designed by Michaelis/Carpelis Design Associates, Inc.

BVG 01

TABLE OF CONTENTS

LIST OF RECIPES

Foreword

"Revolution," according to Webster, is defined as "an extensive change in condition, method, or idea." With the introduction of the food processor, the kitchen has become a most unlikely battlefield, destroying old concepts and opening new horizons for the inexperienced as well as the experienced cook. Recipes that were once thought too difficult have become routine and are now prepared in record time.

Less than a decade ago, the Cuisinart was the only food processor on the market. Today, you the consumer can choose from a variety of machines, ranging in price from $40 to $250. These versatile appliances grind, grate, chop, mix, knead, slice, pulverize, and purée in a matter of seconds.

The first section of my book is devoted to technical information. Read it carefully for a greater understanding of how to operate your food processor. In Tips and Hints (pages 23–29) you may find answers to questions you didn't realize you had.

While teaching food processor classes, I discovered that many people are intimidated by this mechanical Merlin. There is only one way to overcome this—*practice*. Buy packages of carrots, since carrots are not very expensive and can easily be stored as processed for future use. Experiment with all your blades—slice, shred, julienne, chop, mince, and purée. (Once you've mastered these techniques your doughs and crusts will be easy as pie.) After a few packages of carrots, you will become more confident, and then the fun begins.

All my recipes have been chosen for their wide appeal and have been tested and tasted. They range from simple to complex, and with a little experience anyone can do them with great success.

Before long you will wonder how you ever managed without your food processor. Before long you will begin to improvise, enjoying the versatility this machine affords you. After all, isn't that what cooking is all about?

Judy Gethers

TABLE OF FOODS

The following Table of Foods lists maximum quantities that should be used in your food processor's work bowl at one time. I have also suggested the amount of pressure to be used on the pusher when slicing foods. This is to be used as a guide until you become more familiar with your processor.

APPLES
To *chop* (STEEL BLADE) up to 1 cup:
Peel, quarter, and then cross-cut quarters. Process with on/off turns to desired texture.
To *slice* (MEDIUM SLICING BLADE; firm pressure):
Core and quarter; peel if desired. Place 1 or 2 quarters in feed tube, flat side on blade.

APRICOTS
To *chop* (STEEL BLADE) up to 2 cups:
Peel, if desired, pit, and quarter (blanch fruit in boiling water and slip skin off). Process with on/off turns to desired texture.
To *slice* (MEDIUM SLICING BLADE; medium pressure):
Peel, if desired, then pit and halve. Place 1 or 2 halves in feed tube, forming a whole fruit.

ARTICHOKE BOTTOMS
To *purée* (STEEL BLADE) up to 2 cups, see To purée (page 28).

AVOCADOS
To *slice* (MEDIUM or WIDE SLICING BLADE; light pressure):
Using firm, though ripe, avocado; halve, peel, and pit. Cut to fit feed tube and arrange in tube, alternating wide and narrow ends, peeled sides back to back. Pack feed tube tightly so avocado does not slip while being sliced. Sprinkle with lemon juice to prevent darkening.
To *purée* (STEEL BLADE) up to 2 cups, see To purée (page 28).
Pit placed in purée prevents darkening.

BANANAS
To *mash* (STEEL BLADE) up to 3 medium bananas:
Peel and cut into 1-inch pieces. Start with 1 or 2 on/off turns and then let machine run to desired texture. (Blender attachments mash finer than STEEL BLADE.)
To *slice* (MEDIUM or WIDE SLICING BLADE; light pressure):
Peel and cut in half. Stack in feed tube, sliced side on blade.

BEANS (GREEN)

To *French-slice* (MEDIUM SLICING BLADE; light pressure):
Cut beans to fit width of pusher. Stack in feed tube, using spatula to aid in stacking.

To *purée* (STEEL BLADE) up to 2 cups, see To purée (page 28).

BEEF

Uncooked

To *chop* or *grind* (STEEL BLADE) up to 1 cup:
Trim fat and gristle and cut into 1-inch cubes. Use on/off turns to desired texture (coarse for hamburger, fine for steak tartare).

To *slice* (MEDIUM SERRATED BLADE; firm pressure):
Cut thick piece to fit feed tube (thin slices should be stacked one atop the other to fit feed tube). Freeze *just* until firm, *not solid.* For best results, pack feed tube.

Cooked

To *chop* (STEEL BLADE) up to 1 cup:
Meat should be chilled. Trim fat and gristle and cut into 1-inch cubes. Use on/off turns to desired texture.

To *slice* (MEDIUM SERRATED BLADE; moderate pressure):
Chill meat and cut to fit feed tube.

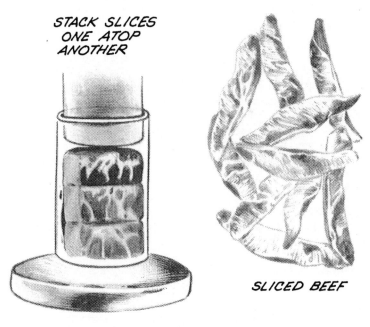

STACK SLICES ONE ATOP ANOTHER

SLICED BEEF

BEETS
Cooked

To *slice* (MEDIUM SLICING BLADE; firm pressure):
For an even slice, use small beets. If beets are large, cut to fit feed tube.

To *shred* or *grate* (MEDIUM SHREDDING BLADE; firm pressure):
Cut beet to fit feed tube.

Uncooked

Wash thoroughly and proceed as for Beets (cooked). Peeling is not necessary. If cooking, leave whole, retaining 1 or 2 inches of top root. Cool, trim, and peel, then proceed as above.

BROCCOLI

To *purée* (STEEL BLADE) up to 2 cups, see To purée (page 28).

CABBAGE (RED OR GREEN)

To *chop* (STEEL BLADE) up to 2 cups:
Quarter and core cabbage, discarding soft, outer leaves. Cut into 1-inch pieces. Process with 2 on/off turns, scrape down sides of work bowl, and continue with on/off turns to desired texture.

To *slice* or *shred* (MEDIUM SLICING BLADE; moderate pressure):
Quarter, core, and fit into feed tube.

CARROTS*

To *chop* (STEEL BLADE) up to 1 cup:
Cut into 1-inch pieces and process with on/off turns to desired texture. Scrape down sides of work bowl as needed.

To *slice* (MEDIUM or WIDE SLICING BLADE; firm pressure):
Cut to fit feed tube, width or length. Stack in feed tube, alternating wide and narrow ends.

To *julienne* (MEDIUM SLICING BLADE; moderate pressure):
(see To julienne, page 27).

To *shred* (MEDIUM SHREDDING BLADE; moderate pressure):
Cut to fit feed tube.

*Peeling is optional.

CAULIFLOWER

To *slice* (MEDIUM SLICING BLADE; moderate pressure):
Break into flowerettes, removing hard stems. Alternate head and stem in feed tube.*

*Crumbled bits can be reserved and used in salads or soups.

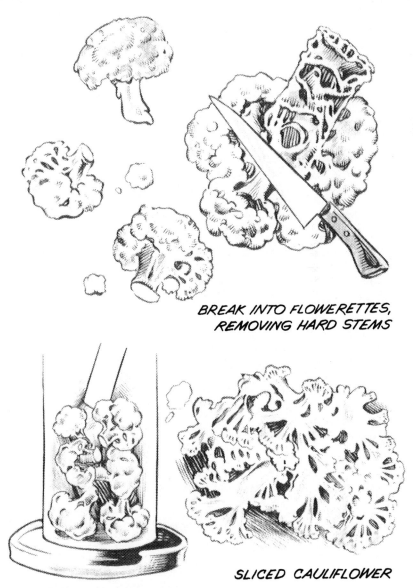

BREAK INTO FLOWERETTES,
REMOVING HARD STEMS

ALTERNATE HEAD AND
STEM IN FEED TUBE

SLICED CAULIFLOWER

5

CELERY*

To *chop* (STEEL BLADE) up to 1 cup:
Cut into 1-inch pieces and process with on/off turns to desired texture.

To *slice* (MEDIUM SLICING BLADE; firm pressure):
Cut stalks into 3 or 4 even lengths. Fit as many as can fit into feed tube.

*Remove strings before processing, using a vegetable peeler.

CHEESES

Hard (Parmesan, Pecorino, etc.)

To *chop* or *grate* (STEEL BLADE):
Have cheese at room temperature and cut into 1-inch pieces. With motor running, drop pieces through feed tube and process to desired texture.

Medium Hard (natural Cheddar, Gruyère, etc.)

To *slice* (MEDIUM SLICING BLADE; moderate pressure):
Remove cheese from refrigerator and cut to fit feed tube.

To *shred* (MEDIUM SHREDDING BLADE; moderate pressure):
Proceed as "To slice," above.

Soft (Roquefort, blue, mozzarella, etc.)

To *crumble* (STEEL BLADE):
Remove cheese from refrigerator and cut or break into 1-inch pieces. With motor running, drop through feed tube. This should take less than 5 seconds.

To *slice* mozzarella (MEDIUM or WIDE SLICING BLADE; firm pressure):
Cut chilled cheese to fit feed tube.

CHICKEN

*Uncooked**

To *chop* or *grind* (STEEL BLADE) up to 1 cup:
Cut well-chilled chicken into 1-inch pieces. Process, using on/off turns, to desired texture.

To *slice* (MEDIUM SERRATED SLICING BLADE; firm pressure):
Slice only larger pieces of chicken. Freeze *just* until firm, *not solid.* Stand in feed tube, rolling up thinner pieces. Pack feed tube for best results.

*Cooked**

To *chop* or *grind* (STEEL BLADE) up to 2 cups:
Cut into 1-inch pieces. Process, using on/off turns, to desired texture.

*Remove skin, bones, and all gristle.

CHINESE CABBAGE
To *slice* (MEDIUM BLADE; moderate pressure):
Stack several layers of cabbage leaves in bundles and wedge into feed tube.

CHOCOLATE
To *grate* (STEEL BLADE) up to 6 one-ounce squares:
Chill chocolate, break each square in half (½ ounce), and process with on/off turns to desired texture. Can also be grated in blender attachment.

CITRUS FRUIT
Peeled
To *slice* (MEDIUM BLADE; light pressure):
Slice off one end of fruit. If small enough, use whole and fit through bottom of feed tube, cut side on blade. If too large, halve, slicing down through stem.
Unpeeled
To *slice* (MEDIUM BLADE; firm pressure):
Slice as for peeled citrus fruit above, but decoratively peel off strips at even intervals with zester before proceeding.

CITRUS RIND
To *chop* or *mince* (STEEL BLADE):
With vegetable peeler, remove rind in strips. With motor running, drop strips through feed tube and process to desired texture. If recipe* calls for sugar, add small amount to work bowl to facilitate chopping.
*Remember to subtract amount of sugar used when continuing with recipe.

COCONUT
To *grate* (STEEL BLADE) up to 1½ cups:
With vegetable peeler, remove inner brown skin. Cut coconut meat into 1-inch pieces and process to desired texture.

CRANBERRIES
To *chop* (STEEL BLADE) up to 2 cups:
Process with 1 or 2 on/off turns. Do not overprocess.

CRUMBS
*Bread** (STEEL BLADE) up to 2 cups:
Use dry bread for best results. Break slices into quarters and process to desired texture.
*Removing crusts is optional.

Cookie (STEEL BLADE) up to 2 cups:
If large, break into pieces. Process to desired texture.

Cracker (STEEL BLADE) up to 12 crackers:
Process to desired texture.

CUCUMBERS*
To *chop* (STEEL BLADE) up to 2 cups:
Halve lengthwise, scoop out seeds, and cut into 1-inch pieces.
Process with on/off turns to desired texture. Do not overprocess.
    To *slice* (MEDIUM BLADE; firm pressure):
Cut to fit feed tube (may use whole or halve lengthwise and scoop
out seeds).
    To *julienne*, see To julienne (page 27).
*Peeled or unpeeled.

EGGPLANT
Uncooked
To *slice* (MEDIUM BLADE; firm pressure):
Cut to fit feed tube and process.
    To *julienne*, see To julienne (page 27).

Cooked
To *chop* (STEEL BLADE) up to 2 cups:
Process with on/off turns to desired texture.

EGGS (HARD-COOKED)
To *chop* (STEEL BLADE) up to 6 eggs:
Halve eggs and chop with on/off turns to desired texture (2 or 3 turns
should be enough).

FISH
Uncooked
To *chop* or *grind* (STEEL BLADE) up to 2 cups:
Cut into 1-inch pieces and chop with on/off turns to desired texture.
Check texture frequently. For a fine chop (*quenelles*, etc.), allow
processor to run up to 60 seconds, stopping to scrape down sides of
work bowl once or twice.
    Cooked
To *chop* (STEEL BLADE) up to 2 cups:
Cut fish into 1-inch pieces and process with on/off turns to desired
texture, checking frequently.

FRUIT (Dried or Candied)
To *chop* (STEEL BLADE) up to 2 cups:
Add small amount of flour from recipe* to work bowl containing

fruit. Process with on/off turns. Do not overprocess.
*Remember to subtract amount of flour used when continuing with recipe.

GARLIC
To *chop* or *mince* (STEEL BLADE):
With motor running, drop peeled garlic through feed tube.

GINGERROOT
To *chop* or *mince* (STEEL BLADE):
Peel and cut into 1-inch pieces. Process the same as for Garlic, above.

GREEN ONIONS (Scallions)*
To *chop* (STEEL BLADE) up to 2 cups:
Cut into 1-inch pieces (if very thick, slice lengthwise into 2 or 3 pieces). Process, allowing machine to run, scraping down sides of work bowl as necessary.
To *slice* (MEDIUM BLADE; firm pressure):
Cut into 3- or 4-inch lengths and stack tightly.
*Trim roots and tops and wash thoroughly.

HERBS (FRESH) (Parsley, Watercress, Tarragon, Basil, etc.)
To *chop* (STEEL BLADE) up to 2 cups:
Wash and dry thoroughly (use paper towels or lettuce spinner). In dry work bowl, process with 3 or 4 on/off turns and then allow machine to run until desired texture is reached.

HORSERADISH*
To *grate* (STEEL BLADE) up to 1 cup:
Peel, then cut into 1-inch pieces and process to desired texture.
*Horseradish root will keep 4 to 6 weeks if set in container, covered with water, and refrigerated. Change water as necessary.

LEEKS
See Green Onions (page 9).

MEAT (Packaged—Ham, Bologna, etc.)
To *chop* (STEEL BLADE) up to 1 cup:
Cut into 1-inch pieces and process to desired texture.
To *slice* (MEDIUM SERRATED BLADE; moderate pressure):
Fold or roll several slices and stack into feed tube. It may be easier to fit through the bottom.
See also Beef (page 3).

ROLL SEVERAL SLICES

STACK ROLLED MEAT
SLICES INTO FEED TUBE

SLICED PACKAGED MEAT

MELON

To *slice* (THIN or MEDIUM SLICING BLADE; moderate pressure):
Cut pieces to fit feed tube, first removing seeds and rind. Pack into feed tube.

To *purée* (STEEL BLADE) up to 2 cups, see To purée (page 28).

MUSHROOMS

To *chop* (STEEL BLADE) up to 2 cups:
Large mushrooms should be halved or quartered to ensure a more even chop. Process with on/off turns to desired texture.

To *slice* (FINE or MEDIUM BLADE; firm pressure):
Slice off small piece from sides of 2 mushrooms and lay on blade. Place cover on work bowl and stack mushrooms, alternating caps and stems.*

*Stems may be removed and used in dishes that call for chopped mushrooms.

NUTS
Hard (almonds, filberts, peanuts, cashews, etc.)
To *chop* (STEEL BLADE) up to 2 cups:
Process to desired texture. If very fine grind is desired for baking, process with ¼ cup flour, otherwise will turn to Nut Butter (see page 212).

Soft (pecans, walnuts, etc.)
To *chop* or *grind* (STEEL BLADE) up to 2 cups:
Process with on/off turns to desired texture. Coarse chop may be obtained in 2 or 3 turns. For fine grinding, allow machine to run about 15 seconds.

OKRA
To *slice* (MEDIUM BLADE; moderate pressure):
Trim ends and cut in lengths to fit feed tube. Pack tightly in feed tube.

OLIVES
To *chop* (STEEL BLADE) up to 1 cup:
Process with on/off turns to desired texture. Stop and scrape down sides of work bowl as necessary.
To *slice* (MEDIUM BLADE; moderate pressure):
Arrange olives on blade, in upright position. Replace cover and slice.

ONIONS
To *chop* (STEEL BLADE) up to 2 cups:
Quarter medium onions; cut larger onions into eighths. Process with on/off turns, checking frequently, to desired texture. Drain, if necessary, before using.
To *slice* (MEDIUM or FINE BLADE; firm pressure):
If small, fit whole onion into feed tube; if large, cut to fit tube.

PARSLEY
See Herbs (page 9).

PARSNIPS
See Carrots (page 4).

PEACHES
To *chop* (STEEL BLADE) up to 2 cups:
Peel, pit, and quarter. Process with on/off turns to desired texture.
To *slice* (MEDIUM BLADE; firm pressure):
Peel, pit, and halve. Place 1 or 2 halves in feed tube and slice.*
*Sprinkle with lemon juice as processed to prevent discoloration.

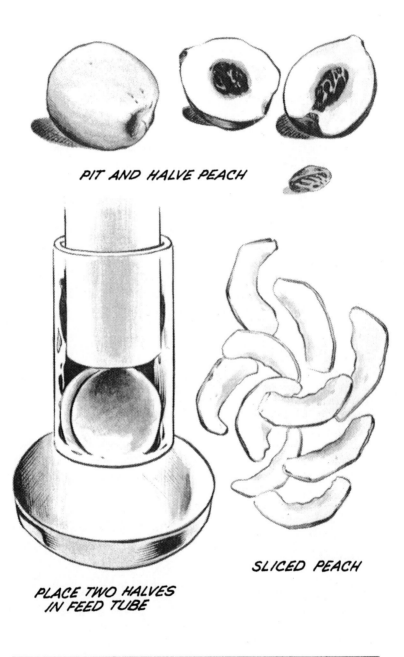

PIT AND HALVE PEACH

PLACE TWO HALVES
IN FEED TUBE

SLICED PEACH

PEARS*
To *slice* (MEDIUM SLICING BLADE; firm pressure):
Quarter lengthwise and core. Stand in feed tube, alternating wide
and narrow ends. Slice, then sprinkle with lemon juice to prevent
discoloration.
*Peeled or unpeeled.

PEPPERS (Red or Green)
To *chop* (STEEL BLADE) up to 2 cups:
Remove tops; core, seed, and quarter. Cut into 1-inch pieces and
process with on/off turns to desired texture. Drain, if necessary,
before using in recipe.
To *slice* (MEDIUM SLICING BLADE; moderate pressure):
If pepper is small enough, remove top, core, seed, and fit into feed
tube. Otherwise, halve, remove tops, core, seed, and fit into feed
tube.

PEPPERONI
To *slice* (MEDIUM SERRATED SLICING BLADE; firm pressure):
Remove casing and cut into lengths to fit feed tube.

PICKLES
To *chop*, see Cucumbers (page 8).
To *slice* (FINE or MEDIUM SLICING BLADE; moderate pressure):
Remove ends, pack into feed tube, and slice.

PINEAPPLE
To *chop* (STEEL BLADE) up to 2 cups:
Peel, quarter, and remove cores. Cut into 1-inch pieces and chop
with on/off turns to desired texture.
To *slice* (FINE or MEDIUM SLICING BLADE; firm pressure):
Peel, quarter, and remove cores. Cut to fit feed tube or wedge small
lengths into tube.

PORK
See Beef (page 3).

POTATOES
*Uncooked**
To *chop* (STEEL BLADE) up to 2 cups:
For large potatoes, peel and cut into 1-inch pieces; for medium
potatoes, peel and quarter. Process with on/off turns to desired
texture, careful that potatoes do not become too soft and mushy.
To *slice* (FINE or MEDIUM SLICING BLADE; firm pressure):
It is best to select potatoes that can fit feed tube whole. Slice small

sliver from one end, and if potato is too large, cut to firmly fit feed tube. Place sliced end on blade and process.

To *shred* (FINE or MEDIUM SHREDDING BLADE; firm pressure): Proceed as "To slice," above. When potatoes are processed, remove to mixing bowl with cold water. This prevents discoloration and removes excess starch.

*Potatoes may be peeled or unpeeled.

RADISHES

To *chop* (STEEL BLADE) up to 2 cups:
Process with on/off turns to desired texture.

To *slice* (MEDIUM SLICING BLADE; firm pressure)
Cut off top and root end. Fill feed tube, cut side down.

RHUBARB

See Celery (page 6).

SAUSAGE*

See Pepperoni (page 13).
*Including hard salami, etc.

SHALLOTS

See Garlic (page 9).

SQUASH

Summer

To *chop* (STEEL BLADE) up to 2 cups:
Trim and cut into 1-inch pieces. Process with on/off turns to desired texture.

To *slice* (FINE or MEDIUM SLICING BLADE; firm pressure):
Cut to fit feed tube and wedge in as many as possible.

Winter

To *purée* (STEEL BLADE) up to 2 cups:
Peel and seed. See To purée (page 28).

STRAWBERRIES

To *chop* (STEEL BLADE) up to 2 cups:
Hull berries and halve larger ones. Process with 1 or 2 on/off turns.

To *slice* (MEDIUM SLICING BLADE; light pressure):
For best results, berries should not be too soft or too ripe. Hull and arrange on sides atop blade.

To *purée* (STEEL BLADE) up to 2 cups, see To purée, (page 28).

TOMATOES

To *chop* (STEEL BLADE) up to 2 cups:
Peel and seed if desired. Quarter medium tomatoes or cut into
1-inch pieces. Process with on/off turns. Do not overprocess.

To *slice* (MEDIUM SLICING BLADE; moderate pressure):
Use tomatoes that can fit feed tube (small or plum tomatoes). Remove stem, set on blade, replace cover, and slice.

To *purée* (STEEL BLADE) up to 2 cups:
Peel and seed, if desired. See To purée (page 28).

TURNIPS

See Potatoes (page 13).

WATER CHESTNUTS

See Radishes (page 14).

WATERCRESS

See Herbs (page 9).

ZUCCHINI

See Squash (Summer) (page 14).

TABLE OF EQUIVALENTS

Frequently Used Foods

FOOD	PROCEDURE*	APPROXIMATE YIELD
Apple (1 medium)	Chopped or sliced	¾ cup
Apricots (8 ounces dried)	Chopped	1½ cups
Avocado (1 medium)	Chopped or sliced	1¼ to 1½ cups
Banana (1 medium)	Sliced	1 cup
	Mashed	¾ cup
Beans, green or wax (6 ounces)	Sliced	1⅓ cup
Beet (1 medium)	Sliced	⅔ cup
Broccoli (1 pound)	Chopped or sliced	2 cups
Cabbage (1 medium; about 2 pounds)	Sliced or shredded	11 cups
Carrot (1 medium)	Chopped or sliced	½ cup
	Puréed	¼ cup
Cauliflower (1 cup flowerettes)	Chopped	¾ cup
Celery (1 large stalk)	Sliced	1 cup
Cheeses		
Cheddar (4 ounces)	Shredded	1 cup
Parmesan (2 ounces)	Grated	½ cup
Swiss or Gruyère (2 ounces)	Chopped or shredded	½ cup
Cranberries, whole (1 cup)	Chopped	1 cup

*1 cup any cooked vegetable or fruit will make ½ cup purée.

FOOD	PROCEDURE	APPROXIMATE YIELD
Cucumber (1 medium)	Chopped Sliced	1 cup 1½ cups

Crumbs
  biscuits (7 ounces)
  bread (1 whole slice)
	Crumbed
	Crumbed
		2 cups
		½ cup

Eggplant (1½ pounds)	Sliced	6 cups
Leeks (2 medium)	Chopped or sliced	1 cup
Meat and Poultry (beef, chicken, ham, lamb, veal; ½ pound, boneless and trimmed)	Chopped Sliced	1 cup 1½ cups
Mushrooms (¼ pound)	Chopped or sliced	1¼ cups
Nuts (almonds, pecans, hazelnuts, walnuts, etc.; 1 cup)	Chopped	1¼ cups

Onion
  yellow (1 large)
  green scallions (6)
	Chopped or sliced
	Sliced
		1 cup
		½ cup

Peach (1 medium)	Chopped Sliced	½ cup 1 cup
Peanuts (2 cups)	Peanut butter	1 cup
Pear (1 medium)	Sliced	1 cup
Pepper (green or red; ½ medium)	Chopped Sliced	½ cup ¾ cup

FOOD	PROCEDURE	APPROXIMATE YIELD
Potato (1 medium)	Chopped or sliced	¾ cup
	Shredded	½ cup
Purées, 1 cup cooked vegetable or fruit	Puréed	½ cup
Scallions (see Onions, green, above)		
Shallots (4 large)	Chopped or minced	¼ cup
Tomato (1 medium)	Chopped	¾ cup
Watercress (1 cup)	Chopped	½ cup
Zucchini (1 medium)	Chopped	1 cup
	Sliced	1⅓ cups
	Julienned	1 cup

GLOSSARY OF COOKING TERMS

BAIN-MARIE (water bath): The French version of a double boiler, it is a combination of two cooking vessels; the smaller one holds the food and the larger one is partially filled with simmering water that must never boil. If the water is about to boil, add 2 or 3 tablespoons of cold water to vessel.

BASTE: To spoon liquid over foods while cooking. Liquid can be pan juices, wine, melted butter, etc.

BLANCH: To drop food into boiling water to partially precook or soften.

BLEND: To combine foods gently.

CARAMELIZE: To combine white sugar and water and cook until mixture becomes a light brown syrup.

CORE: To remove the center of certain fruits or vegetables containing one or more pits or seeds.

CROUSTADES: Toasted bread cups that are filled as desired and generally served as hors d'oeuvres or appetizers.

CRUMB: To break bread or crackers into small pieces and then pulverize.

DEGLAZE: To add liquid to a pan after meat or poultry has been cooked. The liquid is stirred through to scrape up all bits adhering to the bottom of the pan and then incorporated into the sauce. Liquid can be wine, brandy, stock, etc.

DEGREASE: To remove all fat from sauces, soups, or stocks. This can be done by skimming fat from top, using a bulb baster for roasts or chilling and then removing fat that accumulates on top.

DREDGE: To coat food with flour or crumb mixture.

EN CROUTE: Applies to a food that is enclosed and baked in a pastry crust.

FORCEMEAT: A puréed mixture of meat, vegetables, or fish that can be used as a stuffing, pâté, or spread.

GARNISH: To decorate a platter of food before serving.

GRATIN: To brown food in a hot oven or under a broiler, usually using crumbs or cheese.

HORS D'OEUVRES: Small foods eaten before the first course of a meal.

NAP: To spoon a small amount of sauce over food when serving.

PAUPIETTE: Thin slices of meat or fish fillets, stuffed and rolled.

POACH: To cook food in a simmering liquid, such as stock, wine, or seasoned water.

PRALINE: A hardened mixture of almonds and caramelized sugar that is then ground or broken into small pieces.

PREHEAT: To turn on oven to desired temperature at least 20 minutes before being used.

PUREE: To reduce solid food to a pulp.

REDUCE: To boil liquid so that it becomes more concentrated. This is a most important process in the preparation of sauces. You must be careful not to oversalt, waiting to season properly when the quantity has "reduced."

REFRESH: To plunge hot foods into cold water immediately after cooking to stop the cooking process.

ROUX: The cooking together of butter and flour to use as a thickening agent for certain sauces.

SAUTE: To cook food in an open saucepan or skillet. For best results there are three basic rules to follow: (1) Heat pan before adding fat; (2) make sure food being added is thoroughly dry; (3) do not overcrowd the pan.

SCORE: To cut across the surface of food with sharp but light strokes.

SIMMER: To cook liquid just below the boiling point.

TIMBALE: A mixture of meat, fish, or vegetables combined with eggs, cream, and seasonings and baked in small individual molds that are unmolded when served.

ZEST: Tiny pieces of citrus rind used to flavor foods.

PROCESSOR EQUIPMENT AND ITS USES

WORK BOWL: The capacity may vary, but all work bowls are made of clear, durable plastic. Most are dishwasher safe. Food is processed in the work bowl.

WORK BOWL COVER: Made of the same durable plastic as work bowl. Processors will not operate unless cover is properly set in place. Cover has a feed tube through which foods are poured or dropped as the processor operates. Solid foods to be sliced or shredded are fitted into feed tube and guided with pusher.

PUSHER: Made of plastic to fit feed tube. It is used to press food into work bowl as food is being sliced or shredded. Amount of pressure used is determined by type of food.

STEEL BLADE: This S-shaped blade is used more frequently than any other blade. It chops, minces, grinds, mixes, purées, and kneads, depending upon food and amount of processing.

SLICING BLADE: The medium slicing blade is standard equipment with most food processors. It is used to slice fruits, vegetables, cheeses, meats, etc. Some processors have a fine slicing blade and a wide slicing blade for thinner or thicker slices.

SHREDDING BLADE: The medium shredding blade is standard equipment. It is used for vegetables, cheeses, etc. Depending upon how food is placed in feed tube, shorter or longer shreds are obtained. Some processors have a fine shredding blade and a wide shredding blade.

PLASTIC BLADE: Least-used blade, but good for eggs and sauces and to purée foods if some texture is desired.

BLENDER: For those processors that have this attachment, used for puréeing.

WHIP: The only processor attachment that whips cream and egg whites to a peak.

FRENCH-FRY BLADE: Slices vegetables decoratively.

JULIENNE BLADE: Juliennes vegetables.

Do's AND DON'TS

1. Carefully read your instruction manual so you will understand particular do's and don'ts of your food processor.

2. Handle all processor blades with great care. Remember, they are like very sharp knife blades.

3. Use pusher to guide food through feed tube for slicing and/or shredding. *Never* use fingers.

4. Do not remove cover from work bowl during processing until blades stop spinning.

5. It is wise to wash, dry, and store blades after each use.

6. Store blades out of reach of young children.

7. If a child is old enough to handle a knife, he or she is old enough to be taught the proper use of the food processor.

8. Unplug food processor when not in use.

9. Do not attempt to whip cream or egg whites to stiff peaks unless your food processor has a "whip" attachment.

10. Hot foods may be added to work bowl only when recipe so specifies.

11. If you want perfectly chopped or sliced vegetables—of uniform size—chop by hand. The food processor cannot guarantee a perfect, even chop.

TIPS AND HINTS

1. This is a machine of seconds, whether used for chopping, slicing, or kneading. *Practice* is the only way to gain confidence in and control of the food processor.

2. The blade used most frequently is the STEEL BLADE. It is used to chop, mince, purée, grind, and make doughs for pastries and bread.

3. The on/off turn is a most important technique. This is the best method to chop, giving the most control. With some machines this is done with a pushbutton; with others, a smooth, quick twist of the feed tube, back and forth. (The Hamilton-Beach processor has a touch system.)

4. To obtain best results in chopping, quarter or cut food into approximately 1-inch slices or pieces. Do not overload work bowl.

5. Remember to stop machine and scrape down sides of work bowl to obtain a more even chop or smoother purée.

6. Fresh herbs should be snipped off at stems and chopped in dry work bowl. Large batches can be processed, refrigerated or frozen, and used as needed.

7. To grind nuts for nut butters, no other ingredient is necessary. To grind nuts for use in cakes, sugar from recipe should be added to work bowl to prevent nuts from becoming a paste.

8. Candied and dried fruit can be chopped only if flour from recipe is added to work bowl, or fruit will not chop well.

9. When slicing, cut foods to fit feed tube. To determine size of food that will conveniently fit feed tube, use pusher as a guide—for length or width. For best results, pack feed tube as tightly as possible.

10. When shredding vegetables, length of shred is determined by whether food is placed in feed tube horizontally or vertically. Stacked horizontally, shred will be longer.

11. Cheeses, vegetables, and fruits should be processed directly from refrigerator. The exceptions are Parmesan and Romano cheeses—these harder cheeses should be at room temperature.

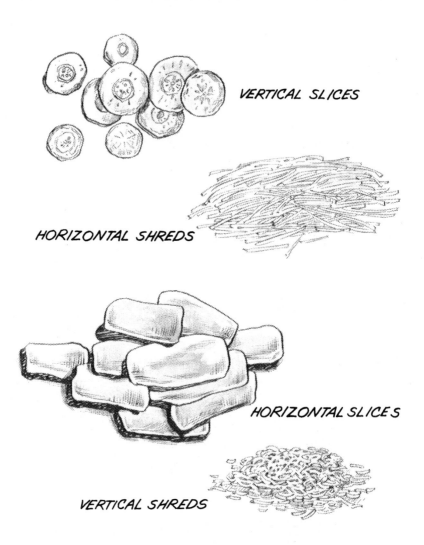

VERTICAL SLICES

HORIZONTAL SHREDS

HORIZONTAL SLICES

VERTICAL SHREDS

12. Meat slices best when partially frozen (see Table of Foods, pages 2–15). Only a serrated slicing blade will slice meat.

13. The amount of pressure used to slice foods depends upon texture of the food itself (see Table of Foods, pages 2–15).

14. When slicing, if food will not fit through top of feed tube, try loading through bottom, since bottom is slightly wider.

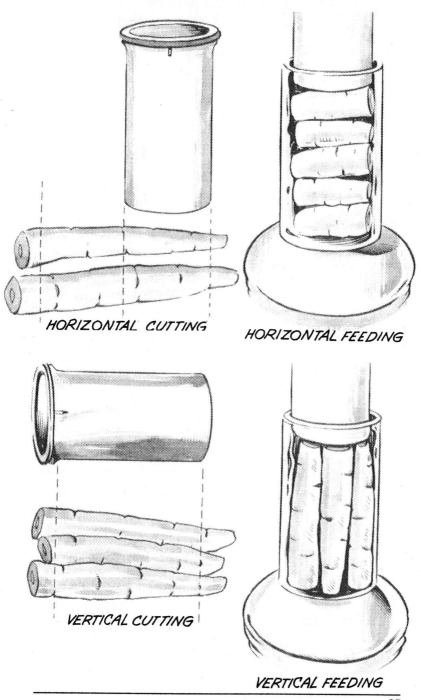

HORIZONTAL CUTTING

HORIZONTAL FEEDING

VERTICAL CUTTING

VERTICAL FEEDING

15. For rounded foods (radishes, mushroom caps), slice a very small piece from one side so food rests directly on slicing blade. Then place remaining items of food in feed tube so as to form a pile.

16. For more even slices, make sure that food lays flat on blade.

17. When slicing long, narrow foods (carrots), pack foods so that wide and narrow ends alternate in feed tube.

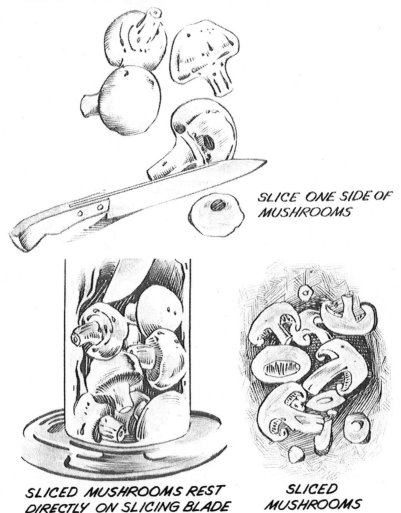

SLICE ONE SIDE OF MUSHROOMS

SLICED MUSHROOMS REST DIRECTLY ON SLICING BLADE

SLICED MUSHROOMS

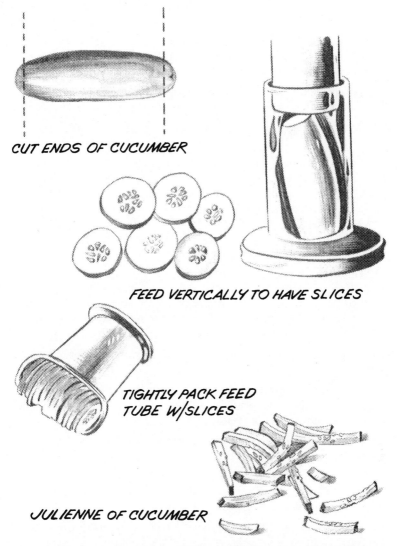

CUT ENDS OF CUCUMBER

FEED VERTICALLY TO HAVE SLICES

TIGHTLY PACK FEED TUBE w/SLICES

JULIENNE OF CUCUMBER

18. To julienne: For those machines that do not have a julienne blade, slice food first, using MEDIUM SLICING BLADE. Remove slices from work bowl and pack feed tube tight, sliced edges at right angles to cover. Slice again.

19. When grating or slicing, food will pile up on one side of the work bowl. This is normal. Remove food to mixing bowl as necessary and continue procedure.

20. When grating or slicing, some foods will remain on top of blade. This is normal. If large enough, these can be reprocessed.

21. A coarse chop usually requires 2 to 4 on/off turns; a finer chop or mince, 6 or 7 on/off turns. Check work bowl to determine degree of doneness.

22. To purée: When puréeing, use STEEL BLADE, and purée up to 2 cups. The technique is the same, whether puréeing fish for mousse, cooked vegetables, raw berries, soups, etc. Start with on/off turns, scrape down sides of work bowl, and then allow processor to run until desired texture is reached (no more than 60 seconds). If processor has blender attachment, blender may be used.

23. When emptying a full work bowl, I recommend sticking your index finger in opening on underside of work bowl, when possible, thus securing STEEL or PLASTIC BLADE. This prevents blade from dropping out. Remove blade when most of food has been emptied from work bowl, scraping out remaining food with spatula.

24. Recipes will denote when flour is to be sifted. Otherwise, unsifted flour is to be used.

25. If recipe calls for too much flour to be processed at one time, cut recipe in half, process in two batches, and then combine on work area, continuing with recipe.

26. When preparing yeast dough, temperature of warm water or milk should be 105° to 115°F.

27. Consult manual to determine liquid and flour capacity. Too much liquid will overflow work bowl; too much flour will cause motor to stop due to overload.

28. Recipes are organized so that there is a minimal amount of cleanup. Recipes will indicate "clean" work bowl as needed. I recommend purchase of second work bowl. It is a good investment, eliminating much of the washup until recipe is completed.

29. If motor shuts off during processing, due to overload, unplug cord and allow machine to rest for 20 or 30 minutes. Reattach cord and proceed with recipe. If processor still does not operate, consult manual to determine correct procedure to follow.

30. I recommend use of a long, narrow brush to clean out parts of work bowl and blades that are difficult to reach. When puréeing fish, you must be especially careful to remove particles that may stick to inside of STEEL BLADE. I usually fill work bowl, blade still attached, with sudsy water, then rinse clean. It is so easily cleaned, I seldom set it in the dishwasher.

31. If a blade is difficult to remove from work bowl, wrap a towel around sides of blade and gently work blade back and forth until it lifts out.

COCKTAIL
FOODS
AND
APPETIZERS

This is the marvelous country French mayonnaise. If you don't like garlic, this recipe isn't for you. The French serve this with fish soup and use it as a dip for raw and cooked vegetables.

AIOLI

Makes about 2 cups

8 to 10 cloves garlic
3 egg yolks
Pinch of salt

Freshly ground pepper
2 to 4 teaspoons lemon juice
2 to 2½ cups olive oil

1. Using STEEL BLADE, process garlic, egg yolks, salt, pepper, and 2 teaspoons lemon juice until combined.

2. With motor running, *slowly* add oil through feed tube. Texture will be smooth and thick. Correct seasoning, adding remaining lemon juice if necessary.

TO PREPARE IN ADVANCE: Through step 2.
TO FREEZE: Do not freeze.

NOTE: If aïoli "breaks" (curdles), transfer to a spouted vessel and wash work bowl. Add 2 egg yolks to work bowl and process lightly. With motor running, *slowly* pour aïoli through feed tube.

In this recipe, the avocado retains its green color.

AVOCADO DIP

Makes about 1⅓ cups

1 medium avocado, halved, peeled,
   pitted, and cut in 1-inch pieces
1 clove garlic
¼ cup sour cream

Juice of ½ small lemon or lime
½ teaspoon salt
Freshly ground pepper
Dash of Tabasco

1. Using STEEL BLADE, combine avocado and garlic and process until puréed, scraping down sides of work bowl as necessary.

2. Add remaining ingredients and process until smooth, scraping down sides of work bowl as necessary. Refrigerate until needed.

3. Serve chilled, with vegetables, tortilla chips, or crackers.

TO PREPARE IN ADVANCE: Through step 3.
TO FREEZE: Do not freeze.

This has just enough tang to be served with drinks before dinner, or it can be served after dinner with fruit.

Spicy cheese dip

Makes about 2½ cups

8 ounces Cheddar cheese, at room
  temperature, cut in 1-inch
  pieces
4 ounces blue cheese, at room
  temperature, cut in 1-inch
  pieces

8 ounces cottage cheese
½ teaspoon salt
1 teaspoon Worcestershire sauce
Dash of Tabasco
1 tablespoon brandy
½ cup heavy cream

1. Using STEEL BLADE, cream Cheddar and blue cheeses. Start with on/off turns and then allow motor to run until smooth, scraping down sides of work bowl as necessary.

2. Add remaining ingredients and process until well combined.

3. Shape mixture into a ball and allow to stand at room temperature 2 to 3 hours. Drain any liquid that may accumulate. Cover and refrigerate until needed.

4. To serve, place on dish and surround with crackers or cocktail bread, vegetable sticks, or fruit.

TO PREPARE IN ADVANCE: Through step 3.
TO FREEZE: Do not freeze.

VARIATION: May be shaped into a log and rolled in chopped pistachio nuts.

DEVILED CHEESE SPREAD

Makes about 1½ cups
Serves 4 to 6

¼ cup pecans
¼ small onion
3 ounces cream cheese, cut in
   1-inch pieces

2 ounces Roquefort cheese, cut in
   1-inch pieces
¼ cup Deviled Ham (page 34), or
   1 small can (2¼ ounces) deviled
   ham

1. Using STEEL BLADE, chop pecans fine. Reserve.

2. Using STEEL BLADE, with on/off turns, coarsely chop onion. Add remaining ingredients and process until smooth, scraping down sides of work bowl as necessary.

3. Remove from work bowl, form into ball, and chill. Roll in chopped nuts.

4. Serve with cocktail breads or plain crackers.

TO PREPARE IN ADVANCE: Through step 3, this will keep up to one week, covered in plastic wrap and refrigerated.
TO FREEZE: Do not freeze.

VARIATION: Roll in chopped parsley instead of nuts.

This is so much better than store-bought.

DEVILED HAM

Makes about 1½ cups

1 cup cooked ham, cut in 1-inch
   pieces
¼ cup ham fat, cut in 1-inch
   pieces
1 teaspoon Quatre-Épices (page
   246)
¼ teaspoon dried thyme
Freshly ground pepper

1 clove garlic
1½ teaspoons Dijon mustard
2 teaspoons red wine vinegar
5 dashes Tabasco
1 anchovy fillet, patted dry
   (optional)

1. Using STEEL BLADE, combine all ingredients and process until mixture is smooth, scraping down sides of work bowl as necessary.

2. Correct seasoning to taste. Store, covered, in jar and refrigerate 48 hours. Use on sandwiches.

TO PREPARE IN ADVANCE: Through step 2.
TO FREEZE: Through step 2.

LOBSTER BALLS

Makes about 24 balls

½ cup cooked lobster meat, cut in
   1-inch pieces
3 ounces cream cheese, at room
   temperature, cut in 6 pieces
1 teaspoon lemon juice

½ teaspoon salt
Freshly ground pepper
½ teaspoon celery seed
Pretzel sticks (optional)
Sizzle Sauce (page 199)

1. Using STEEL BLADE, combine all ingredients, except pretzel sticks, in work bowl. Start with on/off turns and process until smooth, scraping down sides of work bowl as necessary.

2. Shape into balls about ¾ inch in diameter.

3. Stick pretzel stick into each ball and use as handle. Serve with Sizzle Sauce.

TO PREPARE IN ADVANCE: Through step 2.
TO FREEZE: Through step 2.

SERBIAN CHEESE WITH RED PEPPER CAVIAR

8 ounces cream cheese, at room
temperature, cut in 1-inch
pieces
¼ pound (1 stick) unsalted butter,
at room temperature, cut in
1-inch pieces

1 pound creamy feta cheese
(preferably Bulgarian or
Yugoslavian), cut in 1-inch
pieces
1 recipe Red Pepper Caviar (page
36), or to taste

1. Using PLASTIC BLADE, combine cream cheese and butter and process until creamy. With motor running, add feta cheese, bit by bit, through feed tube and continue to process until smooth, scraping down sides of work bowl as necessary.

2. Remove to large mixing bowl and combine thoroughly with Red Pepper Caviar. Refrigerate in tightly covered container until needed.

3. Serve with thin-sliced buttered rye or pumpernickel bread.

TO PREPARE IN ADVANCE: Through step 2.
TO FREEZE: Do not freeze.

RED PEPPER CAVIAR

8 large sweet red peppers (or 4
green and 4 red)
1 small clove garlic

Juice of ½ lemon
Salt and freshly ground pepper
2 to 4 tablespoons olive oil

1. Over an open flame or under a broiler, char skins of peppers until blistered and blackened, turning to char all sides.

2. Place in a closed plastic bag for 1 hour to help loosen skin. Clean under cold running water to remove blackened skin.

3. Cut peppers in half, remove seeds and membranes, and cut in large strips. Using STEEL BLADE, with on/off turns, coarsely chop peppers in several batches. Add garlic with last batch. Remove to mixing bowl and toss with lemon juice. Season with salt and pepper to taste.

4. Slowly add oil, 1 tablespoon at a time, until peppers are moist but not too oily.

5. Refrigerate until needed.

6. May be served as is or combined with Serbian Cheese (page 36).

TO PREPARE IN ADVANCE: Through step 5.
TO FREEZE: Do not freeze.

My advice is to double this recipe. Rillettes can be refrigerated for up to 4 weeks and are delicious with an aperitif.

Rillettes of Pork

Makes 2 cups

---

2 tablespoons vegetable oil
1 pound fresh pork belly, cut in
   1-inch pieces
1 pound pork shoulder, cut in
   1-inch pieces (do not remove fat)
1 carrot, sliced lengthwise
2 celery stalks, sliced lengthwise
1 bay leaf

Pinch of dried thyme
Pinch of dried sage
1 tablespoon fresh savory (or 1
   teaspoon dried)
1 teaspoon salt
¼ teaspoon freshly ground pepper
2 cups white wine

1. In large skillet, heat oil. Add pork belly and pork shoulder and sauté on moderate flame until golden, 30 to 35 minutes, turning meat to cook on all sides. *Do not brown.* Remove meat to large saucepan.

2. In a piece of cheesecloth, wrap together carrot, celery, bay leaf, thyme, sage, and savory. Add to meat. Add salt, pepper, wine, and enough water to reach three-quarters way to top of meat. Cover saucepan and cook about 2 hours over moderate flame, or until meat shreds easily when pierced with fork.

3. Discard cheesecloth package and drain meat, reserving any fat that has accumulated.

4. Using STEEL BLADE, shred meat, 1 cup at a time, processing with on/off turns. (With very fast on/off turns, it may take 13 or 14 turns.) The meat must come out shredded, *not a paste.*

5. Remove meat to mixing bowl, add reserved fat, and combine thoroughly. Cool and refrigerate until ready to use, stirring occasionally to distribute fat.

6. Serve in crock or bowl with crackers or party rye bread.

TO PREPARE IN ADVANCE: Through step 5.
TO FREEZE: Through step 5. Defrost overnight in refrigerator.

NOTE: The addition of ½ teaspoon green peppercorns in step 4 will provide additional zest.

Refrigerating overnight enhances the flavor; try tasting the pâté when you prepare it and note the improvement the next day. Pâté will thicken as it chills.

CHICKEN LIVER PATE

Makes about 2 cups

1 pound chicken livers
6 tablespoons unsalted butter
½ teaspoon salt
¼ teaspoon white pepper
2 tablespoons Cognac
1 clove garlic
2 tablespoons heavy cream

Pinch of Quatre-Épices (page 246)
Pinch of dried thyme
Pinch of dried basil
½ teaspoon Madeira
1 or 2 tablespoons Clarified Butter (page 205)

1. Pat chicken livers dry and cut in half. In medium skillet melt 3 tablespoons of the butter over moderate flame. When foam subsides, add livers to pan and sauté on both sides until light brown but still pink on the inside, about 10 minutes. Season with salt and pepper and remove to work bowl fitted with STEEL BLADE.

2. Pour Cognac into skillet and stir to mix pan juices. Add garlic clove and cook 1 or 2 minutes to reduce liquid slightly, then pour into work bowl containing chicken livers.

3. Cut remaining 3 tablespoons butter into 3 pieces and add to work bowl with heavy cream, *Quatre-Épices*, thyme, basil, and Madeira. Process with 4 or 5 on/off turns, scraping down bits that cling to sides, then allow machine to run until texture is smooth, about 60 seconds. Correct seasoning to taste.

4. Spoon mixture into a 2-cup serving crock or dish and cover with a layer of Clarified Butter. Chill 12 to 24 hours.

5. Serve with crackers and/or pumpernickel bread.

TO PREPARE IN ADVANCE: Through step 4, it will keep at least 1 week refrigerated.
TO FREEZE: Through step 4. Defrost overnight in refrigerator.

Pâtés are fun to make. This and the two that follow are just a little different and are perfect with cocktails.

*B*USY DAY PATE
Makes about 2 cups

¼ *small onion, cut in half*
1 *pound liverwurst, cut in 1-inch*
   pieces

¼ *cup brandy*
½ *cup sour cream*
1 *teaspoon Dijon mustard*

1. Using STEEL BLADE, chop onion with 2 or 3 on/off turns. Add remaining ingredients and process until smooth.

2. Pack into 2-cup mold and refrigerate until needed.

3. Serve with rounds of rye bread and cornichons.

TO PREPARE IN ADVANCE: Through step 2.
TO FREEZE: Through step 2. Defrost overnight in refrigerator.

VARIATION: Saute ½ cup minced mushrooms in 1 tablespoon butter and process with liverwurst.

SHRIMP PATE

½ pound cooked, shelled shrimp
4 tablespoons (½ stick) unsalted
  butter, softened, cut
  in 4 pieces
1 tablespoon cream cheese

2 tablespoons Cognac
½ teaspoon lemon juice
½ teaspoon fresh dill leaves
Salt and freshly ground pepper
Dash of Tabasco

1. Using STEEL BLADE, combine all ingredients in work bowl and process until smooth, scraping down sides of bowl as necessary.

2. Correct seasoning to taste.

3. Transfer to serving bowl and refrigerate at least 1 hour.

4. Serve with thin slices of toast.

TO PREPARE IN ADVANCE: Through step 3.
TO FREEZE: Do not freeze.

SMOKED SALMON PATE

Makes about 2 cups
Serves 6 to 8

1-inch piece of fresh horseradish
  root, peeled
6 whole green onions, cut in
  1-inch pieces
4 teaspoons fresh dill

½ pound smoked salmon, cut in
  1-inch pieces
¾ cup sour cream
1 tablespoon Mayonnaise (page
  182)
Salt and freshly ground pepper

1. Using STEEL BLADE, grate horseradish fine.

2. Add green onions and dill to work bowl and process until chopped fine.

3. Add remaining ingredients and process until smooth, scraping down sides of work bowl as necessary.

4. Season with salt and pepper to taste. Spoon into serving dish and refrigerate.

5. Serve chilled, with buttered thinly sliced rye or pumpernickel bread.

TO PREPARE IN ADVANCE: Through step 4.
TO FREEZE: Do not freeze.

NOTE: Horseradish root can be submerged in a container of water and stored in the refrigerator 4 to 6 weeks.

SWEDISH MEATBALLS

Makes about 50
appetizer meatballs

2 slices white bread, torn in small
 pieces
1 cup milk
½ medium onion, cut in half
1 clove garlic
½ stick unsalted butter
½ pound lean beef, cut in 1-inch
 pieces
½ pound pork shoulder, cut in
 1-inch pieces

1 egg
1 teaspoon salt
¼ teaspoon freshly ground
 pepper
⅛ teaspoon ground allspice
2 tablespoons vegetable oil
All-purpose flour
1 cup chicken or beef stock

1. Using STEEL BLADE, process bread into fine crumbs. In a large mixing bowl, soak crumbs in ½ cup of the milk. Reserve.

2. Using STEEL BLADE, with on/off turns, coarsely chop onion and garlic. Drain, as necessary. In a small skillet, over medium heat, melt 2 tablespoons butter and sauté onion and garlic until tender, 2 to 3 minutes.

3. Using STEEL BLADE, with on/off turns, chop beef and pork fine, in separate batches. Add to crumbs in mixing bowl.

4. Skim out cooked onion and garlic and add to mixing bowl with egg, salt, pepper, and allspice. Combine thoroughly. Heat remaining ½ cup milk and slowly add to mixture. Refrigerate 1 hour, until firm.

5. Form meat mixture into small meatballs about 1 inch in diameter.

6. In a large skillet, over moderate flame, melt remaining 2 tablespoons butter and the oil. Sauté meatballs, browning on all sides, 10 to 15 minutes. Remove meatballs from skillet and sprinkle them lightly with flour.

7. Pour off fat from skillet and deglaze pan with stock, scraping particles of meat into liquid as it simmers. Return meatballs to skillet and cook over low flame 15 to 20 minutes longer. Correct seasoning to taste.

8. Serve meatballs hot in gravy.

TO PREPARE IN ADVANCE: Through step 7.
TO FREEZE: Through step 7. Defrost overnight in refrigerator and heat through on low flame.

From Madame Wong's Long–Life Chinese Cookbook, *the best shrimp toast recipe I have ever tasted.*

Shrimp Toast

Yield: 32 pieces

9 slices extra-thin bread, crusts
   removed (day-old bread is
   preferred)
¼ medium onion, halved
1 whole scallion, cut in 1-inch
   pieces
4 water chestnuts
1 pound fresh shrimp, shelled and
   deveined

1 egg
1 tablespoon cornstarch
1 teaspoon dry sherry
1 teaspoon salt
Freshly ground pepper to taste
3 to 4 cups vegetable oil for deep
   frying

1. Cut each bread slice into 4 squares (36 squares). Soak 4 of the squares in water 1 second. Squeeze out liquid and reserve soaked bread.

2. Using STEEL BLADE, chop onion, scallion, and water chestnuts with 4 or 5 on/off turns. Add shrimp and soaked bread and chop with 3 or 4 more on/off turns. Add remaining ingredients, except for oil, and process just until well combined.

3. Place 1 teaspoon shrimp mixture on each bread square, mounding slightly in center.

4. In wok or deep-fryer, heat oil to 375°F. Slip bread squares into oil, a few at a time, shrimp side down. Fry about 1 minute, turn, and fry other side until golden brown. Repeat procedure until all bread squares are cooked.

5. Drain on paper towels. Serve hot, either plain or with duck sauce and Chinese mustard.

TO PREPARE IN ADVANCE: Through step 3.
TO FREEZE: Do not freeze.

This is generally served as an hors d'oeuvre, but two or three may be served as a vegetable accompanying an entrée.

SPINACH CROUSTADES

Yield: 24 pieces

Softened unsalted butter
24 slices thin white bread
2 tablespoons unsalted butter
1 pound spinach, washed and
  stemmed
1 ounce Parmesan cheese, cut in
  1-inch pieces

1 egg
½ teaspoon salt
6 grinds fresh pepper
2 tablespoons all-purpose flour
½ cup half-and-half
2 dashes of nutmeg

1. Preheat oven to 400°F.

2. Using pastry brush, generously butter insides of small muffin tins. Using a 3-inch cookie cutter, cut a circle from each slice of bread. Carefully mold a bread circle into each muffin tin, shaping with your finger or a small rounded object, to make a perfect cup.

3. Bake about 12 minutes, or until croustades are lightly browned and crisp. Remove to rack and cool.

4. Over moderate flame, melt butter in medium saucepan. Add spinach, cover pan, and cook until wilted, about 3 to 5 minutes. Press juice from spinach and reserve. Cool spinach.

5. Using STEEL BLADE, and with motor running, drop Parmesan cheese through feed tube and grate fine. Reserve.

6. Using STEEL BLADE, chop spinach fine. Add egg, salt, and pepper and process until just combined.

7. Heat spinach juice. On low flame, stir in flour. Gradually stir in half-and-half and cook until slightly thickened, 2 to 3 minutes. Add spinach and continue cooking until mixture is homogenous, about 2 minutes. Add nutmeg and correct seasoning to taste.

8. Generously mound spinach into croustades, sprinkle with cheese, and return to oven. Bake 8 to 10 minutes. Serve hot.

TO PREPARE IN ADVANCE: Through step 7.
TO FREEZE: Through step 8, baking only 3 or 4 minutes before freezing. Remove from freezer 30 minutes before baking. To reheat, place on baking tray and bake approximately 10 minutes.

VARIATIONS: 1. Whole-wheat bread may be substituted for white bread.
2. Substitute *Duxelles* (page 158) for spinach filling and follow recipe as above.

This is an easy-to-prepare appetizer that has universal appeal.

QUESADILLAS

Yield: 24 pieces

4 ounces Cheddar cheese, chilled
4 ounces Jack cheese, chilled
1 can (4 ounces) green chiles or
  Green Chile Sauce (page 190)

12 six-inch flour tortillas
2 tablespoons melted unsalted
  butter

1. Preheat oven to 350°F.

2. Using MEDIUM SHREDDING BLADE, grate Cheddar and Jack cheeses. Clean work bowl.

3. Using STEEL BLADE, with on/off turns, coarsely chop chiles.

4. Place each tortilla on unbuttered pastry sheet and sprinkle with

grated cheeses. Place small amount of chopped green chiles (or Green Chile Sauce) over cheese and fold tortilla in half. Brush with melted butter.

5. Bake 10 to 12 minutes, or until golden brown.

6. Cut each quesadilla in half and serve hot.

TO PREPARE IN ADVANCE: Through step 4.
TO FREEZE: Do not freeze.

This is simple fare made elegant by being wrapped in phyllo leaves.

VEGETABLE KNISHES WRAPPED IN PHYLLO LEAVES

Yield: About 48
three-and-one-half-inch knishes

1½ medium onions, quartered
1 clove garlic
1 carrot, peeled
4 celery stalks, strings removed
1 pound mushrooms
½ green pepper, cored and seeded
¾ cup safflower oil
1 cup cooked rice (white or brown)

1 cup cooked kasha, following package directions
1 large egg
1 teaspoon salt
10 grinds fresh pepper
½ cup (1 stick) unsalted butter, melted
24 phyllo leaves

1. Using STEEL BLADE, with on/off turns, coarsely chop onions and garlic. Drain and reserve.

2. Using MEDIUM SHREDDING BLADE, grate carrot, celery, mushrooms, and green pepper.

3. In a large skillet, over moderate flame, heat ¼ cup of the oil. Add onions and garlic and sauté until translucent, 5 to 7 minutes. Add carrot, celery, mushrooms, and green pepper and cook until vegetables are tender but still slightly crisp, about 5 minutes.

4. Stir in rice, kasha, egg, salt, and pepper. Correct seasoning to taste and cool.

---

5. Combine melted butter and remaining ½ cup oil and keep warm. (Use to brush on phyllo leaves.)

6. Preheat oven to 350°F.

7. Dampen a tea towel with cold water and lay flat on work area. Cover towel with waxed paper and place phyllo leaves being used on paper. (Cover unused leaves to prevent drying as you work.)

8. Cut each phyllo leaf in half, crosswise, giving you two 8½ x 11-inch pieces. Brush with melted butter and fold in half again,

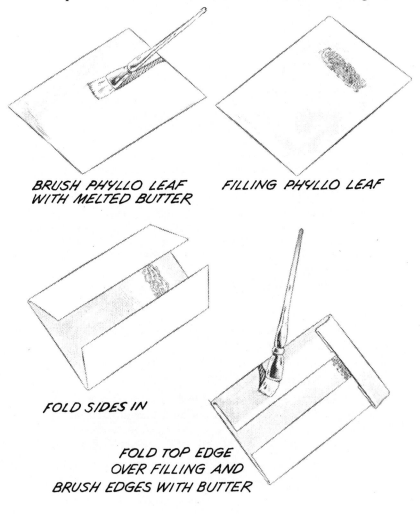

BRUSH PHYLLO LEAF
WITH MELTED BUTTER

FILLING PHYLLO LEAF

FOLD SIDES IN

FOLD TOP EDGE
OVER FILLING AND
BRUSH EDGES WITH BUTTER

giving you an 8½ x 5½-inch leaf. Brush again with melted butter. (I use a small paint brush.)

9. Place a heaping teaspoonful of filling on the 5½-inch end. Fold in sides and turn top edge over filling. Brush edges with butter and roll, as a jelly roll, until you reach the other end, being careful to enclose filling.

10. Place rolled knish, seam side down, on an ungreased baking sheet, brush with melted butter, and cover with aluminum foil as you prepare the remaining leaves.

11. Repeat procedure until all the filling is used.

12. Bake 20 to 25 minutes, until golden brown. Serve hot.

TO PREPARE IN ADVANCE: Through step 12, baking 15 minutes.
TO FREEZE: Through step 12, baking 15 minutes. Remove from freezer 30 minutes before baking and bake in preheated oven 10 to 15 minutes.

NOTE: Each knish can be cut in half to make bite-size pieces. Using a serrated knife, lightly score unbaked knish, bake as above, and slice before serving.

ROLLED KNISH

This is another "freezer favorite," since I can bring out a batch and have it ready with very little notice.

GOUGERE

Makes 60 cheese puffs or
2 eight-inch rings

4 ounces sharp Cheddar cheese or
  Gruyère, cut in 1-inch pieces
2 ounces smoked ham, cut in
  1-inch pieces
1 bouillon cube, dissolved in 1 cup
  boiling water

¼ pound (1 stick) unsalted butter,
  cut in 6 pieces
1 cup all-purpose flour
4 eggs
2 teaspoons Dijon mustard
1 egg, lightly beaten, for egg wash

1. Using STEEL BLADE, with on/off turns, coarsely grate cheese. Reserve.

2. Using STEEL BLADE, with on/off turns, chop ham fine. Reserve and clean work bowl.

3. Preheat oven to 425°F.

4. In medium saucepan, combine dissolved bouillon cube and butter and bring to rolling boil. When butter is completely melted, remove pan from flame and add flour, all at once. Stir vigorously with wooden spoon until flour is absorbed. Return to low flame and cook for 1 or 2 minutes, stirring all the while, until dough comes away from sides of pan and forms a ball. Dump into work bowl fitted with STEEL BLADE.

5. With motor running, add 4 eggs, all at once, to work bowl and process until dough is smooth and shiny, scraping down sides of work bowl as necessary. Add two-thirds of the reserved cheese, the reserved ham, and mustard and process until just combined.

6. Butter baking sheet and sprinkle with cold water, pouring off any excess water.

7. To make puffs, fill pastry tube fitted with #6 plain tip and pipe into 1-inch mounds, 2 inches apart, or drop puffs off a rounded teaspoon onto prepared baking sheet. Brush egg wash over tops, taking care that egg does not drip down on pan. Gently press down tips of dough to prevent burning. Sprinkle with reserved grated cheese.

8. Bake 10 minutes, then lower heat to 350°F. and bake 20 minutes longer, or until puffed and golden brown. Gently pierce sides and bake 5 minutes to dry insides. Serve warm.

TO PREPARE IN ADVANCE: Through step 8, baking 10 minutes at 425°F. and 10 minutes at 350°F.
TO FREEZE: As above. Remove from freezer 30 minutes before baking and bake at 350°F. approximately 20 minutes.

VARIATION (GOUGERE RING): Prepare pastry sheet according to instructions above. Press 8-inch round cake pan onto sheet to form outline of circle; remove. Using pastry tube with #6 tip, press out mounds one next to the other around edge of circle. Use spatula to shape mounds into smooth circle. Brush with egg wash and sprinkle with cheese. Bake in preheated 350°F. oven for 1 hour, or until golden brown.

FIRST
COURSES
AND
LUNCHEON
ENTREES

COUNTRY PATE

½ cup Madeira
¼ cup Cognac
1 shallot, cut in half
1 tablespoon salt
½ teaspoon freshly ground pepper
½ teaspoon ground allspice
Pinch of dried thyme
¼ pound salt pork, cut in 1-inch
pieces

1 pound pork shoulder, cut in
1-inch pieces
1 pound pork fatback, cut in
1-inch pieces
6 chicken livers, cut in half
6 ounces pork fatback, cut in thin
slices
1 bay leaf

1. In large mixing bowl, combine Madeira, Cognac, shallot, salt, pepper, allspice, and thyme. Add salt pork, pork shoulder, 1 pound pork fatback, and chicken livers and stir through. Marinate 4 or 5 days, refrigerated, turning every other day.

2. Preheat oven to 350°F.

3. To prepare forcemeat, drain meats and, using STEEL BLADE, with on/off turns, grind medium fine, 1 cup at a time.

4. Line 8½ x 4½ x 2½-inch loaf pan or pâté mold with thinly sliced pork fatback, leaving enough overlapping edge of pan to enclose meat. Pack forcemeat into prepared pan and place bay leaf on top. Fold fatback over top.

5. Set pan in bain-marie and bring water just to a boil. Cover pan with aluminum foil and transfer to oven. Bake 60 to 70 minutes, being careful that water does not boil. To test for doneness, insert knife into center of meat and carefully slide flat edge of knife along your mouth; if blade is hot, pâté is cooked.

6. Cool and refrigerate at least 24 hours before serving.

7. To serve, invert on platter and accompany with cornichons or Mushrooms à la Grecque (page 171).

TO PREPARE IN ADVANCE: Through step 6.
TO FREEZE: Through step 6. Defrost overnight in refrigerator.

VARIATION (TERRINE OF DUCK): Substitute duck livers for

chicken livers, and bone 1 duck, reserving bones for soup or stock. Slice duck breast into small strips and marinate in port. (Reserve duck legs and wings for a separate meal.) Prepare pork forcemeat above and combine with 1 tablespoon green peppercorns. Line mold with fatback slices and pack with ½-inch layer of forcemeat for first layer. Top with strips of duck, cover with forcemeat, and repeat layers until all meat is used. Continue with recipe as above.

This is my favorite fish pâté, served regularly at Ma Maison restaurant in Los Angeles.

TERRINE DE SAUMON
Salmon Terrine

Serves 10 to 12 as appetizer,
6 to 8 as entrée

1 bunch tarragon, leaves only
Juice of 1 lemon
1 teaspoon salt
1 teaspoon freshly ground pepper
1 cup dry white wine
1 pound salmon, filleted and sliced
   into ¼-inch-wide strips
1 leek, white part only, cut in
   1-inch pieces
2 carrots, peeled, cut in 1-inch
   pieces
3 tablespoons unsalted butter

1 pound scallops
1 egg
Cayenne pepper
2 cups heavy cream
6 asparagus, scraped with
   vegetable peeler
1 pound fresh spinach, washed and
   stemmed
Watercress Mayonnaise (page 185)
   and/or Mayonnaise Concassée
   (page 185)

1. Using STEEL BLADE, chop tarragon leaves fine. Reserve.

2. Combine lemon juice, ½ teaspoon of the salt, ½ teaspoon of the pepper, wine, and 3 tablespoons of the chopped tarragon in a glass bowl. Marinate salmon in mixture for 2 hours, unrefrigerated.

3. Preheat oven to 350°F. Generously butter pâté mold or 8½ x 4½ x 2½-inch loaf pan.

4. Using STEEL BLADE, with on/off turns, chop leek and carrots fine. Clean work bowl. In small skillet, melt butter and sauté leek and carrot for 5 minutes. Cool.

5. To prepare mousse: Using STEEL BLADE, purée scallops with egg, remaining ½ teaspoons salt and pepper, a few dashes of cayenne, and 2 tablespoons chopped tarragon. Purée until very fine, scraping down side of work bowl as necessary. Through feed tube, and with motor running, slowly add chilled cream until thoroughly combined. Remove to large mixing bowl. Fold in leek and carrot. Refrigerate until ready to use. (To test for seasoning, poach a small amount in salted simmering water. Correct seasoning to taste.)

6. To cook asparagus, bring pot of heavily salted water to boil. Add asparagus and bring water back to boil. Cook 5 to 8 minutes, until tender but still firm. Refresh under cold water and reserve. Slice off bottom of asparagus as necessary to fit pâté mold or loaf pan.

7. Cook spinach in lightly salted water until wilted, about 5 minutes. Refresh under cold water, press out all the water, and reserve.

8. To layer terrine, arrange spinach leaves on bottom and sides of pan, leaving a slight overhang, and spread with layer of fish mousse. Arrange half the salmon fillets over mousse and cover with second layer of mousse. Place asparagus over mousse, top with remaining fillets, and cover with remaining mousse (3 layers of mousse, 2 layers of salmon, 1 layer of asparagus). Fold over spinach leaves that are still visible.

9. Butter a large piece of aluminum foil and, buttered side down, loosely cover terrine. Set terrine in a bain-marie and bake 1 hour, or until knife inserted into center is hot to touch. Cool and then refrigerate 24 hours.

10. To serve, invert on serving platter and slice. Serve with either or both mayonnaises.

TO PREPARE IN ADVANCE: Through step 9.
TO FREEZE: Do not freeze.

VARIATION: Mousse may be used to make Quenelles (page 57).

For that special dinner party, this is very special.

SMOKED FISH MOUSSE

Makes about 2½ cups

4 ounces smoked sturgeon, cut in
   1-inch pieces
4 ounces smoked salmon, cut in
   1-inch pieces*

1 cup heavy cream, whipped
Salt and freshly ground pepper
Juice of ½ medium lemon
1 to 2 ounces caviar, red or black

1. Using STEEL BLADE, purée sturgeon, scraping down sides of work bowl as necessary. Remove to medium mixing bowl. Clean work bowl.

2. Using STEEL BLADE, purée salmon, scraping down sides of work bowl as necessary. Remove to a separate mixing bowl.

3. Divide the whipped cream in half and fold into each puréed fish. Season with salt, pepper, and lemon juice to taste.

4. Into a chilled serving bowl, preferably glass, spoon sturgeon mousse and sprinkle with caviar. Top with salmon mousse and decorate with caviar. Chill overnight.

5. Serve with thin slices of warm toast.

TO PREPARE IN ADVANCE: Through step 4.
TO FREEZE: Do not freeze.

VARIATION: Smoked haddock may be substituted for sturgeon.

*I use salmon ends since this is puréed.

MOUSSELINE OF WHITEFISH WITH OYSTERS

Serves 6

12 oysters
6 shallots
¾ pound (3 sticks) unsalted
  butter, at room temperature,
  each stick cut in 8 pieces
1 pound whitefish, filleted, cut in
  1-inch pieces

2 eggs
1 sprig fresh tarragon leaves
Salt and freshly ground pepper
1 cup heavy cream, lightly
  whipped and chilled
1 cup chicken stock
3 tablespoons dry sherry

1. Preheat oven to 350°F. Butter bottom and sides of 6 small custard cups. Chill large mixing bowl.

2. Open oysters and poach in their own juice, about 5 minutes. Allow to cool in the liquid, unrefrigerated.

3. Using STEEL BLADE, and with motor running, drop shallots through feed tube and chop fine. Reserve one-third of shallots. Clean work bowl.

4. Heat 1 piece of the butter in small skillet and sauté two-thirds of the shallots until translucent. Cool.

5. Chill work bowl and blade by placing several ice cubes in bowl for a few minutes, rotating by hand, emptying and drying. Using STEEL BLADE, purée whitefish and tarragon, scraping down sides of work bowl as necessary. Add eggs, 8 pieces of the butter, the sautéed shallots, salt, and pepper and purée until homogenous. Transfer to chilled bowl and fold in whipped cream. To test, poach a teaspoonful of mousseline in simmering salted water. Correct seasoning to taste.

6. Half fill prepared cups with mousseline. Top each with 2 oysters and cover with remaining mousseline. Set cups in a bain-marie and cover with buttered aluminum foil, buttered side down. Bake 15 to 20 minutes, until mousseline is firm to touch.

7. To prepare sauce: In small saucepan, combine oyster liquid, stock, sherry, and remaining raw chopped shallots. Cook over high heat until ½ cup liquid remains.

8. Remove to side of stove and whisk in remaining 15 pieces of butter, a piece at a time. As sauce cools, return to low flame, then

continue to whisk in remaining butter. Do not permit sauce to boil. Season to taste with salt and pepper. (You may strain sauce, if you like, to remove shallots.) Keep warm in Thermos or bain-marie.

9. To serve, unmold mousselines on serving plate and nap with sauce.

TO PREPARE IN ADVANCE: Through step 5 (or fill custard cups and refrigerate).
TO FREEZE: Do not freeze.

VARIATIONS: 1. Cooked spinach may be substituted for oysters. 2. Mussels may be substituted for oysters.

You can substitute fish or veal for the chicken and be equally delighted with the ease with which this is prepared.

CHICKEN QUENELLES   Makes 16 or 17 quenelles

8 ounces skinned, boned chicken   1 whole egg
   breast, cut in 1-inch pieces   1 egg white
½ teaspoon salt   1 cup heavy cream, chilled
¼ teaspoon white pepper   Mustard Sauce (page 195) or
Dash of nutmeg   Madeira Sauce (page 194)

1. Place several ice cubes in work bowl containing STEEL BLADE and rotate bowl by hand for several minutes to chill. Empty and dry bowl.

2. To prepare chicken mousse: Using STEEL BLADE, combine chicken, salt, pepper, and nutmeg in chilled work bowl and process until smooth.

3. Add whole egg and egg white and continue to process until puréed, scraping down sides of work bowl as necessary.

4. With motor running, pour cream through feed tube and process until cream is completely absorbed and mixture is very smooth. Scrape down sides of work bowl as necessary.

5. To test, drop a teaspoonful of mousse into simmering salted water and cook about 2 minutes. Correct seasoning to taste.

6. Butter skillet large enough to hold quenelles. Dip two table-spoons into small bowl of hot water. Scoop up mousse on one spoon and smooth top and sides with second spoon, scraping away excess. Slide off into skillet and repeat with remaining mousse.

7. Butter one side of a piece of aluminum foil large enough to cover quenelles and place buttered side down. Carefully pour boiling salted water around quenelles until quenelles are just covered and gently poach them 4 minutes on one side. Turn and poach 4 minutes on other side.

8. Remove to warm serving plate with slotted spoon and serve with sauce of your choice.

TO PREPARE IN ADVANCE: Through step 5, refrigerating until needed.
TO FREEZE: Do not freeze.

NOTE: For sharper flavor, cayenne pepper may be substituted for nutmeg.

Served with a salad, this makes a nourishing lunch.

SPINACH-CHEESE SOUFFLE

Serves 8

2 sheets unsalted matzohs
2 tablespoons unsalted butter
2 to 2½ pounds spinach, washed
  and stemmed
2 ounces Parmesan cheese, cut in
  1-inch pieces
2 ounces Romano cheese, cut in
  1-inch pieces

1 cup (5 ounces) feta cheese
2 cups small-curd cottage cheese
10 extra-large eggs, separated
Salt and freshly ground pepper
2 or 3 dashes of nutmeg

1. Preheat oven to 350°F. Butter a 9 x 1½ x 11-inch ovenproof dish.

2. Soak matzohs in warm water until soft. Drain.

3. In a large saucepan, over moderate flame, melt butter. Add spinach and cook, covered, until wilted, about 5 minutes. Drain and reserve.

4. Using STEEL BLADE, with motor running, drop Parmesan and Romano cheeses through feed tube and grate. Transfer to large mixing bowl.

5. Using STEEL BLADE, with on/off turns, coarsely chop spinach. Add to cheese in mixing bowl.

6. Using STEEL BLADE, process feta and cottage cheese until smooth. Add to mixing bowl.

7. Using STEEL BLADE, beat egg yolks until frothy. Add drained matzohs and combine with 2 or 3 on/off turns. Add to mixing bowl and combine all ingredients. Season with salt, pepper, and nutmeg.

8. Using wire whisk or rotary beater, whip egg whites until stiff but not dry. Stir one-third into spinach mixture to lighten it, then with large spatula, fold in remaining egg whites as quickly as possible. Pour into prepared dish.

9. Bake 40 to 45 minutes. Serve immediately.

TO PREPARE IN ADVANCE: Through step 7.
TO FREEZE: Do not freeze.

This is an interesting and much lighter variation of the classic quiche.

CREPE QUICHE

Yield: 12 individual quiches

CREPES:

1 medium leek, white part only
2 eggs
1 cup milk
1 tablespoon melted unsalted
   butter
1 cup all-purpose flour
Pinch of salt
Butter for crêpe pan

FILLING:

6 ounces mushrooms
1 tablespoon unsalted butter
4 ounces Swiss cheese, chilled
3 eggs
2 cups half-and-half
1 tablespoon dry sherry
1¾ teaspoon salt
½ teaspoon white pepper
½ bunch chives, snipped

1. To prepare crêpes: Wash leek thoroughly and cut into 1-inch pieces. Using STEEL BLADE, chop coarsely, with on/off turns, scraping down sides of work bowl as necessary.

---

2. Add eggs, milk, and butter to work bowl and process until foamy. Add flour and salt and process until just combined. Texture will resemble thick cream. Pour into mixing bowl for easier crêpe preparation. Clean work bowl.

3. Heat 6-inch crêpe pan and butter lightly. (I find this easier to do with paper towel and soft butter.) Using a ¼-cup measure for each crêpe, dip cup into batter and pour batter into pan. Tilt pan immediately until bottom surface is covered. Cook until underside of crêpe is lightly browned, about 1 minute. Turn and lightly brown other side. Remove to platter and cover with foil or towel, stacking crêpes until all batter is used (you should have 12 crêpes). Butter pan, as necessary, for each crêpe.

4. Preheat oven to 350°F. Butter 12 individual brioche tins or tin for 12 large cupcakes. Carefully press each crêpe to fit fluted or rounded sides of prepared tins.

5. To prepare filling: Using MEDIUM SLICING BLADE, slice mushrooms. Clean work bowl.

6. Heat butter in medium skillet and sauté mushrooms over moderate flame until liquid has evaporated, about 5 minutes.

7. Using MEDIUM SHREDDING BLADE, grate cheese. Reserve.

8. Using STEEL BLADE, combine eggs, half-and-half, sherry, salt, and pepper and process until incorporated.

9. Divide cheese and mushrooms into each crêpe. Fill with egg mixture. Sprinkle with chives.

10. Bake 20 to 25 minutes, or until custard is golden brown and firm to the touch.

11. Remove from tins and serve immediately.

TO PREPARE IN ADVANCE: Through step 7.
TO FREEZE: Through step 3. Defrost crêpes, wrapped, in refrigerator.

VARIATION: Chopped cooked ham and/or bacon may be added to or substituted for mushrooms.

QUICHE LORRAINE

1 pound Puff Pastry (page 257) or
   1 recipe Single-Crust Pie Shell
   (page 252)
2 ounces Gruyère cheese, chilled
½ pound bacon, cooked until crisp
   and cut in 1-inch pieces
6 ounces ham, cut in 1-inch pieces

¼ cup snipped fresh chives
5 large eggs
1½ cups milk
1½ cups heavy cream
¼ teaspoon salt
½ teaspoon white pepper
¼ teaspoon nutmeg

1. Preheat oven to 350°F. Butter a 10-inch quiche pan.

2. On a lightly floured board, roll out pastry slightly larger than quiche pan. Gently fit in pan, but do not trim any overhang. Line with foil, fill with beans or rice, and bake 15 minutes. Remove from oven, carefully remove beans, and discard foil.

3. Using MEDIUM SHREDDING BLADE, grate cheese. Reserve.

4. Using STEEL BLADE, with on/off turns, coarsely chop bacon and ham separately. Sprinkle into pastry shell. Add chives and cheese.

5. Using STEEL BLADE, combine eggs, milk, heavy cream, salt, pepper, and nutmeg in work bowl and process just until frothy. Pour over ingredients in pastry shell and trim edges.

6. Bake 40 to 50 minutes, or until quiche has puffed and browned.

7. Remove from oven and let rest 10 minutes. Slice and serve.

TO PREPARE IN ADVANCE: Through step 6.
TO FREEZE: Through step 2. Pastry may be filled directly from freezer.

A perfect brunch or supper dish. This is my version of Torta Milanese.

HAM AND SPINACH TORTE

PASTRY:

3 cups all-purpose flour
1 teaspoon salt
½ pound unsalted butter, chilled,
   cut in 12 pieces
1 egg yolk
5 to 6 tablespoons ice water

FILLING:

8 ounces Parmesan cheese, cut in
   1-inch pieces
1 pound smoked ham or pork, cut
   in 1-inch pieces
2 large onions, quartered
4 tablespoons vegetable oil
2 pounds fresh spinach, washed
   and stemmed
5 eggs
1 cup ricotta cheese
Salt and freshly ground pepper
Pinch of nutmeg

1. To prepare pastry: Using STEEL BLADE, combine flour, salt, butter, and egg yolk. Process until flour resembles coarse meal. Through feed tube, with motor running, add water until dough begins to form a ball on blade. (If necessary, add a bit more water.) Wrap dough in waxed paper and refrigerate while preparing filling. Clean work bowl.

2. Preheat oven to 425°F.

3. Using STEEL BLADE, with motor running, drop Parmesan cheese through feed tube and process until finely grated. Remove to large mixing bowl.

4. Using STEEL BLADE, with on/off turns, chop ham in 2 batches until just shredded. Add to Parmesan cheese. Clean work bowl.

5. Using STEEL BLADE, with on/off turns, chop onions fine in 2 batches. Drain. Heat 3 tablespoons of the oil in large skillet and sauté onion over moderate flame until translucent, about 5 minutes. Add to mixing bowl.

6. Heat remaining 1 tablespoon oil in skillet. Add spinach leaves;

cover and steam 5 minutes. Drain. Using STEEL BLADE, with on/off turns, chop spinach, being careful not to purée it. Cool slightly and add to mixing bowl. Clean work bowl.

7. Using STEEL BLADE, beat eggs until frothy. Reserve small amount for egg wash and add remaining eggs to mixing bowl. Add ricotta cheese and thoroughly combine entire mixture. Season with salt, pepper, and nutmeg. Correct seasoning to taste.

8. Divide pastry in half. On lightly floured board, roll out one half, large enough to line a 9- or 10-inch tart pan, leaving a slight over-hang. Brush with egg wash and pour filling into shell. Roll out remaining pastry and place over filling, trimming as necessary. Seal, turning edges under, and brush with egg wash. Decorate as desired with scraps of dough cut into fancy shapes and again brush with egg wash. Poke steam hole in center.

9. Bake 40 minutes, or until pastry is golden brown. Remove from oven and allow to rest 10 to 15 minutes before slicing.

TO PREPARE IN ADVANCE: Through step 9, baking only 20 minutes. Bake 20 minutes longer when ready to serve.

TO FREEZE: Through step 9. I recommend slicing, wrapping, and freezing so that individual proportions or entire torte may be used as needed. Place on baking tray and bake in preheated oven, individual slices 20 minutes, whole torte 45–50 minutes.

This is easy to put together, and the result is a delicious meatless dish.

ZUCCHINI TORTE
Serves 6 to 8

4 ounces Cheddar cheese, cut in
  1-inch pieces
1 medium onion, quartered
1 pound zucchini
2 tablespoons unsalted butter or
  vegetable oil

½ recipe Concassée (page 191)
Salt and freshly ground pepper
6 eggs
1 cup plain yogurt
Cheddar Cheese Pastry (page 253),
  fitted into pan and refrigerated

1. Preheat oven to 400°F.

---

2. Using STEEL BLADE, process cheese with on/off turns until coarsely grated. Reserve. Clean work bowl.

3. Using STEEL BLADE, with on/off turns, chop onion fine. Drain, as necessary. Melt butter in large skillet and, over moderate flame, sauté onion until lightly browned.

4. Using MEDIUM SLICING BLADE, slice zucchini. Add to onion and cook about 5 minutes, stirring frequently. Add *Concassée* and salt and pepper to taste and cook 1 to 2 minutes longer. Correct seasoning to taste. Cool slightly. Clean work bowl.

5. Using STEEL BLADE, beat together eggs and yogurt. Remove to large mixing bowl and add cheese and zucchini mixture, blending with spatula.

6. Remove pastry from refrigerator and fill with egg mixture, distributing the zucchini decoratively throughout and on top of the torte. Bake 10 minutes, lower oven temperature to 350°F., and bake 40 minutes longer, or until torte is golden brown and firm to the touch.

TO PREPARE IN ADVANCE: Through step 4.
TO FREEZE: Do not freeze.

GOUGERE WITH TOMATO-CRAB FILLING

Serves 6 to 8

2 tablespoons parsley leaves
2 one-inch pieces Parmesan or
 Romano cheese, at room
 temperature
1 medium onion, cut in half
2 tablespoons unsalted butter
2 tablespoons all-purpose flour
⅓ cup Fish Stock (page 85)
¾ cup Concassée (page 191)

4 ounces cooked crabmeat, in
 bite-size chunks
4 drops Tabasco
½ teaspoon salt
¼ teaspoon white pepper
½ teaspoon herbs de Provence
1 recipe Gougère (page 48)
1 egg, lightly beaten

1. Using STEEL BLADE, chop parsley fine. Reserve.

2. Using STEEL BLADE, grate cheese fine, dropping pieces through feed tube with motor running. Reserve and clean work bowl.

3. Using THIN SLICING BLADE, slice onion. In large skillet, over moderate flame, melt butter. Sauté onion until soft, about 10 minutes.

4. Stir in flour, add stock, and bring to a boil. Add *Concassée* and cook until mixture thickens slightly, about 3 minutes. Add crabmeat, Tabasco, salt, pepper, and *herbs de Provence*. Cook just until crabmeat heats through. Correct seasoning to taste.

5. Preheat oven to 400°F.

6. Pour one-half *Gougère* recipe into oval 10-inch baking dish. Spread evenly to cover bottom of dish. Fill pastry bag with remaining one-half *Gougère* using ½-inch plain tip, and pipe an edging around outside of *Gougère*, forming a "bowl" or "case."

7. Fill center with crabmeat mixture and sprinkle with reserved grated cheese.

8. Bake 35 to 40 minutes, until pastry is golden brown.

9. Sprinkle finished *Gougère* with chopped parsley and serve immediately.

TO PREPARE IN ADVANCE: Through step 6, refrigerating until needed.
TO FREEZE: Through step 4, defrosting overnight in refrigerator. Through step 6, remove from freezer and continue with recipe.

VARIATIONS: 1. Cooked shrimp or leftover fish may be substituted for crabmeat. Use chopped dill instead of *herbs de Provence*. 2. Recipe may be prepared in individual dishes. Reduce cooking time to 20 minutes.

CRABMEAT PROFITEROLES
Yield: About 30 small puffs

¼ pound unsalted butter, at room temperature, cut in 8 pieces
1 clove garlic
½ cup lump crabmeat
1 tablespoon sour cream

Dash of Tabasco
Dash of Worcestershire sauce
Salt and freshly ground pepper
30 to 32 profiteroles (see **Pâte à Choux**, *page 249)*

1. Using STEEL BLADE, cream butter until smooth. With motor running, drop garlic through feed tube and combine with butter.

2. Add crabmeat, sour cream, and seasonings and process until crabmeat is coarsely shredded. Start with on/off turns, scrape down sides of work bowl, then allow machine to run 4 or 5 seconds. Correct seasoning to taste.

3. Fill pastry bag, fitted with ¼-inch plain tip, and pipe filling into each profiterole.

TO PREPARE IN ADVANCE: Through step 2.
TO FREEZE: Through step 2. Defrost overnight in refrigerator.

VARIATIONS: 1. Cooked shrimp may be used instead of crabmeat.
2. At step 2, substitute 3 tablespoons Pernod and 1 teaspoon tarragon leaves (or 1 teaspoon dried tarragon) for Tabasco and Worcestershire sauce and process until smooth.
3. This fill, at room temperature, can be used as a spread on crackers or thinly sliced rye or pumpernickel bread.

PROFITEROLES WITH PARMESAN CHEESE FILLING

Makes 30 small puffs

1 ounce Parmesan cheese, at room temperature, cut in 1-inch pieces
3 tablespoons unsalted butter
3 tablespoons all-purpose flour
1 cup milk, heated almost to a boil

1 teaspoon salt
1 teaspoon white pepper
Few dashes of nutmeg
30 profiteroles (see Pâte à Choux, page 249)

1. Preheat oven to 350°F.

2. Using STEEL BLADE, with motor running, drop Parmesan cheese through feed tube and grate fine. Reserve.

3. In medium saucepan, melt butter. Stir in flour and cook over moderate flame for 3 minutes, stirring constantly. Do not allow roux to color.

4. Remove pan from heat, add hot milk, and whisk to make a smooth paste. Add salt, pepper, cheese, and nutmeg, stirring until cheese melts.

5. Return to heat and cook 2 minutes, stirring all the while.

6. Fill puffs and refrigerate until needed.

7. Bake 10 to 12 minutes. Serve immediately.

TO PREPARE IN ADVANCE: Through step 6.
TO FREEZE: Through step 5. Defrost overnight in refrigerator.

---

*R*OQUEFORT PROFITEROLES   Makes 30 small puffs

4 ounces Roquefort or blue cheese,
   at room temperature
1½ teaspoons Cognac
12 grinds fresh pepper

1½ tablespoons unsalted butter,
   at room temperature
30 profiteroles (see Pâte à Choux,
   page 249)

1. Using STEEL BLADE, combine all ingredients except puffs in work bowl and process until smooth.

2. Fill prepared puffs and refrigerate until needed.

3. Serve hot or cold. To serve warm, heat in 375°F. oven about 10 minutes.

TO PREPARE IN ADVANCE: Through step 2.
TO FREEZE: Through step 2. To reheat, place on baking tray and bake in preheated oven 10 to 15 minutes.

VARIATIONS: 1. Any cheese that sticks out between top and bottom half of puff may be dusted with chopped walnuts.
2. Recipe can be doubled and used as a spread.

PROFITEROLES WITH SARDINE FILLING

Makes 30 small puffs

1 can (3½ ounces) sardines,
   drained
4 tablespoons (½ stick) unsalted
   butter, at room temperature, cut
   in 6 pieces

2 teaspoons Worcestershire sauce
3 tablespoons heavy cream
Juice of ½ lemon
30 profiteroles (see Pâte à Choux,
   page 249)

1. Preheat oven to 350°F.

2. Using STEEL BLADE, combine all ingredients in work bowl and process until smooth.

3. Fill prepared puffs and refrigerate until needed.

4. Bake 10 to 12 minutes.

TO PREPARE IN ADVANCE: Through step 2 or 4.
TO FREEZE: Through step 3. To reheat, place on baking tray and bake in preheated oven 10 to 15 minutes.

VARIATION: Recipe can be doubled and used as a spread.

This can be used as an appetizer, hors d'oeuvre, or vegetable. Great for picnics.

CABBAGE STRUDEL

Makes 4 three-inch pieces,
6 two-inch pieces

1 pound green cabbage, cored and
   cut in 1-inch pieces
4 tablespoons (½ stick) unsalted
   butter
1 teaspoon salt
10 grinds fresh pepper

1 teaspoon snipped fresh dill
1 tablespoon brown sugar
10 phyllo leaves
2 tablespoons safflower oil
Sour cream and snipped fresh dill
   for garnish

1. Using STEEL BLADE, with on/off turns, coarsely grate cabbage.

2. In medium skillet, over moderate flame, heat 2 tablespoons of the butter. Add cabbage, salt, pepper, dill, and brown sugar and gently sauté until cabbage is tender and just beginning to brown, about 10 minutes. Cool.

3. Preheat oven to 400°F.

4. Heat together oil and remaining 2 tablespoons butter and keep warm as you work with phyllo leaves.

5. Working very quickly, stack leaves on waxed paper or clean towel, brushing every second leaf with warm oil and butter mixture. Spread cooled cabbage along long side of leaves, leaving 2 inches on either end. Fold short sides over cabbage and then start rolling from longer side, using towel to help if necessary, as you would for jelly roll, being careful to enclose all the cabbage.

6. With long spatula, gently transfer cabbage strudel to baking sheet and brush with oil and butter. With serrated knife, lightly score portions. Bake 15 to 20 minutes, then remove from oven, slice through with serrated knife, and continue baking 10 to 15 minutes longer, until golden brown.

7. After removing from oven, let rest 5 minutes.

8. Slice and serve with a dollop of sour cream and snipped dill.

TO PREPARE IN ADVANCE: Through step 6, baking 20 minutes.
TO FREEZE: Through step 6, baking 20 minutes. Remove from freezer 30 minutes before using. To reheat, place on baking tray and bake in preheated oven 10 minutes, slice, and continue to bake 10 minutes longer.

Finns love these with ice-cold milk. You may prefer them with white wine. As part of a meal, serve with cold meats or salads. This is from Jerry Di Vecchio, Southwest editor of Sunset *magazine. She has developed many cookbooks for* Sunset *magazine.*

CARROT PIRRAKKA

Makes 60 small pastries,
24 large pastries

FILLING:

12 to 16 medium carrots, peeled
  and cut to fit feed tube
  lengthwise
6 ounces (1½ sticks) unsalted
  butter
1 large onion, quartered
Salt and freshly ground pepper
1 tablespoon sugar

PASTRY:

1 cup rye or whole-wheat flour
⅓ cup all-purpose flour
6 tablespoons sweet butter, at
  room temperature, cut in 4
  pieces
⅓ cup sour cream
1 egg

1. To prepare filling: Using FINE SHREDDING BLADE, shred enough carrots to make 6 cups, firmly packed.

2. In large skillet, over moderate flame, melt butter. Add carrot and sauté.

3. Using STEEL BLADE, chop onion fine with on/off turns. Drain and add to carrot in skillet. Add salt, pepper, and sugar and cook, uncovered, about 30 minutes, or until carrot is tender and beginning to brown lightly. Correct seasoning to taste and cool.

4. Preheat oven to 350°F.

5. To prepare pastry: Using STEEL BLADE, combine all ingredients and process until ball begins to form. Turn dough out of work bowl and divide into desired number of portions (24 or 60). Keep dough that is not being used covered with plastic wrap.

6. Shape each piece into smooth ball by rolling dough between palms of your hands. Roll out dough on lightly floured board; for large pastries, make a circle about 5 inches in diameter; for appetizer-size, make each circle about 2 inches in diameter.

7. For large pastries, spoon 2 tablespoons carrot filling into center of dough and spread to about ¾ inch of rim; for appetizers, spoon about 2 teaspoons filling into center of dough and spread to about ½ inch of the rim. Fold opposing rims of circle over filling, creating an oval with the filling exposed in the center. With your fingers, pinch edges of dough alongside the filling.

OPEN DOUGH WITH FILLING

FOLDING

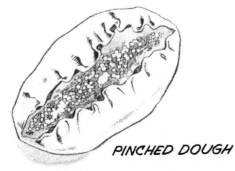

PINCHED DOUGH

8. As pastries are formed, place on ungreased baking sheet, about 1 inch apart. Cover with plastic wrap until sheet is filled.

9. Bake 30 to 35 minutes, until well browned.

10. Serve hot, with Egg Butter (see below).

TO PREPARE IN ADVANCE: Through step 9. Cool on rack and reheat, about 10 minutes.
TO FREEZE: Through step 9, baking 20 minutes. Defrost overnight in refrigerator. To reheat, place on baking tray and bake in pre-heated oven 15 to 20 minutes.

VARIATION: Shredded cabbage may be substituted for carrots, following the same recipe.

EGG BUTTER

Makes about 1½ cups

3 hard-cooked eggs, shelled and
    halved

6 ounces (1½ sticks) unsalted
    butter, at room temperature, cut
    in 6 pieces

1. Using STEEL BLADE, with on/off turns, chop eggs. Add butter and process until well combined.

2. Serve, at room temperature, spooned over hot Pirrakkas (page 70).

TO PREPARE IN ADVANCE: Through step 1. Cover and refrigerate as needed.
TO FREEZE: Do not freeze.

TURKEY TURNOVERS

Yield: About 24
small turnovers

TURNOVER PASTRY:

2 cups all-purpose flour
1 teaspoon salt
⅔ cup shortening or unsalted
    butter, chilled, cut in 1-inch
    pieces
3 to 4 tablespoons ice water

FILLING:

1 pound uncooked turkey meat,
    cut in 1-inch pieces
1 tablespoon unsalted butter
1 small onion, quartered
1 teaspoon salt
Freshly ground pepper
1 medium potato, cooked, peeled,
    and quartered
½ pound spinach, cooked and
    drained
¼ cup ketchup
1 egg, lightly beaten, for egg wash
Mustard Sauce (page 195)

1. To prepare pastry: Using STEEL BLADE, combine flour and salt in work bowl with 2 on/off turns. Add butter and process with on/off turns until mixture resembles coarse meal. With motor running, slowly add water through feed tube just until ball begins to form on blade. Remove dough from work bowl, wrap in waxed paper, and refrigerate. Clean work bowl.

2. To prepare filling: Using STEEL BLADE, with on/off turns, grind turkey meat fine. In large skillet, over moderate flame, melt butter. Brown turkey, stirring occasionally, about 10 minutes.

3. Using STEEL BLADE, chop onion with 3 or 4 on/off turns. Drain, as necessary. Add to skillet and brown well, about 5 minutes. Turn down flame and season with salt and pepper. Clean work bowl.

4. Using PLASTIC BLADE, with 2 or 3 on/off turns, mash potatoes. Add to skillet with spinach and ketchup. Remove from flame.

5. Preheat oven to 375°F.

6. Divide pastry in half, refrigerating unused portion. On lightly floured board, roll out pastry to 12 x 9-inch rectangle. Cut into 3-inch squares and spoon 1 teaspoonful of turkey mixture in center of each square.

7. Brush edges of pastry squares with egg, fold in half, and press down edges with tines of fork to seal. Cut 2 slits on top to allow steam to escape. Place on baking sheet and brush with egg wash.

8. Repeat procedure with remaining pastry and filling.

9. Bake 20 to 25 minutes or until pastry is golden brown.

10. Serve hot or cold, with Mustard Sauce.

TO PREPARE IN ADVANCE: Through step 9.
TO FREEZE: Through step 9, baking 15 minutes. To reheat, place on baking sheet and bake in preheated oven, 20 minutes.

VARIATION: Meat (beef or pork) may be substituted for turkey.

These make wonderful appetizers, a buffet dish, or, when served with Ana's Spanish Salad (page 176) a filling lunch. The pastry should be prepared the day before.

EMPANADAS CHILENAS

Makes 24 three-and-one-half-inch empanadas

PASTRY:

3½ cups all-purpose flour
¼ teaspoon salt
1 egg
¼ teaspoon red wine vinegar
⅔ cup cold water
1 pound (4 sticks) unsalted butter,
   chilled and cut in 16 pieces

FILLING:

½ cup fresh parsley leaves
2 medium onions, quartered
1 red pepper, seeded and cut in
   1-inch pieces
1 green pepper, seeded and cut in
   1-inch pieces
¾ cup vegetable oil
1½ pounds lean meat, cut in
   1-inch pieces
⅓ cup dark, seedless raisins
1 teaspoon salt
½ teaspoon freshly ground pepper
½ teaspoon paprika
3 or 4 dashes cayenne pepper
3 hard-cooked eggs, peeled and cut
   in half
1 egg, lightly beaten, for egg wash

1. To prepare pastry: Using STEEL BLADE, combine 3 cups of the flour, the salt, egg, and vinegar in work bowl and process 2 or 3 seconds. With motor running, pour water through feed tube until ball forms on blade. Turn out on lightly floured board and knead 1 minute. Roll out into 8 x 15-inch rectangle, with 8-inch side in front of you. Fold dough in thirds, wrap in plastic wrap, and refrigerate 30 minutes.

2. Using STEEL BLADE, process remaining ½ cup flour and butter until butter forms a mass on blade. Remove from work bowl, form into 4 x 6-inch block, wrap in plastic wrap, and place in freezer until pastry is ready. (Do not freeze more than 20 minutes.)

3. Remove pastry from refrigerator and, on lightly floured board, roll out into rectangle larger than butter block, about 8 x 10 inches. Remove butter from freezer, place in center of pastry, and fold edges

of pastry over butter to completely enclose. Turn seam side down and gently press with rolling pin to soften butter, being careful that butter does not break through pastry. Roll out to a rectangle approximately 8 x 15 inches, lightly sprinkling with flour as necessary. Starting at 8-inch side nearest you, fold pastry into thirds, rewrap in plastic wrap, and refrigerate 30 minutes. (This is the second turn.) Follow directions for Puff Pastry (page 257) until 6 turns are completed.

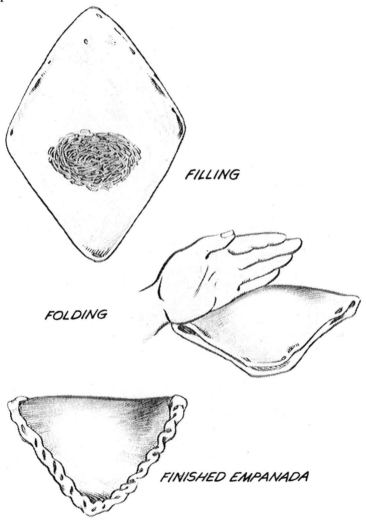

FILLING

FOLDING

FINISHED EMPANADA

4. Remove pastry from refrigerator after last turn and cut into 4 equal pieces. Work with one quarter at a time, refrigerating unused pastry until needed.

5. Preheat oven to 350°F.

6. To prepare filling: Using STEEL BLADE, chop parsley fine. Reserve.

7. Using STEEL BLADE, with on/off turns, coarsely chop onions and green and red peppers separately, one at a time. In large skillet, over high flame, heat oil. Sauté onions and peppers 2 or 3 minutes.

8. Using STEEL BLADE, with on/off turns, coarsely chop meat, 1 cup at a time. Add to skillet and cook, stirring occasionally, 20 minutes. Add raisins and reserved parsley after 15 minutes. Clean work bowl.

9. Season with salt, pepper, paprika, and cayenne pepper. Correct seasoning to taste. Cool.

10. Using STEEL BLADE, with 2 or 3 on/off turns, coarsely chop eggs. Reserve.

11. On lightly floured board, roll each pastry quarter into 10 x 12-inch rectangle and divide into 6 pieces. Roll each piece to about ¼-inch thickness. Spoon 1 tablespoon meat filling at one end, top with 1 teaspoon chopped egg, brush edges with egg wash, and fold dough over to enclose, pressing filling in to secure. Cut away excess pastry and press edges together (see illustration). Place on ungreased baking sheet and refrigerate 30 minutes. Repeat procedure until all dough is rolled, cut, and filled, adding scraps of dough to unused pastry.

12. Brush tops with egg wash, being careful that egg does not drip down onto baking sheet. Bake 25 minutes, until golden brown. (If top is still not brown, place under broiler flame for a few minutes.)

13. Serve hot, with mustard.

TO PREPARE IN ADVANCE: Through step 12.
TO FREEZE: Through step 12. To reheat, place on baking tray and bake in preheated oven for 20 minutes.

FEUILLETE D'ASPERGE

Serves 6

(Asparagus in Puff Pastry)

18 large asparagus, scraped with
   peeler to remove rough spots
1 pound Puff Pastry (page 257)
1 egg, lightly beaten, for egg wash
2 medium shallots
4 or 5 chives, cut in 1-inch pieces
2 tablespoons heavy cream
3 tablespoons water

½ pound (2 sticks) unsalted
   butter, at room temperature, cut
   in 16 pieces
Juice of 1 lemon
Salt and white pepper
Chopped parsley or chervil
   (optional)

1. Preheat oven to 375°F.

2. In large saucepan, bring 4 quarts of heavily salted water to rolling boil. Add asparagus, bring water back to boil, and cook 5 to 7 minutes, until vegetable is cooked but still firm to the bite—al dente. Refresh asparagus rapidly under cold water. Reserve.

3. Divide Puff Pastry in half, refrigerating one half until needed. On lightly floured board, roll pastry out into 18-inch square. With sharp point of a knife, cut into 6 three-inch squares. Place on ungreased baking sheet.

4. Brush pastry with egg wash, being careful that egg does not drip down on tray. Place 3 asparagus spears on each square.

5. Roll out and cut reserved pastry as in step 4 of Puff Pastry recipe. Cover asparagus with second piece of pastry and brush with egg wash.

6. Bake 30 to 35 minutes, until golden brown.

7. While pastry is baking, prepare sauce. Using STEEL BLADE, chop shallots and chives, dropping shallots through feed tube with motor running. In medium saucepan over high flame, combine cream, water, shallots, and chives and bring to a boil. Remove from heat and slowly add butter, whisking all the while, until all the butter has been incorporated. As sauce cools, return to low flame. Do not permit sauce to boil.

8. Add lemon juice and salt and pepper to taste. Strain.

9. To serve, spoon small amount of sauce on individual plate, top with puff pastry, and nap with additional sauce. Sprinkle with chopped parsley or chervil, if desired.

TO PREPARE IN ADVANCE: Through step 6, refrigerating until needed.
TO FREEZE: Do not freeze.

VARIATIONS: 1. Cooked spinach may be substituted for asparagus.
2. Sautéed shrimp may be substituted for vegetable.

LEE'S SPINACH ROULADE

Makes 12 to 14 one-inch slices, or 4 three-and-one-half-inch pieces

1 pound spinach, washed and
  stemmed
½ pound mushrooms
½ medium onion, cut in half
2 tablespoons unsalted butter
1 egg
1 cup ricotta cheese
½ teaspoon dried tarragon or
  leaves from 1 sprig fresh
  tarragon

⅛ teaspoon nutmeg
Pinch of dried basil
1 teaspoon salt
Freshly ground pepper
1 pound Puff Pastry (page 257),
  chilled
1 egg, lightly beaten, for egg wash

1. Preheat oven to 425°F.

2. Using STEEL BLADE, coarsely chop spinach, mushrooms, and onion, separately, with on/off turns. Drain onion as necessary. Reserve separately. Clean work bowl.

3. In large skillet, over moderate flame, melt butter. Sauté onion until translucent, about 10 minutes. Add mushrooms and cook 5 minutes longer. Add spinach and cook just until wilted, 3 to 4 minutes. Remove to large mixing bowl and cool slightly.

4. Using STEEL BLADE, combine egg, ricotta, tarragon, nutmeg, and basil in work bowl and process, with 3 or 4 on/off turns. Transfer to mixing bowl, combine thoroughly with spinach mixture, and season with the salt and pepper to taste.

5. On lightly floured board, roll out Puff Pastry to a 10 x 16-inch rectangle. Brush edges with egg wash. Spoon spinach mixture *along one 16-inch edge* of pastry, leaving 1 inch on either end.

6. Fold ends over filling and roll pastry as for jelly roll, being careful to enclose all filling as you roll.

7. Place roll on baking sheet and brush with egg wash, being careful that egg does not drip onto baking sheet. (Pastry will not rise evenly.) Bake 30 minutes, or until golden brown.

8. Slice with serrated knife into 3½-inch pieces for a first course or 1-inch pieces for hors d'oeuvres, and serve warm. If serving as a first course, serve with *Beurre Blanc* (page 193).

TO PREPARE IN ADVANCE: Through step 7, reheating as necessary.
TO FREEZE: Through step 7. To reheat, place on baking tray and bake 20 minutes in preheated oven. Reduce temperature to 375°F. and bake 10 minutes longer.

Spinach Timbales

Serves 6

2 pounds fresh spinach, washed
1 tablespoon unsalted butter
½ cup heavy cream
Salt and freshly ground pepper

Juice of ½ small lemon
3 eggs
Dash of nutmeg
Concassée (page 191)

1. Preheat oven to 350°F. Thoroughly butter insides of 6 half-cup timbales.

2. Remove any large stems from spinach. In medium saucepan, melt butter and cook spinach, covered, until wilted, about 5 minutes.

3. Using STEEL BLADE, combine heavy cream, salt, pepper, lemon juice, eggs, and nutmeg. Process until eggs are foamy. Add spinach and continue to process 20 seconds longer. (If you want a purée, process to desired texture.) Correct seasoning to taste. Divide spinach mixture and spoon into timbales.

4. Place timbales in bain-marie and bake 30 to 40 minutes, or until knife inserted into center of timbale comes out clean.

5. Unmold and serve as is or topped with *Concassée*.

TO PREPARE IN ADVANCE: Through step 3.
TO FREEZE: Do not freeze.

SOUPS

VEAL STOCK

Makes about 2½ quarts

2 medium carrots
2 medium onions
1 large leek
2 stalks celery
4 pounds veal bones, shanks, and
   trimmings
½ teaspoon dried thyme

2 cloves garlic
1 bay leaf
½ teaspoon whole peppercorns
1 cup white wine
4 quarts warm water
1 teaspoon salt

1. Preheat oven to 450°F.

2. Using WIDE SLICING BLADE, slice carrots, onions, leek, and celery stalks.

3. Arrange meat and vegetables in large roasting pan. Roast in oven, turning to brown evenly, about 35 to 40 minutes. Drain off fat and remove all ingredients to 6- to 8-quart stock pot. Add thyme, garlic, bay leaf, and peppercorns.

4. Set roasting pan on stove and, over moderate flame, deglaze pan with white wine, scraping up bits of meat. Pour into stock pot with 4 quarts water and bring to boil. Skim, then lower flame and let simmer, uncovered, 5 to 6 hours, until reduced to approximately 2½ quarts. Continue skimming while cooking.

5. Strain stock through fine sieve and correct seasoning, adding salt to taste.

6. Cool and refrigerate overnight. Discard hardened fat layer that forms, transfer to covered containers, and store. Use as needed.

TO PREPARE IN ADVANCE: Through step 5.
TO FREEZE: Through step 6. To reheat, place in saucepan and heat through over low flame.

NOTE: Freeze in ice-cube trays or small containers. When cubes harden, unmold and place in plastic bags in freezer so you can use as much or as little as you need.

CHICKEN STOCK

5 pounds chicken bones and
  carcasses
1 stewing chicken (5 pounds),
  quartered
Giblets from chicken
6 medium carrots, cut in 1-inch
  pieces
2 large onions, quartered
1 small turnip, quartered
2 leeks, white part only, cut in
  1-inch pieces

3 stalks celery, cut in 1-inch pieces
1 tablespoon salt
Bouquet garni (10 white
  peppercorns, 2 bay leaves, 1
  large bunch parsley, fresh
  tarragon sprigs, 6 cloves garlic
  [optional], pinch of dried
  thyme, tied in cheesecloth)

1. In 12- to 16-quart stock pot, cover bones, stewing chicken, and giblets with cold water. Over moderate heat, bring to boil and skim.

2. Using STEEL BLADE, with on/off turns, coarsely chop carrots, onions, turnip, leeks, and celery, separately. Add to stock pot with salt and bouquet garni.

3. Lower flame and simmer stock 6 to 8 hours, skimming often. Add boiling water as stock evaporates.

4. Strain stock into large bowls, cool, and refrigerate overnight. Discard hardened fat layer that forms, transfer to covered containers, and store.

5. Use as needed.

TO PREPARE IN ADVANCE: Through step 4.
TO FREEZE: Through step 4. To reheat, place in saucepan and heat through over low flame.

Browning the meat and bones in the oven gives this stock its brown color and rich flavor. Recipe can easily be doubled or tripled if desired.

*B*EEF STOCK
(Brown Stock)

Makes about 2½ quarts

3 medium carrots, cut in 1-inch
   pieces
1 large onion, quartered
3 pounds beef shin, trimmings,
   and bones, cracked
3 pounds veal bones, shank and/or
   knuckle, cracked
1 cup boiling water

2 green onions, cut in 1-inch
   pieces
2 stalks celery, cut in 1-inch pieces
2 leeks, cut in 1-inch pieces
Bouquet garni, (10 peppercorns, 1
   large bay leaf, 1 small bunch of
   parsley, pinch of dried thyme,
   tied in cheesecloth)

1. Preheat oven to 425°F.

2. Using STEEL BLADE, with on/off turns, coarsely chop carrots and onions, separately.

3. In shallow roasting pan, roast meat, bones, carrots, and onion, uncovered, 45 minutes to 1 hour, turning meat to brown on all sides. Drain fat and transfer all ingredients to 8- to 10-quart stock pot.

4. Pour 1 cup boiling water into roasting pan and stir to scrape up all juices. Pour into stock pot. Completely cover meat and bones with cold water and bring to rolling boil over moderate flame. Skim, bring back to boil, and skim again.

5. Using STEEL BLADE, with on/off turns, coarsely chop green onions, celery, and leeks, separately. Add to stock pot with bouquet garni. Lower flame and simmer stock 5 to 6 hours, skimming as necessary. As water evaporates below meat level, replace with boiling water.

6. Strain stock into bowls, cool, and refrigerate overnight. Discard hardened fat layer that forms. Return to stock pot and reduce to 2½ quarts. Transfer to covered containers, and store. Use as needed.

TO PREPARE IN ADVANCE: Through step 6.
TO FREEZE: Through step 6. To reheat, place in saucepan and heat through over low flame.

NOTE: Freeze in ice-cube trays and then place cubes in plastic bags for freezer storage. This is convenient for using small as well as large amounts.

For additional flavor, use this for poaching fish.

*F*ISH STOCK

Makes 1 to 1½ quarts

1 medium onion, cut in half	¼ teaspoon salt
1 medium carrot	3 to 4 white peppercorns
2 pounds fish bones and heads*	2 cloves garlic (optional)
¼ pound mushroom stems	1 cup dry white wine
Pinch of dried thyme	6 cups water

1. Using MEDIUM SLICING BLADE, slice onion and carrot.

2. In 8- to 10-quart saucepan, over high flame, combine all ingredients and bring to boil. Skim, lower flame, and simmer 20 to 25 minutes.

3. Strain through fine sieve. Correct seasoning to taste.

4. Use as needed.

TO PREPARE IN ADVANCE: Through step 3. If refrigerated, must be reboiled every 2 days.
TO FREEZE: Through step 3. To reheat, place in saucepan and heat through over low flame.

*Use any fish bones for stock except salmon.

The trick in breaking apart a live lobster is to hold it very firmly. This is a rich soup. The addition of rice makes it a hearty and filling dish.

LOBSTER SOUP

3 live lobsters (1 to 1½ pounds each)
¼ cup olive oil
2 medium carrots, cut in 1-inch pieces
3 stalks celery, cut in 1-inch pieces
5 cloves garlic
5 shallots
3 medium tomatoes, quartered
3 sprigs fresh tarragon

3 tablespoons Cognac, warmed
2 cups white wine
3 or 4 tablespoons tomato paste
Salt and freshly ground pepper
Cayenne pepper
Pinch of dried thyme
1 bay leaf
Fish Stock (page 85), bouillon, or water to cover
1 cup heavy cream

1. Holding lobsters firmly, break off tails, then claws. Break body.

2. *Heat* large, wide saucepan over moderate flame and add oil. Sauté lobster pieces until red, turning on all sides.

3. Using STEEL BLADE, with on/off turns, coarsely chop carrots and celery, separately. Add to saucepan.

4. Using STEEL BLADE, with on/off turns, coarsely chop garlic, shallots, tomatoes, and tarragon. Add to saucepan and continue to sauté 5 minutes longer.

5. Pour Cognac into pan and ignite. Immediately deglaze with white wine.

6. Add tomato paste and season with salt, pepper, and cayenne. Add thyme and bay leaf. Cover with Fish Stock, bring to a boil, and cook 15 minutes.

7. In separate pan, heat cream and reduce by half.

8. Remove lobster pieces from pan. Break open tails and claws and extract meat. Slice into bite-size pieces and reserve. Discard body and, using STEEL BLADE, grind legs, one at a time. Return to pan and cook 5 minutes longer. Strain, pressing out as much soup as possible.

9. Stir in cream, add reserved lobster meat, and heat through.

10. To serve, ladle soup into heated bowls.

TO PREPARE IN ADVANCE: Through step 8.
TO FREEZE: Through step 8. To reheat, place in saucepan and heat through over low flame, then continue with recipe.

VARIATION: For a thicker soup, add 1 cup cooked rice or dissolve 1 or 2 slices French bread or brioche in the soup.

POTATO AND LEEK SOUP

Serves 6 to 8

1 pound leeks, white parts only,
   trimmed and washed, cut in
   1-inch pieces
2 tablespoons unsalted butter
1 pound potatoes, peeled, cut to
   fit feed tube

8 cups boiling water
1 tablespoon salt
½ teaspoon white pepper
1 cup heavy cream
Chopped chives (optional)

1. Using STEEL BLADE, with on/off turns, coarsely chop leeks.

2. In 4- to 6-quart saucepan, over moderate flame, melt butter. Add leeks and sauté about 5 minutes.

3. Using MEDIUM SLICING BLADE, slice potatoes. Add to saucepan with water, salt, and pepper. Partially cover pan and cook 40 to 50 minutes, until vegetables are tender. Clean work bowl.

4. Using STEEL BLADE, purée soup in batches, scraping down sides of work bowl as necessary. (If a finer purée is desired, strain through fine sieve.) Return to saucepan, stir in cream, and heat through over moderate flame.

5. To serve, ladle soup into heated bowls and sprinkle with chives.

TO PREPARE IN ADVANCE: Through step 4.
TO FREEZE: Through step 4. To reheat, place in saucepan and heat through over low flame.

VARIATIONS: 1. Substitute 4 medium sliced carrots for all but 1 potato and proceed as above.

2. Vichyssoise: Use Chicken Stock (page 83) instead of water and proceed as above through puréeing of soup. Cool and refrigerate to chill. Serve chilled in chilled bowls, sprinkled with chopped chives and a dollop of sour cream.

For a hastily put-together first course that has a gourmet look and taste, try this.

CONSOMME JULIENNE

Serves 6

2 medium carrots, peeled, cut to fit width of pusher
2 celery stalks, strings removed, cut to fit width of pusher
1 leek, white part only, cut to fit width of pusher

½ pound small mushrooms
10 cups cold Chicken Stock (page 83)
1 pound Puff Pastry (page 257)
1 or 2 eggs, lightly beaten, for egg wash

1. Have ready 6 ovenproof onion-soup bowls.

2. Using JULIENNE or MEDIUM SHREDDING BLADE, julienne carrots, celery, leek, and mushrooms.

3. In large skillet, over moderate flame, melt butter. Sauté vegetables until tender but still crisp, 3 to 4 minutes. Divide among the soup bowls.

4. Fill bowls two-thirds up sides with stock.

5. Roll out Puff Pastry ⅛ inch thick. Cut out 6 pieces, large enough to cover bowl one-third down outer sides. Brush sides of bowls with egg wash and cover with pastry, careful that there are no tears in pastry. Refrigerate until needed.

6. Preheat oven to 450°F.

7. Brush pastry with egg wash and place bowls on baking sheet with sides for easier handling. Bake 25 minutes, or until pastry is golden brown and has puffed up into round domes.

8. Serve immediately.

TO PREPARE IN ADVANCE: Through step 5.
TO FREEZE: Do not freeze.

VARIATION: Add shredded cooked chicken to vegetables in bowls.

This and the next four cream soup recipes can be used as the basis for any number of variations, depending on the ingredients you have in the house and your own preferences.

ASPARAGUS SOUP

Serves 6 to 8

1½ pounds fresh asparagus, scraped with peeler to remove rough spots
2 teaspoons salt
1 medium onion, cut in half
9 tablespoons unsalted butter

1 medium potato, peeled and cut in half
6 cups boiling water
1 cup heavy cream
Sour cream (optional)

1. Cut asparagus into 1-inch pieces. Reserve tips.

2. In medium saucepan, bring 4 cups water to rolling boil. Add asparagus tips and 1 teaspoon salt. Cook until tender, about 3 minutes. Drain asparagus, then refresh under cold running water and reserve for garnish.

3. Using MEDIUM SLICING BLADE, slice onion. In 4-quart saucepan, over moderate flame, melt 4 tablespoons of the butter. Sauté onion until translucent, about 5 minutes. Add remaining 1 teaspoon salt.

4. Using MEDIUM SLICING BLADE, slice potato. Add to onion with boiling water and asparagus stalks. Cook, uncovered, over high heat until vegetables are tender, about 30 minutes.

5. Add heavy cream, lower flame, and cook 5 minutes longer.

6. Using STEEL BLADE, purée soup, in batches. (If you prefer finer purée, strain through fine sieve.) Return to pan and add 4 tablespoons butter. Heat through. (If too thick, thin with milk.)

7. Heat asparagus tips in remaining 1 tablespoon butter.

8. To serve, ladle soup into heated bowls. Top with dollop of sour cream and asparagus tips.

TO PREPARE IN ADVANCE: Through step 6.
TO FREEZE: Through step 6. To reheat, place in saucepan and heat through over low flame, then continue with recipe.

BROCCOLI SOUP

Serves 8

4 tablespoons (½ stick) unsalted
  butter
2 leeks, white part only, washed
  and cut in 1-inch pieces
1 large bunch broccoli, cut in
  small flowerettes, stems removed
1 quart Chicken Stock (page 83) or
  water

2 potatoes, peeled and cut in
  1½-inch pieces
1 teaspoon salt
¼ teaspoon white pepper
1 cup heavy cream
1 teaspoon sour cream or Crème
  Fraîche (page 205)

1. In 4-quart saucepan, melt 2 tablespoons of the butter. Add leeks and broccoli and sauté about 10 minutes, stirring occasionally. Add stock, bring to a boil, and add potatoes. Over moderate flame, continue to boil until all vegetables are cooked, about 20 minutes.

2. Strain soup and remove all vegetables to work bowl fitted with STEEL BLADE. Process until finely puréed, scraping down sides of work bowl as necessary. Return soup and vegetables to saucepan. Add salt and pepper.

3. Stir in heavy cream, sour cream, and remaining 2 tablespoons butter. Over moderate flame, heat through.

4. Soup may be served hot or cold. If served cold, correct seasoning to taste.

TO PREPARE IN ADVANCE: Through step 3. Reheat when ready to serve.
TO FREEZE: Through step 2. To reheat, place in saucepan and heat through over low flame, then continue with recipe.

VARIATION: One large bunch watercress can be substituted for broccoli.

NOTE: Garnish is optional. Try sautéed croutons or chopped parsley or dollops of sour cream.

This is equally delicious cold or hot.

CREAM OF CELERY SOUP

¼ cup fresh parsley leaves
2 pounds celery, strings removed,
  cut in 4-inch lengths
1 bunch green onions, cut in
  4-inch lengths
3 tablespoons unsalted butter

1 clove garlic
Salt and freshly ground pepper
3 tablespoons all-purpose flour
4 cups Chicken Stock (page 83)
Juice of ½ small lemon
½ cup heavy cream

1. Using STEEL BLADE, chop parsley fine. Reserve.

2. Using MEDIUM SHREDDING BLADE, chop celery and green onions.

3. Melt butter in medium saucepan and add celery, onions, garlic, and salt and pepper to taste. Cover pan and cook over low flame until mixture is very soft, about 10 minutes.

4. Remove from heat, stir in flour and stock, and return to low flame. Bring soup to boil and simmer 10 minutes. Add lemon juice.

5. Using STEEL BLADE, purée soup in batches, being careful that soup does not overflow machine (about 1½ cups at a time). Purée until smooth. (Allow machine to run 60 seconds, check texture, and purée longer if necessary.)

6. Return purée to saucepan and add cream. Heat through but do not boil. Sprinkle with reserved parsley and serve.

TO PREPARE IN ADVANCE: Through step 5.
TO FREEZE: Through step 5. To reheat, place in saucepan and heat through over low flame, then continue with recipe.

VARIATION: Zucchini may be substituted for celery with excellent results.

If I were to choose my favorite soup, this would be it.

CREAM OF MUSHROOM SOUP

¼ cup fresh parsley leaves	½ teaspoon salt
1 large shallot	Freshly ground pepper
1 tablespoon unsalted butter	1½ cups Chicken Stock (page 83)
1 pound mushrooms	1½ cups heavy cream
Juice of 1 medium lemon	1 teaspoon cornstarch
Pinch of dried thyme	2 tablespoons water
1 bay leaf	

1. Using STEEL BLADE, chop parsley fine. Reserve.

2. Using STEEL BLADE, with motor running, drop shallot through feed tube and coarsely chop. Heat heavy 4-quart saucepan, then melt butter and lightly sauté shallot.

3. Using STEEL BLADE, with on/off turns, coarsely chop mushrooms, 1 cup at a time. Sprinkle mushrooms with lemon juice as chopped. Add to saucepan with thyme, bay leaf, salt, and pepper. Sauté until liquid evaporates, about 10 minutes.

4. Add chicken stock and cream and simmer 20 minutes.

5. Dissolve cornstarch in 2 tablespoons water and add to soup. Simmer 10 minutes longer. Correct seasoning to taste. Remove bay leaf.

6. To serve, ladle soup into heated bowls and sprinkle with reserved chopped parsley.

TO PREPARE IN ADVANCE: Through step 5, keeping warm in a bain-marie.
TO FREEZE: Through step 5. To reheat, place in saucepan and heat through over low flame.

The Coach House is one of the few 3-star restaurants in New York City and has been singled out for praise by magazines and newspapers throughout the world. It is a reflection of its dedicated owner, Leon Lianides. Here is Mr. Lianides' recipe for black bean soup, a Coach House specialty.

BLACK BEAN SOUP

Serves 8

2 cups dried black beans
2 cloves garlic
2 large onions, quartered
3 leeks, white part only, cut in
    1-inch pieces
1 celery stalk, strings removed, cut
    in 1-inch pieces
4 tablespoons (½ stick) unsalted
    butter
2 bay leaves
2 or 3 cloves

Shank of ham, split in half
3 pounds beef bones
Freshly ground pepper
2 tablespoons all-purpose flour
4 or 5 quarts water
½ cup fresh parsley leaves
3 hard-cooked eggs, peeled and cut
    in half
1 or 2 small lemons
½ cup Madeira

1. Soak beans in water to cover overnight.

2. Using STEEL BLADE, with on/off turns, coarsely chop garlic, onions, leeks, and celery. In 8-quart saucepan, over moderate flame, melt butter and sauté vegetables until slightly wilted, about 3 minutes. Clean work bowl.

3. Add bay leaves, cloves, ham, and beef bones and cook 3 to 4 minutes. Grind fresh pepper into pan, sprinkle with flour, and stir to blend. Cook 2 or 3 minutes, then add water and bring to boil. Lower flame and simmer, partially covered, 6 hours, skimming as necessary.

4. Drain beans, add to saucepan, and continue to simmer 2 hours longer, stirring occasionally to prevent sticking. Add boiling water if soup thickens too much. Correct seasoning to taste.

5. Using STEEL BLADE, chop parsley fine. Reserve.

6. Using STEEL BLADE, with on/off turns, chop eggs fine. Reserve.

7. Using THIN SLICING BLADE, with firm pressure, slice lemon. Reserve. Clean work bowl.

8. Discard all bones from soup and, using STEEL BLADE, purée soup, in batches. Return to saucepan and, over moderate flame, bring to boil. Stir in Madeira and heat through.

9. Serve in heated bowls garnished with reserved parsley, chopped egg, and lemon slices.

TO PREPARE IN ADVANCE: Through step 8.
TO FREEZE: Through step 8. To reheat, place in saucepan and heat through over low flame.

This is served in Ratner's, New York, as a refreshing cold soup. My family likes it hot as well.

BORSCHT

Serves 8

½ cucumber, peeled, seeded, and
   cut in 1-inch pieces
2 bunches beets, peeled
3 quarts water
1½ to 2 tablespoons salt

Juice of 1 medium lemon
½ to ¾ cup sugar
3 eggs
2 cups sour cream, plus additional
   for garnish

1. Using STEEL BLADE, with on/off turns, chop cucumber coarsely. Reserve.

2. Using MEDIUM SHREDDING BLADE, grate beets. Clean work bowl.

3. In large saucepan, combine beets, water, 1½ tablespoons salt, lemon juice, and ½ cup sugar. Bring to boil, then lower flame and simmer 20 minutes, or until beets are tender. Correct seasoning to taste, adding remaining salt and sugar as needed.

4. Using PLASTIC BLADE, beat together eggs and sour cream until well blended. Remove to large mixing bowl.

5. Gradually whisk in 2 cups hot borscht. Return mixture to saucepan and simmer until hot. Do not boil.

6. Serve hot or cold with dollop of sour cream. Sprinkle reserved chopped cucumber over top.

TO PREPARE IN ADVANCE: Through step 5.
TO FREEZE: Do not freeze.

On a cold day, nothing tastes better than a bowl of hearty onion soup. I always have a batch in my freezer.

ONION SOUP

Serves 6

3 pounds medium onions, cut in
    half
3 tablespoons unsalted butter
3 tablespoons vegetable oil
4 cups Chicken Stock (page 83)
4 cups Beef Stock (page 84)

½ cup white wine
2 tablespoons Madeira
8 ounces Gruyère cheese, chilled
8 thick slices French bread, toasted
Freshly-ground pepper

1. Have ready 6 ovenproof onion-soup bowls.

2. Using FINE SLICING BLADE, slice onions. Clean work bowl.

3. Heat butter and oil in large skillet. Add onions and cook, over low flame, until golden brown, stirring occasionally. (This may take 1 hour or longer.)

4. Pour chicken and beef stock into 4-quart saucepan. Add onions.

5. Deglaze skillet with white wine and Madeira, scraping up any particles remaining in pan. Add to stock and cook over moderate flame for 45 minutes.

6. Preheat oven to 400°F.

7. Using MEDIUM SHREDDING BLADE, grate cheese.

8. To serve, put 1 slice French bread into each ovenproof soup bowl and sprinkle with small amount of cheese. Fill each bowl with soup and sprinkle with remaining cheese.

9. Bake 10 to 15 minutes, or until soup is piping hot and cheese has browned. Serve immediately.

TO PREPARE IN ADVANCE: Through step 7.
TO FREEZE: Through step 5. To reheat, place in saucepan and heat through over low flame, then continue with recipe.

This soup may be served hot or cold.

FRESH TOMATO SOUP WITH BASIL

Serves 6

12 leaves fresh basil
1 medium carrot, peeled, cut in
  1-inch pieces
½ medium onion, halved
3 cloves garlic
2 tablespoons olive oil
6 ripe tomatoes, peeled, seeded,
  and quartered

1 bay leaf
1½ tablespoons tomato paste
1 teaspoon salt
¼ teaspoon white pepper
7 cups Chicken Stock (page 83) or
  water (or half of each)

1. Using STEEL BLADE, mince basil leaves. Reserve.

2. Using STEEL BLADE, chop carrot with on/off turns until coarsely chopped. Reserve.

3. Coarsely chop onion and garlic with on/off turns, dropping garlic through feed tube while motor is running.

4. In 4-quart saucepan, heat olive oil. Add chopped vegetables and cook, over moderate flame, 5 minutes.

5. Using STEEL BLADE, coarsely chop tomatoes with on/off turns. Add to soup pot with bay leaf, tomato paste, salt, pepper, and Chicken Stock. Simmer over moderate flame, partially covered, for 20 minutes. Remove bay leaf. Clean work bowl.

6. Using STEEL BLADE, purée soup, in batches. (If clear soup is desired, strain through fine mesh strainer.) Correct seasoning to taste.

7. If soup is to be served cold, refrigerate and taste before serving. When cold, soup may require additional seasoning. To serve, ladle into bowls and top with minced basil leaves.

TO PREPARE IN ADVANCE: Through step 6.
TO FREEZE: Through step 6. To reheat, place in saucepan and heat through over low flame. If serving cold, defrost in refrigerator and continue with recipe.

A marvelous luncheon dish. Michel Maupuy, associate chef at Ma Maison, first showed me how to prepare this.

COLD AVOCADO SOUP WITH CAVIAR Serves 6

2 cups Chicken Stock (page 83)
¼ small onion, halved
2 or 3 large, very ripe avocados,
   peeled, pitted, and cut in 1-inch
   pieces

Juice of 1 lemon
2 cups heavy cream
Salt and freshly ground pepper
Caviar for garnish (optional)

1. In medium saucepan, bring chicken stock to simmer. Remove from flame.

2. Using STEEL BLADE, with on/off turns, chop onion fine. Add to Chicken Stock.

3. Using STEEL BLADE, purée avocados, adding lemon juice to prevent darkening. Stir into Chicken Stock. Add heavy cream and salt and pepper. Correct seasoning to taste. Cool, then refrigerate.

4. To serve, ladle soup into individual chilled bowls and top with a sprinkling of caviar.

TO PREPARE IN ADVANCE: Through step 4.
TO FREEZE: Do not freeze.

VARIATION: Soup may be topped with a dollop of sour cream and a sprinkling of red caviar.

This has a very tart taste and is extremely refreshing on a warm day.

CUCUMBER-YOGURT SOUP Serves 6 to 8

½ pound spinach, washed and
   stemmed
2 large cucumbers, peeled
2 cups plain yogurt

1½ cups Chicken Stock (page 83)
Salt and freshly ground pepper
Sour cream for garnish (optional)

1. With water that clings to spinach leaves after washing, cook in covered medium saucepan just until wilted, about 5 minutes.

2. Slice cucumbers lengthwise and seed. Cut into 1-inch pieces. Using STEEL BLADE, combine spinach and cucumbers and process until finely puréed, scraping down sides of work bowl as necessary. Remove to large mixing bowl.

3. Stir in yogurt, Chicken Stock, and salt and pepper to taste. Refrigerate 2 to 3 hours, until chilled.

4. To serve, ladle soup into chilled bowls and top with a dollop of sour cream.

TO PREPARE IN ADVANCE: Through step 3.
TO FREEZE: Do not freeze.

Simple to prepare, this may become a summer favorite.

GAZPACHO

Serves 8 to 10

1 medium green pepper, cored, seeded, and cut in 1-inch pieces
3 large tomatoes, peeled, seeded, and quartered
1 medium cucumber, peeled, seeded, and cut in 1-inch pieces
1 medium onion, quartered
1 large can (46 ounces) tomato juice

2 tablespoons olive oil
3 tablespoons safflower oil
⅓ cup red wine vinegar
½ cup vodka (optional)
2 dashes Tabasco
1 to 1½ teaspoons salt
Freshly ground pepper
Croutons* (optional)

1. Using STEEL BLADE, combine half each of the green pepper, tomatoes, cucumber, and onion in work bowl. Process until very finely chopped. Add ½ cup tomato juice and continue processing until vegetables are puréed. Pour into large mixing bowl. Clean work bowl.

2. Add to mixing bowl remaining tomato juice, olive oil, safflower oil, vinegar, vodka, Tabasco, and 1 teaspoon salt. Cover and refrigerate overnight. When thoroughly chilled, correct seasoning to taste, adding more salt if needed. Soup thickens as it stands.

3. Using STEEL BLADE, chop coarsely reserved green pepper, tomatoes, cucumber, and onion separately, with on/off turns. Reserve, refrigerated, in small mixing bowl.

4. To serve, ladle soup into chilled individual bowls. Sprinkle with chopped vegetables and croutons.

TO PREPARE IN ADVANCE: Through step 3.
TO FREEZE: Do not freeze.

*To make croutons, remove crusts from bread and cut into tiny squares. Sauté in butter until golden brown.

4.

MAIN
DISHES

STEAMED PIKE WITH CHIVE BUTTER

CHIVE BUTTER:

Leaves from 1 bunch fresh
  tarragon
2 bunches chives, cut in 1-inch
  pieces
6 shallots
1 cup white wine
¼ cup heavy cream
1 pound (4 sticks) unsalted butter,
  cut in small pieces
Juice of 1 medium lemon
Salt and freshly ground pepper

FISH:

1 pound pike fillets, cut in 6
  serving portions
Salt and freshly ground pepper
1 teaspoon dried thyme
2 medium carrots, peeled
2 medium zucchini, ends removed
3 stalks celery, strings removed
1 tablespoon unsalted butter
½ cup white wine

1. To prepare chive butter: Using STEEL BLADE, coarsely chop tarragon, chives, and shallots, dropping shallots through feed tube with motor running. Clean work bowl.

2. In medium saucepan, over high flame, combine shallots, tarragon, chives, and white wine and reduce until approximately one-quarter of liquid remains.

3. Add cream and continue to reduce until mixture thickens. Remove from heat and slowly whisk in butter, bit by bit. The trick is to keep the sauce at the same temperature; when sauce begins to cool, return to low heat and repeat procedure until all butter is incorporated.

4. Add lemon juice and season with salt and pepper to taste. Strain and reserve herbs. Keep sauce warm in bain-marie.

5. Season fish with salt, pepper, and thyme. Reserve.

6. Using JULIENNE BLADE, julienne carrots, zucchini, and celery. In medium skillet, over moderate flame, melt butter and cook vegetables just until wilted, 2 or 3 minutes. Reserve.

7. Fill bottom of steamer with water and ½ cup white wine. Add herbs that have been strained from chive butter and bring to boil. Place fish on rack and steam about 5 minutes. Arrange vegetables on fish and steam 5 minutes longer.

8. Place fish on heated plates, nap with chive butter, and serve.

TO PREPARE IN ADVANCE: Through step 6.
TO FREEZE: Do not freeze.

VARIATION: Any firm-fleshed fish fillets may be used, such as sea bass or red snapper.

NOTE: Sauce can be used with any poached or steamed fish.

Whitefish, Italian Style
Serves 6

TOMATO SAUCE:

½ *medium onion, cut in half*
5⅓ *tablespoons unsalted butter*
4 *large tomatoes, peeled, seeded, and quartered*
2 *tablespoons tomato paste*

FISH:

2½ *pounds whitefish fillets*
Salt and freshly ground pepper
¼ *cup fresh parsley leaves*
2 *shallots*
¼ *pound medium mushrooms*
1 *tablespoon unsalted butter*
Juice of ½ medium lemon
½ *cup dry white wine*

1. Make sauce first. Using STEEL BLADE, with on/off turns, chop onion fine.

2. In medium skillet, over moderate flame, melt butter. Lightly sauté onions, 2 to 3 minutes.

3. Using STEEL BLADE, with on/off turns, chop tomatoes fine. Add to skillet with tomato paste and cook 3 to 5 minutes. Clean bowl.

4. Season fish with salt and pepper.

5. Using STEEL BLADE, chop parsley fine. Reserve.

6. Using STEEL BLADE, chop shallots fine, dropping them through feed tube. Reserve.

7. Using MEDIUM SLICING BLADE, slice mushrooms.

8. In large skillet, over moderate flame, melt butter. Arrange shallots and fish in skillet and top with mushrooms, lemon juice, and wine. Cover and cook about 10 minutes. Transfer fish and mushrooms to warm platter.

9. Over high heat, reduce liquid in skillet by half, 1 or 2 minutes. Add tomato sauce and cook 2 to 3 minutes longer. Pour over fish and sprinkle with reserved parsley. Serve immediately.

TO PREPARE IN ADVANCE: Through step 7.
TO FREEZE: Do not freeze.

This is an elegant but inexpensive main dish from my friend Alice Herson Elliot.

SCANDINAVIAN FISH PUDDING

Serves 8

½ slice white bread, crusts
   removed, cut in half
1 pound cod or haddock, cut in
   1-inch pieces
¼ pound (1 stick) unsalted butter,
   at room temperature, cut in 8
   pieces
4 eggs, separated

3 tablespoons all-purpose flour
1 cup milk
1 teaspoon salt
⅛ teaspoon white pepper
2 dashes cayenne pepper
1 cup heavy cream, whipped
Lemon slices for garnish

1. Preheat oven to 350°F.

2. Using STEEL BLADE, process bread to make fine crumbs. Butter a 2-quart mold and dust with crumbs, inverting dish to remove any excess. Clean bowl.

3. Using STEEL BLADE, purée fish. Add butter, egg yolks, flour, milk, salt, and white and cayenne peppers and process until smooth. Transfer to large mixing bowl and refrigerate.

4. With rotary beater or whip, beat egg whites until stiff but not dry. Fold into fish purée. Fold in whipped cream. To test for seasoning, poach a small amount of purée in salted simmering water. Correct seasoning to taste.

5. Pour mixture into prepared mold and cover with buttered waxed paper, buttered side down. (Mixture should come about three-quarters up sides of mold.)

6. Set mold in bain-marie and bake 1 hour, or until knife inserted in center of pudding is hot to touch.

7. Unmold on serving plate and serve with slices of lemon (see note below).

TO PREPARE IN ADVANCE: Through step 5, refrigerating and removing 30 minutes before baking.
TO FREEZE: Do not freeze.

NOTE: You can also serve this with Béchamel Sauce (page 193) to which chunks of cooked lobster, crabmeat, or shrimp have been added.

A lovely luncheon entrée or first course for dinner.

SALMON MOUSSE WITH DILL SAUCE
Serves 6 to 8

1 cup fresh dill leaves
1 cup Classic Mayonnaise (page 182)
2 cups plain yogurt
1 envelope unflavored gelatin
½ cup boiling water
¼ medium onion, cut in half

1 tablespoon lemon juice
1 pound boned, poached salmon,*
    cut in 1-inch pieces
Paprika
Tabasco
Freshly ground pepper

1. To prepare dill sauce: Using STEEL BLADE, chop dill fine. Remove one-third of dill and reserve. Add ½ cup mayonnaise and 1 cup of the yogurt to remaining dill in work bowl. Process until combined, scraping down sides of work bowl as necessary. Remove to serving bowl, cover with plastic wrap, and refrigerate until needed. Clean work bowl.

2. To prepare mousse: Using STEEL BLADE, return reserved dill to work bowl. Add gelatin, boiling water, onion, and lemon juice. Process 60 seconds to dissolve gelatin. Add remaining ½ cup mayonnaise, 1 cup yogurt, and the salmon. Process until smooth. Season with a few dashes paprika, Tabasco, and grinds of pepper. Correct seasoning to taste.

3. Rinse a 4-cup mold in cold water. Pour out water but do not dry. Pour salmon mixture into mold and refrigerate until firm, 3 to 4 hours.

4. To unmold mousse, dip mold in warm water for a few seconds, then slide knife around mousse to loosen and unmold onto serving platter. Serve with dill sauce.

TO PREPARE IN ADVANCE: Through step 3.
TO FREEZE: Do not freeze.

*One 1-pound can of salmon, well drained, may be substituted.

Growing up in and around the Ratner's kitchen, I have always loved gefüllte fish. Since my association with Ma Maison restaurant, I adapted the recipe, French style, at the urging of Chef Wolfgang Puck.

GEFULLTE FISH MA MAISON

Serves 4 to 6

1 tablespoon unsalted butter
4 green onions, white part only, cut in 1-inch pieces
2 slices, ¾ inch each, Challah (page 221), crusts removed
1 cup heavy cream
1½ pounds whitefish, cut in 1-inch pieces
1 egg plus 1 egg yolk
1 teaspoon salt
Freshly ground pepper (white, if possible)

Cayenne pepper
6 large cabbage leaves
1 cup white wine
Fish Stock (page 85) to cover
1 small carrot, peeled and cut to fit width of pusher
1 leek, white part only, cut to fit width of pusher
2 celery stalks, strings removed, cut to fit width of pusher

1. In small skillet, over moderate flame, melt butter. Lightly sauté green onions, about 2 minutes. Reserve.

2. Break Challah into pieces and soak in heavy cream.

3. Using STEEL BLADE, grind fish. Add sautéed green onions and process until chopped fine.

4. Add egg, egg yolk, salt, pepper, and cayenne and process until smooth. Correct seasoning (fish should be peppery). Refrigerate.

5. In small saucepan, blanch each cabbage leaf for about 1 minute. Drain on paper towels and cut away hard core.

6. Using moistened hands, divide and shape fish into 6 ovals. Wrap 1 cabbage leaf securely around each oval and arrange, seam side down, in large skillet. Pour in wine and enough hot, strained Fish Stock to cover. Poach fish, over moderate heat, 30 minutes.

7. Using JULIENNE BLADE or MEDIUM SHREDDING BLADE, julienne carrot, leek, and celery. Add to fish 15 minutes before it has cooked.

8. Using slotted spoon, transfer fish to platter and top with drained vegetables. Serve hot or cold.

TO PREPARE IN ADVANCE: Through step 8.
TO FREEZE: Do not freeze.

A gourmet dish made particularly easy by the processor.

PAUPIETTES DE SAUMON
Serves 6 to 8

½ *pound boned pike, cut in 1-inch*
  pieces
2 *pounds salmon fillet*
1 *whole egg plus 1 egg yolk*
2 *cups heavy cream, chilled*
Salt and freshly ground pepper

1 *cup dry white wine*
1 *jigger Pernod*
6 *tablespoons unsalted butter, at*
  room temperature, cut in 6
  pieces
Chopped fresh parsley (optional)

1. To prepare mousse: Chill work bowl and steel blade. Using STEEL BLADE, purée pike, 4 ounces of the salmon, egg, and egg yolk. Start with on/off turns, then allow machine to run until purée is smooth, scraping down sides of work bowl as necessary. With motor running, pour 1 cup heavy cream through feed tube and process just until cream is incorporated. Do not overbeat. Season with salt and pepper. Test for seasoning by cooking small amount in salted simmering water, about 5 minutes. Correct seasoning to taste. Refrigerate until needed.

2. Preheat oven to 375°F.

3. To prepare paupiettes: Slice remaining salmon into thin scallops and season with salt and pepper. Divide mousse and place small amount on top of each salmon scallop. Roll salmon over mousse to make paupiettes.

4. Arrange paupiettes in buttered casserole, spacing them so that they do not touch. Pour white wine over salmon and bring to boil on top of stove. Remove to oven and bake 5 to 8 minutes.

5. Transfer pan from oven to top of stove and deglaze with Pernod. Arrange paupiettes on platter and keep warm.

6. Gradually add remaining 1 cup cream to pan and reduce by half. With wire whip, whisk butter into sauce, 1 piece at a time, to smooth texture.

7. To serve, arrange paupiettes on serving platter, cover with sauce, and sprinkle with chopped parsley.

TO PREPARE IN ADVANCE: Through step 3. Refrigerate until needed.
TO FREEZE: Do not freeze.

JOAN'S POACHED TROUT WITH DUXELLES

Serves 6

2 medium carrots, peeled
1 small onion, cut in half
2 stalks celery, 1 small and 1
    large, strings removed
1 bay leaf
⅛ teaspoon dried thyme
4 or 5 whole peppercorns
1 cup dry vermouth
½ cup water
4 large shallots
6 whole trout, boned and skinned

1½ cups Duxelles (page 158)
Salt and freshly ground pepper
Juice of 1 medium lemon
1 medium zucchini
1 tablespoon unsalted butter
2 egg yolks
1 cup heavy cream
4 tablespoons (½ stick) unsalted
    butter, softened and cut in small
    pieces

1. To prepare poaching liquid: Using MEDIUM SLICING BLADE, slice 1 carrot, the onion, and small stalk celery. In stainless steel or enameled medium saucepan, combine sliced vegetables with bay leaf, thyme, peppercorns, vermouth, and water. Bring to boil, then lower flame and let simmer 20 to 30 minutes.

2. Using JULIENNE BLADE, julienne remaining carrot, large celery stalk, and zucchini. In a small skillet, melt 1 tablespoon unsalted butter and, over medium heat, sauté vegetables until barely tender, about 2 minutes. Reserve. Clean work bowl.

3. Using STEEL BLADE, drop shallots through feed tube with motor running and chop fine. Reserve.

4. Preheat oven to 350°F. Butter a 9 x 13-inch baking dish.

5. Stuff each trout with ¼ cup of the *Duxelles* and arrange in prepared baking dish. Season with salt, pepper, and lemon juice.

6. Strain poaching liquid over fish and cover with buttered waxed paper, buttered side down. Bake 8 to 10 minutes, then transfer fish to heated serving platter and keep warm while preparing sauce.

7. Strain pan juices into medium saucepan and add shallots. Bring to boil over high flame and reduce by half.

8. In small mixing bowl, lightly beat egg yolks and ¼ cup of the cream. Reserve.

9. Add remaining ¾ cup cream to saucepan, again bring to boil, and reduce until sauce begins to thicken, about 5 minutes. Add reserved julienne of vegetables, turn flame down to low, and, stirring constantly, add egg yolk mixture. Cook 2 to 3 minutes, being careful that sauce does not boil. Remove from heat and whisk in softened butter, 1 piece at a time.

10. Spoon sauce over fish and arrange a few vegetables on top of each trout. Serve immediately.

TO PREPARE IN ADVANCE: Through step 5.
TO FREEZE: Do not freeze.

VARIATION: Filets of sole may be used. Roll filets over *Duxelles*, secure with toothpicks, and proceed as above.

Ma Maison, the most talked about restaurant on the West Coast, is owned by Patrick Terrail and Chef Wolfgang Puck. Mr. Puck combines the best of American ingredients with his marvelous modern French cuisine. Trout en croûte is served regularly at this popular restaurant.

FILET DE TROUT EN CROUTE
Serves 8 to 12

(Stuffed Fillet of Trout in Pastry)

½ *pound fresh salmon, cut in 1-inch pieces, or scallops*
1 egg
2 teaspoons salt
1 teaspoon white pepper
Dash of cayenne pepper
Leaves from 1 sprig tarragon
½ *cup heavy cream, chilled*

6 trout (10 ounces each), skinned, boned, and filleted
2 pounds Puff Pastry (page 257)
1 or 2 eggs, lightly beaten, for egg wash
Beurre Blanc (page 193)

1. To prepare mousse: Using STEEL BLADE, combine salmon, egg, ½ teaspoon of the salt, ¼ teaspoon of the white pepper, the cayenne, and tarragon leaves and process until smooth, scraping down sides of work bowl as necessary.

2. With motor running, slowly pour cream through feed tube and process until completely incorporated. Test for seasoning by poaching a small amount of mousse in salted simmering water. Correct seasoning to taste. Refrigerate until needed. Clean work bowl.

3. Preheat oven to 350°F.

4. Season trout fillets with remaining 1½ teaspoons salt and ¾ teaspoon white pepper. Place half the trout on work table, skin side down. Divide mousse and spread equally over each fillet. Top with remaining fillets, skin side up.

5. Divide pastry into 6 pieces. On lightly floured board, roll out each piece large enough to enclose one trout. Lay trout on one end of pastry. Brush edges with egg wash and fold over pastry, wrapping the fish, and pressing to seal all around fish. With pastry cutter, cut away excess pastry, forming a fish in the procedure, reserving scraps.

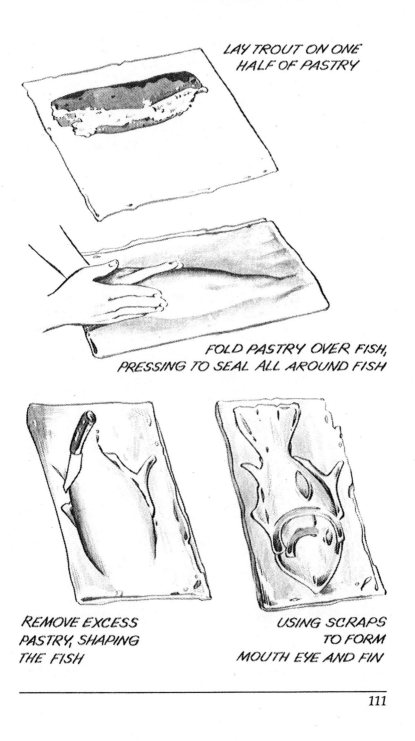

LAY TROUT ON ONE
HALF OF PASTRY

FOLD PASTRY OVER FISH,
PRESSING TO SEAL ALL AROUND FISH

REMOVE EXCESS
PASTRY, SHAPING
THE FISH

USING SCRAPS
TO FORM
MOUTH EYE AND FIN

USE PASTRY TUBE AND
DECORATE FISH WITH SCALES

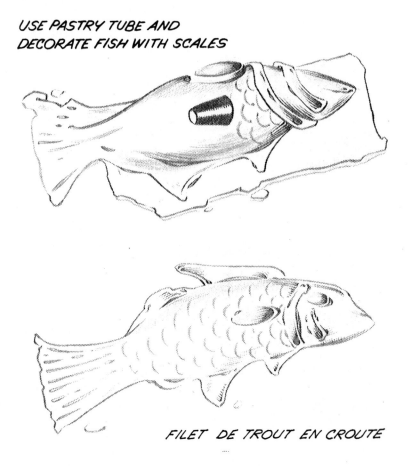

FILET DE TROUT EN CROUTE

6. Place trout on pastry sheet and brush entire fish with egg wash, being careful that egg does not drip down on pan. Bend top of pastry tube and decorate fish with scales. Use scraps to form mouth, eye, and fin. Brush with egg wash.

7. Bake 30 to 35 minutes, or until pastry is golden brown.

8. Serve with *Beurre Blanc* (page 193).

TO PREPARE IN ADVANCE: Through step 6. Refrigerate until needed.
TO FREEZE: Do not freeze.

SHRIMP IN BEER BATTER

1 pound large raw shrimp
1 cup all-purpose flour
½ teaspoon salt
Dash of Tabasco
1 teaspoon vegetable oil plus oil for
  deep frying

1 cup beer
Tomato Sauce (page 201), spiked
  with capers or horseradish, or
  Sizzle Sauce (page 199)

1. Peel and devein shrimp, leaving tails intact.

2. Using STEEL BLADE, with 2 or 3 on/off turns, process flour, salt, Tabasco, and 1 teaspoon oil. With motor running, pour beer through feed tube and process until mixture is smooth. Transfer batter to a mixing bowl, cover, and let stand 2 to 3 hours, unrefrigerated.

3. In a wok or deep saucepan, heat oil for deep frying. Coat shrimp with batter, dipping 2 or 3 times, and fry until golden brown. Drain on paper towels.

4. Serve with sauce of your choice.

TO PREPARE IN ADVANCE: Through step 2.
TO FREEZE: Do not freeze.

SHRIMP CREOLE

Serves 6

2 cloves garlic
2 medium onions, quartered
1 green pepper, halved, cored, and
  seeded
3 stalks celery, strings removed
¼ cup olive oil or vegetable oil
1 can (16 ounces) peeled tomatoes,
  undrained

3 tablespoons tomato paste
Dash of cayenne pepper
Pinch of dried thyme
1 bay leaf
Salt and freshly ground pepper
1½ pounds shrimp, cooked and
  shelled
Hot, cooked rice

1. Using MEDIUM SLICING BLADE, slice garlic, onions, and green

pepper. Cut celery to fit feed tube and slice. Heat oil in large skillet and sauté vegetables for 15 minutes.

2. Using STEEL BLADE, chop tomatoes.

3. Add tomatoes and juice, tomato paste, cayenne pepper, thyme, and bay leaf to vegetables in skillet. Season with salt and pepper. Correct seasoning to taste. Simmer over medium flame 30 to 40 minutes, stirring occasionally. Remove bay leaf.

4. Add shrimp and cook just until heated, 2 to 3 minutes. Serve over rice.

TO PREPARE IN ADVANCE: Through step 3.
TO FREEZE: Through step 3. To reheat, place in saucepan, heat through over low flame, then continue with recipe.

VARIATION: Sausage or chicken may be substituted for shrimp, or you can use a combination of everything for Jambalaya.

This is an excellent buffet dish.

CHICKEN BARCELONA

Serves 4 to 6

1 cup loosely packed fresh parsley leaves
Rind of 2 oranges, cut in 1-inch strips
2 medium onions, quartered
2 cloves garlic
6 medium tomatoes, peeled, seeded, and quartered, or one can (16 ounces) peeled tomatoes, drained

2 tablespoons vegetable oil
1 tablespoon unsalted butter
2 frying chickens (about 2½ pounds each), quartered
Juice of 4 medium oranges (1½ cups)
Juice of ½ lemon

1. Using STEEL BLADE, chop parsley fine. Reserve.

2. Using STEEL BLADE, with motor running, drop orange rind through feed tube and process until coarsely chopped. Reserve.

3. Using STEEL BLADE, with on/off turns, chop onions fine, one at a time (4 quarters). Drop garlic through feed tube while chopping second onion. Drain as necessary and reserve. Clean work bowl.

4. Using STEEL BLADE, coarsely chop tomatoes, 2 at a time (if using fresh). Reserve.

5. In large skillet, over moderate flame, heat oil and butter. Season chicken with salt and pepper and brown well on both sides. Remove to baking pan.

6. In same skillet, over moderate flame, sauté onions and garlic until golden. Add tomatoes, orange juice, and ¼ cup of the chopped parsley. Cover and cook over low heat until sauce thickens, about 30 minutes. Correct seasoning to taste.

7. Preheat oven to 350°F.

8. Pour sauce over chicken and sprinkle with chopped orange rind. Cover and bake 20 minutes.

9. To serve, pour sauce over chicken arranged on a platter and sprinkle with reserved parsley.

TO PREPARE IN ADVANCE: Through step 6.
TO FREEZE: Through step 8. To reheat, place in preheated oven and bake approximately 30 minutes.

This is a variation of a galantine of chicken wrapped in phyllo leaves. It is an impressive buffet dish, made very simple with the food processor.

CHICKEN BOMBE

Serves 12 to 14

¼ cup fresh parsley leaves
¼ cup pistachio nuts, shelled and peeled
4 ounces cooked tongue, cut in 1-inch pieces
4 ounces shallots
2 cloves garlic
4 tablespoons (½ stick) unsalted butter
2 tablespoons Cognac
2 chickens (3½ pounds each), boned, skinned, and cut in 1-inch pieces

2 egg whites
1 cup heavy cream, chilled
1 teaspoon salt
¼ teaspoon white pepper
¼ teaspoon dried thyme
Dash of cayenne pepper
2 or 3 dashes of nutmeg
6 phyllo leaves
½ cup melted unsalted butter

---

1. Using STEEL BLADE, chop parsley fine. Reserve.

2. Using STEEL BLADE, with on/off turns, coarsely chop pistachio nuts and tongue, separately. Reserve.

3. Using STEEL BLADE, chop shallots and garlic fine, dropping them through feed tube. In small skillet, over moderate flame, sauté shallots and garlic until translucent. Do not brown. Pour Cognac into skillet and cook 1 to 2 minutes. Clean work bowl.

4. Preheat oven to 350°F.

5. Divide chicken in half. Using STEEL BLADE, chop first half until fine. Add half each shallot mixture and parsley and continue to process. With motor running, through feed tube, add 1 egg white and ½ cup heavy cream. Process until smooth, scraping down sides of work bowl as necessary. Remove to large mixing bowl.

6. Repeat with remaining chicken, shallot mixture, parsley, egg white, and cream. Add to mixing bowl with pistachio nuts and tongue and combine thoroughly. Season with salt, pepper, thyme, cayenne, and nutmeg. Correct seasoning to taste.

7. To assemble bombe, brush 3 phyllo leaves with melted butter and use to line a 4-cup round mold. Fill with chicken mixture and fold leaves over filling. Brush remaining 3 leaves with butter and fold in half. Place over bombe, tucking ends in around bombe to enclose. Brush top with melted butter.

8. Bake 45 minutes, brushing with butter every 15 minutes. Remove from oven, invert on baking tray, brush with butter, and return to oven to bake 45 minutes longer. Phyllo leaves will be golden brown.

9. Bombe may be served hot or cold. If served hot, allow to rest 15 minutes after removing from oven before slicing.

TO PREPARE IN ADVANCE: Through step 8. To serve hot, bake only 45 minutes.
TO FREEZE: Through step 8, baking 45 minutes. To reheat, invert on baking tray and bake in preheated oven 30 minutes. Brush with melted butter and continue to bake 30 minutes longer, brushing with melted butter after 15 minutes.

VARIATION: Turkey may be used instead of chicken. Ham may be used instead of tongue.

CORNISH GAME HENS WITH ZUCCHINI STUFFING

3 Cornish hens, cut in half,
  backbones removed and reserved
  for broth
½ teaspoon salt
½ teaspoon freshly ground pepper
½ teaspoon dried marjoram
2 ounces Parmesan cheese, at room
  temperature, cut in 1-inch
  pieces
1 pound zucchini, cut to fit width
  of pusher
1 medium onion, cut to fit width
  of pusher
8 to 10 medium mushrooms, cut
  in half
6 tablespoons unsalted butter
⅓ cup ricotta cheese
1 teaspoon Italian seasoning
1 egg, lightly beaten
½ cup white wine
Game Hen Broth (see below),
  strained

1. Preheat oven to 350°F.

2. Rub insides of hens with salt, pepper, and marjoram.

3. Using STEEL BLADE, grate Parmesan cheese fine. Reserve.

4. Using JULIENNE or MEDIUM SHREDDING BLADE, julienne zucchini, onion, and mushrooms. In large skillet, over moderate flame, melt 2 tablespoons butter. Sauté zucchini, onion, and mushrooms until tender, but still crisp, 3 to 4 minutes. Drain and cool slightly.

5. Stir in ricotta, Italian seasoning, and egg. Correct seasoning, adding salt and pepper to taste. Divide and fill cavity of each hen.

6. In shallow roasting pan, over moderate flame, melt remaining 4 tablespoons butter. Set hens in pan, skin side down, raise flame, and saute 2 minutes. Transfer to oven and bake 45 minutes.

7. Remove hens to heated platter and let rest 10 minutes.

8. To prepare sauce, deglaze pan with wine and broth and reduce slightly, to enhance flavor. Correct seasoning.

9. To serve, lightly nap plate with sauce and top with one-half hen, skin side up. Pass remaining sauce.

TO PREPARE IN ADVANCE: Through step 6.
TO FREEZE: Do not freeze.

VARIATION: Use filling to stuff red or green peppers and serve as a vegetable.

GAME HEN BROTH

Back bones, giblets, and neck from
　Cornish game hens
1 one-inch piece carrot
2 one-inch pieces celery stalk

2 sprigs fresh parsley
4 peppercorns
¼ medium onion
2 garlic cloves, unpeeled

1. Combine all ingredients in medium saucepan and add water to cover.

2. Bring to boil, skim, and lower flame. Simmer 20 minutes, skimming as necessary. Strain and use as needed.

Though I advise using Madeira Sauce, I have served this substituting port wine, and the sauce is wonderful.

CHICKEN WRAPPED IN LETTUCE

Serves 4 to 6

3 whole chicken breasts, skinned
　and boned, cut in half
Salt and freshly ground pepper
6 large butter lettuce leaves or
　spinach leaves
3 medium mushrooms

1 medium carrot, peeled
1 medium leek, white part only
1 stalk celery, strings removed
5 tablespoons unsalted butter
Madeira Sauce (page 194)

1. Partially slice each half chicken breast lengthwise so that breast can be opened and stuffed. Pound lightly. Season with salt and pepper.

2. Wash and blanch lettuce leaves, 3 to 4 seconds. Dry on paper towel and reserve.

3. Using FINE SHREDDING BLADE, or JULIENNE BLADE, shred mushrooms, carrot, leek, and celery. (If using SHREDDING BLADE, cut vegetables to fit width of pusher.) In small skillet, over moderate flame, melt 1 tablespoon butter and sauté vegetables about 1 minute. Season with salt and pepper to taste.

4. Divide vegetables and place on each chicken breast, folding over to enclose stuffing. Wrap each breast in 1 lettuce leaf.

5. In medium skillet, melt remaining 4 tablespoons butter and, over low heat, sauté wrapped chicken breasts until tender, about 15 minutes, turning to brown each side.

6. Serve on heated plates and nap with Madeira Sauce.

TO PREPARE IN ADVANCE: Through step 4.
TO FREEZE: Through step 5, cooking 10 minutes.

VARIATIONS: 1. Chopped, cooked ham may be added to stuffing with vegetables.
2. Green peppercorns may be added to sauce.

These need no sauce—just a bit of lemon juice over the cutlets at serving time.

CUTLET POJARSKY

Serves 6

8 slices white bread, crusts
   removed, torn in pieces
½ cup heavy cream
1½ pounds uncooked chicken,
   skinned and boned, cut in
   1-inch pieces

1 egg
1 teaspoon salt
½ teaspoon white pepper
½ teaspoon paprika
3 to 4 tablespoons unsalted butter
Lemon slices for garnish

1. Using STEEL BLADE, process bread into fine crumbs.

2. In medium bowl, combine 1 cup crumbs with heavy cream and reserve remaining crumbs.

3. Using STEEL BLADE, with on/off turns, coarsely grind chicken, 1 cup at a time. Add to mixing bowl and repeat procedure until all the chicken is ground.

4. Add egg, salt, pepper, and paprika to mixing bowl and thoroughly combine all ingredients. Mixture will be sticky.

5. With moistened hands, divide chicken into 6 patties, 5 ounces each, and shape into cutlets approximately ¾ inch thick. Immediately roll in reserved bread crumbs, coating all sides and edges. (This will facilitate shaping.) Refrigerate at least 30 minutes, or until needed.

6. In a large skillet, over low flame, melt 3 tablespoons butter. Sauté cutlets, 5 minutes on one side, 4 minutes on second side, using additional butter if necessary. Cutlets will be golden brown outside and still moist inside.

7. To serve, arrange cutlets on heated platter and garnish with slices of lemon.

TO PREPARE IN ADVANCE: Through step 5.
TO FREEZE: Through step 5. Defrost overnight in refrigerator, then continue with recipe.

NOTE: Chicken can be divided into 12 cutlets, with cooking time reduced by 1 minute on each side.

VARIATION: Veal may be substituted for chicken.

CHICKEN CREPES

Serves 6 to 8

1 ounce Swiss cheese, chilled
8 medium mushrooms
1 or 2 teaspoons lemon juice
2 shallots
4 tablespoons (½ stick) unsalted butter, plus butter for dotting sauce (optional)
2 cups cooked chicken, chilled, cut in 1-inch pieces
⅔ cup dry sherry

2 teaspoons arrowroot
½ cup Chicken Stock (page 83) or canned broth
2 cups heavy cream
1 cup milk
1 teaspoon salt
½ teaspoon white pepper
1 or 2 dashes of nutmeg
12 to 16 Basic Crêpes (page 233)

1. Using MEDIUM SHREDDING BLADE, grate cheese. Reserve.

2. Using THIN SLICING BLADE, slice mushrooms. Transfer to medium mixing bowl and sprinkle with lemon juice.

3. Using STEEL BLADE, with motor running, drop shallots through feed tube and chop fine. In large skillet, melt 4 tablespoons butter. Turn flame to high and sauté mushrooms and shallots until liquid evaporates, about 5 minutes.

4. Using STEEL BLADE, with on/off turns, coarsely chop chicken, 1 cup at a time. Add to skillet and stir to combine. Transfer to medium mixing bowl.

5. Deglaze skillet with sherry and reduce until approximately 2 tablespoons remain.

6. Dissolve arrowroot in chicken broth and, using wooden spoon, stir into skillet with heavy cream and milk. Cook, over moderate flame, until sauce thickens, 3 to 4 minutes. Season with salt,* pepper, and nutmeg. Correct seasoning, adding lemon juice to taste.

7. Pour one-third of sauce into chicken mixture. Add reserved cheese and combine. Dot remaining sauce with butter to prevent a film from forming (or place buttered waxed paper directly over sauce).

8. Preheat oven to 425°F. Butter a 9 x 13-inch baking dish.

9. To assemble, place heaping tablespoon of filling on lower third of each crêpe and roll. Place in buttered baking dish, seam side down. Continue until all the filling is used. Pour sauce over crêpes.

10. Bake 15 to 20 minutes, until heated through.

TO PREPARE IN ADVANCE: Through step 9.
TO FREEZE: Do not freeze.

VARIATIONS: 1. Combine 1 cup chopped ham, 1 cup chopped chicken, and ¼ cup chopped parsley and proceed as above.
2. Sprinkle sauce in step 9 with additional grated cheese and bake until golden brown.

*If using canned broth, sauce may require less salt.

Croquettes are fun to prepare, and a good way to use leftover turkey or chicken.

TURKEY CROQUETTES

2 slices bread, crusts removed,
    torn into pieces
2 tablespoons fresh parsley leaves
2 cups cooked turkey, chilled and
    cut into 1-inch pieces
1 medium onion, quartered
1 clove garlic
¼ pound (1 stick) plus 2
    tablespoons unsalted butter

1 egg
½ cup sour cream
Salt and freshly ground pepper
Dash of cayenne pepper
Sizzle Sauce (page 199) or
    Mushroom Sauce (page 196)

1. Using STEEL BLADE, process bread into fine crumbs. Reserve.

2. Using STEEL BLADE, chop parsley fine. Remove to large mixing bowl.

3. Using STEEL BLADE, with on/off turns, grind turkey fine, 1 cup at a time. Add to mixing bowl.

4. Using STEEL BLADE, with on/off turns, chop onion and garlic fine. Drain. In small skillet, over moderate flame, melt the 2 tablespoons butter and sauté onion and garlic until golden, about 5 minutes. Add to mixing bowl. Clean work bowl.

5. Using STEEL BLADE, with 2 or 3 on/off turns, process egg and sour cream until smooth. Add to mixing bowl and thoroughly combine all ingredients. Season to taste with salt, pepper, and cayenne pepper. Refrigerate 30 minutes.

6. To form croquettes, remove turkey mixture from refrigerator and with dampened hands mold into pyramids about 2 inches high. Roll in bread crumbs, coating all sides, and refrigerate.

7. In large skillet, over moderate flame, melt the ¼ pound butter. Arrange croquettes in pan and brown on all sides, about 15 minutes. Gently insert point of knife to make certain croquette is hot in the center. Drain on paper towels.

8. Serve with sauce of your choice.

TO PREPARE IN ADVANCE: Through step 6.

TO FREEZE: Through step 6. To reheat, place on baking tray in a preheated 350°F. oven. Bake 10 minutes, brush with melted butter and bake 15 minutes longer, brushing with butter as necessary.

A variation of chili con carne, using turkey meat.

CHILI CON PAVO

Serves 12

3¼ pounds turkey breast, skinned
    and boned, cut in 1-inch pieces
5 tablespoons vegetable oil
2 medium onions, quartered
4 cloves garlic
4 tablespoons chili powder
1½ teaspoons dried oregano
1½ teaspoons ground cumin
1 teaspoon crushed red pepper, or
    to taste

1 can (6 ounces) tomato paste
2 cups Beef Stock (page 84)
1 can (1 pound 13 ounces)
    tomatoes, undrained
1 tablespoon salt
1 teaspoon sugar
1 to 2 tablespoons cornmeal
1 cup cooked or canned kidney
    beans

1. Using STEEL BLADE, and in 3 batches, coarsely chop turkey with on/off turns.

2. Heat 3 tablespoons of the oil in large (4-quart) saucepan and brown turkey, one-third at a time. Remove to large mixing bowl as it browns.

3. Using STEEL BLADE, chop onion coarsely with on/off turns. Drop garlic through feed tube as motor is running. Drain as necessary. Heat remaining 2 tablespoons oil in saucepan and brown onions and garlic.

4. Stir chili powder, oregano, cumin, and crushed red pepper into saucepan. Add tomato paste, stock, tomatoes with their juice, salt, and sugar.

5. Return turkey to pan, cover, and simmer 1 hour. Uncover and simmer 40 to 50 minutes longer, until meat is tender.

6. Stir in cornmeal to thicken. Add kidney beans, heat through, and serve.

TO PREPARE IN ADVANCE: Through step 6.
TO FREEZE: Through step 6. Defrost overnight in refrigerator. To reheat, place in saucepan and heat through over low flame.

Brenner's Park Hotel in Baden-Baden is among the top hotels in the world. It has maintained its grand tradition of luxury and fine food since 1872. Here is its kitchen's recipe for Russian Meat Pie, a hearty dish, well worth the effort.

Russian Meat Pie

Serves 8

It is important that filling be well seasoned for pie to be tasty.

2 ounces Parmesan cheese, at room temperature, cut in 1-inch pieces
1 small bunch fresh parsley, leaves only
3 medium carrots, cut in 1-inch pieces
3 medium onions, quartered
2 cloves garlic
2 tablespoons vegetable oil
¾ pound veal shoulder, in one piece
¾ pound pork butt, in one piece
Salt and freshly ground pepper

Cayenne pepper
½ cup port
1 cup rice
2 cups bouillon or Beef Stock (page 84)
¼ pound (1 stick) unsalted butter
1 pound cabbage, quartered and cored
2 hard-cooked eggs, peeled and cut in half
1 pound Puff Pastry (page 257)
1 egg, lightly beaten, for egg wash

1. Using STEEL BLADE, grate Parmesan cheese fine. Reserve.

2. Using STEEL BLADE, chop parsley. Reserve.

3. Using STEEL BLADE, with on/off turns, coarsely chop carrots. Reserve.

4. Using STEEL BLADE, with on/off turns, coarsely chop onions, one at a time (4 quarters), dropping garlic through feed tube with last onion. Drain and reserve. Clean work bowl.

5. In medium skillet, over moderate flame, heat oil. Sear meat on all sides. Add chopped carrots and 1 onion and season with salt,

pepper, and a few dashes of cayenne pepper. Cover, lower flame, and simmer 45 to 55 minutes, until meat is tender, turning often to brown all sides.

6. Transfer meat to medium mixing bowl and deglaze pan with port. Strain gravy in skillet over meat and let cool. Cut meat into bite-size pieces.

7. In medium saucepan, over high flame, bring to boil rice and bouillon. Lower flame and cook until tender, 20 to 25 minutes, adding more liquid if necessary.

8. In small skillet, over moderate flame, melt half the butter. Sauté 1 chopped onion until translucent, about 5 minutes. Stir into cooked rice with grated cheese, 2 tablespoons of the chopped parsley, and salt and pepper to taste. Reserve.

9. Using MEDIUM SLICING BLADE, with firm pressure, slice cabbage. In medium skillet, over moderate flame, melt remaining butter. Sauté remaining onion until translucent, about 5 minutes. Add cabbage and continue to cook until cabbage is tender but still crunchy, about 15 minutes. Season with salt and pepper and reserve. Clean work bowl.

10. Using STEEL BLADE, with 2 or 3 on/off turns, coarsely chop eggs. Reserve.

11. Preheat oven to 400°F. Lightly butter 8-inch springform pan.

12. On lightly floured board, roll out pastry large enough to fit into pan and completely fold over filling. Carefully lay in prepared pan, leaving a generous overhang.

13. Fill pie as follows: 1 layer rice, 1 layer cabbage, 1 layer meat. Sprinkle with parsley and chopped egg and repeat the layers a second time, again sprinkling with parsley and chopped egg, adding 1 layer of rice and 1 layer of cabbage as the final layers.

14. Fold over pastry to enclose filling, allowing for a small overlap. Brush with egg wash and decorate as desired. Poke 3 small air holes in pie to allow steam to escape.

15. Bake 1 hour, or until pastry is golden brown. Let rest 10 minutes, slice, and serve.

TO PREPARE IN ADVANCE: Through step 14 or 15.
TO FREEZE: Through step 14, defrost 2 or 3 hours in refrigerator. To reheat, place in preheated oven and bake 1 hour. Lower oven to

350°F. and bake 15 minutes longer. Through step 15, place in pre-heated 400°F. oven and bake 15 minutes. Lower oven to 350°F. and bake approximately 30 minutes longer.

VARIATION: Use individual bowls (I use onion-soup bowl) and prepare as above, poking only 1 hole in center and baking 30 to 35 minutes, until golden brown.

BEEF AND PEPPERS
Serves 4 to 6

1 pound flank steak, cut to fit feed tube
1 medium red pepper, halved, cored, and seeded
1 medium green pepper, halved, cored, and seeded
2 teaspoons cornstarch

1 egg white
2 tablespoons soy sauce
½ teaspoon sugar (optional)
½ teaspoon salt
4 tablespoons vegetable oil
Steamed rice

1. See Tips and Hints on slicing beef (page 24). Using MEDIUM SERRATED SLICING BLADE, slice steak. Reserve.

2. Using MEDIUM SLICING BLADE, slice peppers. Reserve.

3. In a medium mixing bowl, marinate steak in cornstarch, egg white, soy sauce, and sugar, using fingers to coat each slice of steak with mixture.

4. Heat 2 tablespoons of the oil in wok. Add peppers and cook over moderate flame, about 3 minutes, stirring constantly. Add salt and stir through. Remove peppers from wok.

5. Heat remaining 2 tablespoons oil in wok over high flame. Slide steak into wok and cook, stirring, 2 minutes. Lower flame, add peppers, and continue cooking and stirring 2 minutes longer. Correct seasoning to taste.

6. Serve immediately with steamed rice.

TO PREPARE IN ADVANCE: Through step 3.
TO FREEZE: Through step 5. Defrost completely in refrigerator.

Heat 2 tablespoons oil. Add beef and peppers and stir to heat through.

VARIATION: Substitute 2 medium onions for peppers.

Beef Wellington

Serves 6

6 tablespoons unsalted butter
6 beef tournedos (6 ounces each)
2 shallots
1 pound mushrooms
¼ cup heavy cream

Salt and freshly ground pepper
2 pounds Puff Pastry (page 257)
1 egg, lightly beaten, for egg wash
Béarnaise Sauce (page 202)

1. In large skillet, over high flame, melt 3 tablespoons butter. Sauté tournedos rapidly, about 1 minute on each side. Cool completely.

2. Using STEEL BLADE, with on/off turns, drop shallots through feed tube and chop fine. Reserve.

3. Using STEEL BLADE, with on/off turns, chop mushrooms fine, 1 cup at a time. In large skillet, over moderate flame, melt remaining 3 tablespoons butter. Sauté shallots and mushrooms until all liquid evaporates, about 10 minutes. Stir in cream and season with salt and pepper. Reduce to thick purée, 3 to 5 minutes. Correct seasoning to taste. Cool. Clean work bowl.

4. Preheat oven to 450°F.

5. Divide pastry and mushroom purée into six portions. On a lightly floured board, roll out pastry large enough to enclose fillet, about ¼ inch thick. Spread mushroom purée on half the pastry, top with fillet, and cover with more purée (see illustration). Brush edges of pastry with egg wash and fold over, molding to shape of fillet. Remove excess pastry and brush with egg wash. Decorate as desired with pastry scraps and again brush with egg wash.

6. Place fillets on greased baking sheet and bake 10 to 12 minutes, until pastry is golden brown. Fillet will be medium rare.

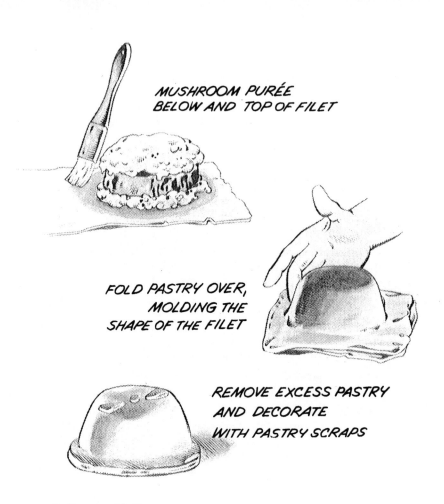

MUSHROOM PURÉE
BELOW AND TOP OF FILET

FOLD PASTRY OVER,
MOLDING THE
SHAPE OF THE FILET

REMOVE EXCESS PASTRY
AND DECORATE
WITH PASTRY SCRAPS

7. Serve with Sauce.

TO PREPARE IN ADVANCE: Through step 5, refrigerating until needed.
TO FREEZE: Through step 3. Defrost overnight in refrigerator and continue with recipe.

VARIATION: Prepare recipe using ground meat. Lightly season meat with salt and freshly ground pepper and form into thick hamburgers, 6 ounces each. Over high flame, sauté hamburgers, about 1 minute on each side. Cool completely and continue as above. Hamburger will be medium rare. Serve with sauce as above.

This was inspired by Chasen's famous chili.

CHILI CON CARNE

Serves 6 to 8

½ pound dried pinto beans
½ cup fresh parsley leaves
2 large onions, quartered
2 cloves garlic
1 green pepper, seeded and cut in
    1-inch pieces
2 tablespoons vegetable oil
3 tablespoons unsalted butter
2 pounds beef chuck, trimmed and
    cut in 1-inch pieces
4 medium tomatoes, peeled,
    seeded, and quartered

1 tablespoon chili powder
1 teaspoon crushed cumin seed
¼ teaspoon cayenne pepper
2 teaspoons salt
Chopped onion for garnish
    (optional)
Grated Cheddar cheese for garnish
    (optional)
Sour cream for garnish (optional)

1. Wash beans and soak overnight in water to cover.

2. In medium saucepan, over moderate heat, simmer beans in soaking water until tender, about 1 hour, adding more water as needed.

3. Using STEEL BLADE, chop parsley fine. Reserve.

4. Using STEEL BLADE, with on/off turns, coarsely chop onions, one at a time (4 quarters), dropping garlic through feed tube with last onion. Drain as necessary.

5. Using STEEL BLADE, with on/off turns, coarsely chop pepper.

6. In large saucepan, over moderate flame, heat oil and butter and sauté onion, garlic, and green pepper until onion is golden. Clean work bowl.

7. Using STEEL BLADE, with on/off turns, coarsely chop beef, one cup at a time. Add to saucepan and cook about 15 minutes, until meat loses its pink color. Break up meat with wooden spoon as you stir it.

8. Using STEEL BLADE, purée tomatoes. Start with on/off turns and then allow machine to run, scraping down sides of work bowl as necessary. Add to saucepan with parsley, chili powder, cumin seed, cayenne pepper, and salt. Drain pinto beans, reserving liquid, and

stir into saucepan. Add 1 cup reserved bean liquid, cover, and simmer over low heat for 1 hour. Uncover and simmer 30 minutes longer. If too thick, add water from bean pot as chili cooks.

9. Skim fat from top and serve in small dishes topped with chopped onions and grated Cheddar cheese or a dollop of sour cream.

TO PREPARE IN ADVANCE: Through step 8.
TO FREEZE: Through step 8. Defrost overnight in refrigerator. To reheat, place in saucepan and heat through over low flame.

For dieters and nondieters alike.

MEAT LOAF

Serves 6 to 8

1 pound lean beef, cut in 1-inch pieces	½ green pepper, quartered and seeded
1 pound veal, cut in 1-inch pieces	2 eggs
2 medium carrots, peeled and cut in 1-inch pieces	½ cup ketchup
	Dash of Tabasco
1 medium onion, quartered	½ teaspoon salt
2 stalks celery, strings removed, cut in 1-inch pieces	5 to 6 grinds fresh pepper

1. Preheat oven to 350°F. Oil 9 x 4½ x 2½-inch loaf pan.

2. Using STEEL BLADE, with on/off turns, chop beef fine, 1 cup at a time. Remove to large mixing bowl.

3. Using STEEL BLADE, with on/off turns, chop veal fine, 1 cup at a time. Add to beef.

4. Using STEEL BLADE, with on/off turns, chop fine carrots, onion, celery, and green pepper, separately. Drain onion, as necessary. Add to mixing bowl as processed.

5. Using STEEL BLADE, add remaining ingredients to work bowl and process until eggs are foamy, 4 to 5 seconds. Pour into mixing bowl and combine ingredients thoroughly. (I find using my hands the most effective method.)

6. Shape to fit loaf pan and bake 45 minutes.

7. Drain slightly, invert on serving platter, slice, and serve.

TO PREPARE IN ADVANCE: Through step 5.
TO FREEZE: Through step 6. Defrost overnight in refrigerator. To reheat, place in preheated oven and bake 20 minutes.

NOTE: Delicious served cold the next day.

ROASTED SHORT RIBS WITH VEGETABLES

Serves 6

4 pounds beef short ribs, cut in
serving portions
¼ cup all-purpose flour
4 or 5 sprigs fresh parsley leaves
3 tablespoons vegetable oil
2 cups Beef Stock (page 84)
12 cloves garlic, unpeeled

3 medium onions, cut in half
3 medium potatoes, cut to fit feed
tube
8 medium carrots, peeled, cut to
fit feed tube, horizontally
1 teaspoon salt
½ teaspoon freshly ground pepper

1. Dredge short ribs lightly with flour.

2. Preheat oven to 350°F.

3. Heat oil in skillet large enough to hold short ribs. Over high flame, brown ribs on all sides very quickly. Remove ribs from skillet. Deglaze pan with 1 cup of the stock, adding the garlic cloves at the same time, and scrape up all remaining particles in the pan.

4. Using STEEL BLADE, chop parsley leaves fine. Reserve.

5. While short ribs are browning, slice onions, potatoes, and carrots, using MEDIUM SLICING BLADE. Place in the bottom of roasting pan. Arrange browned ribs on vegetables and pour stock from skillet plus remaining 1 cup over all. Season with salt and pepper and cover pan with lid or aluminum foil.

6. Roast 45 minutes, then remove lid and bake 45 minutes longer, basting occasionally, until meat is fork-tender.

7. To serve, arrange short ribs on serving platter, surround with vegetables, and sprinkle with parsley.

TO PREPARE IN ADVANCE: Through step 6, roasting only 45 minutes.

TO FREEZE: Through step 6, roasting only 45 minutes. To reheat, place in roasting pan in preheated oven and roast 1 hour.

This recipe comes from Frank McHugh, long-time film star. It's been our family favorite for many years.

TAMALE PIE

Serves 8

FILLING:

¼ cup fresh parsley leaves
2 pounds lean beef, cut in 1-inch
  pieces
3 tablespoons vegetable oil
2 medium onions, quartered
2 cloves garlic
½ pound mushrooms
1 can (16 ounces) peeled tomatoes,
  undrained
1½ teaspoons salt
2 tablespoons chili powder
1 teaspoon crushed cumin seed
1½ cups pitted black olives, cut in
  half
1 cup seedless raisins
3 ounces Cheddar cheese, chilled

CORNMEAL CRUST:

2 cups cold water
2 cups yellow cornmeal
2 teaspoons salt
6 cups boiling water
1½ teaspoons chili powder
3 tablespoons unsalted butter

1. Using STEEL BLADE, chop parsley fine. Reserve.

2. Using STEEL BLADE, coarsely grind beef, 1 cup at a time. In large skillet, on moderate flame, heat oil and brown meat, stirring occasionally.

3. Using STEEL BLADE, with on/off turns, coarsely chop onions, one at a time (4 quarters), dropping garlic through feed tube as onion is being chopped. Drain onion as necessary. Add to skillet. Cook until golden, 12 to 15 minutes.

4. Using MEDIUM SLICING BLADE, slice mushrooms. Add to skillet with tomatoes and their juices, salt, chili powder, cumin seed, olives, raisins, and reserved parsley. Cook over low heat for 1½ hours, stirring occasionally. Correct seasoning to taste. Cool slightly. Clean work bowl.

5. Using MEDIUM SHREDDING BLADE, grate Cheddar cheese. Reserve.

6. Preheat oven to 350°F.

7. Prepare cornmeal crust. In heavy 3-quart saucepan, stir cornmeal and salt into 2 cups cold water. Gradually pour in 6 cups boiling water and sprinkle with chili powder. Cook over moderate flame, stirring constantly with wooden spoon, until thick, about 10 minutes. Place pan over boiling water (or on an asbestos pad) and cook 10 minutes longer, stirring occasionally. Add butter and stir until melted. Pour into 13 x 8½ x 1½-inch pan and cool completely to make handling easier.

8. Lightly butter bottom and sides of 2-quart ovenproof baking dish, leaving top inch unbuttered. (Cornmeal will cling better if top of dish is unbuttered.)

9. Line baking dish with two-thirds of the cornmeal, using your fingers to press up the sides. (This will be a thick crust.) Carefully ladle filling into prepared crust. Cover meat completely with reserved cornmeal (cut cornmeal into squares, arrange on top, and smooth with spatula), being careful to cover rim of baking dish. Poke an air hole in center to allow steam to escape.

10. Bake 45 minutes, then sprinkle with reserved cheese, and continue to bake 15 minutes longer. Serve hot.

TO PREPARE IN ADVANCE: Through steps 9 or 10.
TO FREEZE: Through step 10, without sprinkling top with cheese. Defrost overnight in refrigerator. To reheat, place in preheated oven and bake 20 minutes, sprinkle with grated cheese, and continue to bake 10 to 15 minutes longer.

Do not prepare this until just before you serve. This must be as fresh as possible.

STEAK TARTARE

Serves 2 as main dish,
4 to 6 as appetizer

½ cup fresh parsley leaves
1 pound filet of beef, trimmed and
   cut in 1-inch pieces
1 small onion, quartered
2 egg yolks
2 or 3 dashes of Worcestershire
   sauce
1 teaspoon Dijon mustard

2 tablespoons capers, drained
1 teaspoon lemon juice
2 teaspoons Cognac
Salt and freshly ground pepper
Watercress for garnish (optional)
Warm toast triangles (optional)
Thinly sliced dark bread (optional)
Sour cream (optional)

1. Using STEEL BLADE, chop parsley fine. Reserve.

2. Using STEEL BLADE, with on/off turns, chop filet fine, 1 cup at a time. Transfer to medium mixing bowl.

3. Using STEEL BLADE, with on/off turns, chop onion fine. Drain and add to chopped filet. Clean work bowl.

4. Using STEEL BLADE, process egg yolks, Worcestershire sauce, mustard, capers, lemon juice, and Cognac until blended. Combine thoroughly with chopped filet, onion, and parsley, using your hands. Season with salt and pepper to taste.

5. To serve as a main dish, shape into 2 large ovals, place on serving plate, and decorate with watercress. Serve with warm toast triangles.

6. To serve as an appetizer, shape into 1 large mound, place on serving plate, and cover with sour cream. Surround with thinly sliced dark bread.

TO PREPARE IN ADVANCE: Do not prepare in advance.
TO FREEZE: Do not freeze for Steak Tartare. To use as hamburgers, freeze in patties through step 4.

VARIATION: To basic recipe, add 2 tablespoons tomato ketchup, 2 tablespoons chopped anchovy fillets, and 1 mashed clove garlic.

NOTE: Additional chopped onions, capers, and chopped egg may be served if desired.

This is one of Rita Leinwand's recipes. Rita is food editor for Bon Appétit magazine and enjoys a reputation as one of our fine cooks and teachers.

PERSILLADE CARRE D'AGNEAU
Serves 4

(Parslied Rack of Lamb)

2 racks of lamb (2½ pounds each)
3 slices bread, torn in pieces
1½ cups fresh parsley leaves
2 shallots
2 cloves garlic

2 teaspoons paprika
6 tablespoons drippings from
 roasted rack of lamb, butter, or
 Chicken Stock (page 83)
Fresh parsley sprigs for garnish

1. Have butcher trim all fat from lamb racks and french bone ends.

2. Preheat oven to 450°F.

3. Set lamb racks on rack in roasting pan and roast 12 to 15 minutes, or until browned outside and pink inside.

4. Using STEEL BLADE, process bread into fine crumbs. Transfer to small mixing bowl.

5. Using STEEL BLADE, chop parsley leaves fine. Add to mixing bowl.

6. Using STEEL BLADE, chop shallots and garlic fine, dropping through feed tube with motor running. Add to mixing bowl with paprika and drippings, butter, or Chicken Stock. Combine thoroughly and spread over meaty side of lamb racks (this is your *persillade*).

7. Preheat broiler and place racks of lamb under the broiler just until lightly browned, checking often to be sure they do not burn.

8. Slice into single chops or noisettes and serve garnished with parsley sprigs.

TO PREPARE IN ADVANCE: Parsley mixture can be prepared ahead, using butter or Chicken Stock.
TO FREEZE: Do not freeze.

This is an elegant presentation for a dish that is very simple to prepare.

LAMB EN CROUTE

Serves 10 to 12

2 tablespoons unsalted butter
2 tablespoons vegetable oil
2 boned racks of lamb, (2 pounds
    each after boning), bones
    reserved for sauce
Salt and freshly ground pepper
1 slice day-old white bread, torn in
    pieces
1 shallot, cut in half

2 cloves garlic
2 pounds spinach, stemmed,
    blanched, and drained well
2 eggs
1 or 2 tablespoons heavy cream or
    Crème Fraîche (page 205)
1½ pounds Puff Pastry (page 257)
1 egg, lightly beaten, for egg wash
Lamb Sauce (see below)

1. In medium skillet, over high flame, heat butter and oil. Brown lamb on all sides, then drain on paper towels and let cool. Season lightly with salt and pepper.

2. Using STEEL BLADE, process bread into fine crumbs. Reserve.

3. Using STEEL BLADE, coarsely mash shallot, garlic, spinach, and eggs. Add cream, 1 tablespoon at a time, just to make mixture spreadable. Divide in half for use with each rack of lamb.

4. Divide pastry in half, refrigerating unused portion until needed. Roll out first half very thin (⅟₁₆ inch), large enough to enclose 1 rack. Sprinkle half the bread crumbs on pastry. Spread a layer of spinach down the center, top with lamb, and cover with spinach. Brush edges of pastry with egg wash and wrap around lamb, trimming excess pastry.

5. Repeat procedure with remaining pastry, lamb, bread crumbs, and spinach. Brush both with egg wash and decorate with pastry cutouts as desired. Refrigerate at least 30 minutes, or until needed.

6. Preheat oven to 425°F.

7. Place racks on baking sheet and brush with egg wash. Roast 20 to 25 minutes for medium rare. (To test for degree of doneness, insert long metal skewer into center of lamb. If it comes out hot to the touch, meat is ready.) Remove from oven and let rest 10 minutes.

8. To serve, nap warm plate with sauce and top with thick slices of meat.

TO PREPARE IN ADVANCE: Through step 5.
TO FREEZE: Do not freeze.

VARIATIONS: 1. Use a butterflied leg of lamb. Brown in 450°F. oven 15 minutes. Proceed with recipe as above, roasting 50 to 55 minutes. 2. Replace spinach stuffing with *Duxelles* (page 158) bound with 2 to 4 tablespoons *Crème Fraîche* (page 205).

LAMB SAUCE

Makes 1½ to 2 cups

2 tablespoons vegetable oil
Lamb bones (from racks of lamb)
½ medium carrot
1 stalk celery, strings removed
½ large onion
1 cup white wine
6 sprigs fresh parsley

2 cloves garlic
6 black peppercorns
½ large bay leaf
Small pinch dried thyme
3 cups Beef Stock (page 84)
2 tablespoons tomato paste
2 tablespoons unsalted butter

1. In a medium saucepan, over high flame, heat oil. Brown bones, turning to brown on all sides.

2. Using MEDIUM SLICING BLADE, slice carrot, celery, and onion. Add to pan and brown lightly.

3. Deglaze pan with white wine and add parsley, garlic, peppercorns, bay leaf, thyme, Beef Stock, and tomato paste. Lower heat and simmer until sauce is reduced by half. Strain.

4. Return sauce to saucepan and, over low heat, simmer until reduced by half. Sauce should be very rich and shiny.

5. Remove pan from heat and whisk in butter, 1 tablespoon at a time. Correct seasoning.

You will find this to be a very tasty dish. Seasoning is very important.

STUFFED BREAST OF VEAL

Serves 4

1 breast of veal (3 to 3½ pounds)
2½ teaspoons salt
1½ teaspoons freshly ground
  pepper
3 cloves garlic, cut in half
5 tablespoons fresh parsley leaves
3 medium onions, quartered
2 tablespoons vegetable oil
1 tablespoon unsalted butter
1 pound veal, in 1-inch pieces,
  chilled

½ cup dried apricots
1 cup port
¼ cup water
¼ teaspoon dried thyme
¼ teaspoon Quatre-Épices (page
  246)
1 cup Veal Stock (page 82) or Beef
  Stock (page 84), plus additional
  stock or water as needed.

1. Have butcher prepare pocket in breast of veal for stuffing. Season with 1½ teaspoons of the salt, 1 teaspoon of the pepper, and rub entire surface with cut sides of garlic cloves. Reserve garlic.

2. Preheat oven to 400°F.

3. Using STEEL BLADE, chop parsley fine. Reserve.

4. Using STEEL BLADE, with on/off turns, chop onions, one at a time (4 quarters). Drain. In large skillet, over moderate flame, heat oil and butter. Sauté one-third of the chopped onion until lightly browned, 12 to 15 minutes.

5. Using STEEL BLADE, with on/off turns, coarsely chop veal, 1 cup at a time. Add to skillet and cook, stirring occasionally, until veal loses pink color, about 10 minutes. Clean work bowl.

6. In small saucepan, over moderate flame, cook apricots in port and water until tender, about 5 minutes. Drain, reserving liquid, and remove to work bowl fitted with STEEL BLADE. With on/off turns, coarsely chop apricots. Add to skillet with remaining 1 teaspoon salt and ½ teaspoon pepper, the thyme, parsley, and *Quatre-Épices*. Cool.

7. Stuff veal breast with mixture and secure with string or skewers.

8. Arrange remaining chopped onion over bottom of baking pan, place veal on top, sprinkle with reserved garlic halves, and add stock and reserved port sauce. Roast 20 minutes, then lower oven to 350°F. and roast 1 hour 40 minutes longer, or until meat is tender. Baste occasionally, adding boiling stock or water as needed.

9. To serve, remove string or skewers, slice, and arrange on hot serving platter. Serve onions over veal. Strain gravy, spoon a small amount over veal, and serve remainder in separate bowl.

TO PREPARE IN ADVANCE: Through step 6.
TO FREEZE: Through step 8. Remove stuffing and freeze separately. Defrost overnight in refrigerator. To reheat, place veal in baking pan in preheated oven and roast 15 to 20 minutes. Heat stuffing in separate pan.

Served with hot German Potato Salad (page 172) and cole slaw, this becomes a hearty and satisfying supper.

SPICED VEAL SAUSAGES
Serves 10 to 12

2 pounds veal shoulder, cut in
  1-inch pieces
3 pounds boneless pork, cut in
  1-inch pieces
¼ pound pork fat, cut in 1-inch
  pieces
4 teaspoons salt

2 teaspoons freshly ground pepper
3 tablespoons crushed coriander
  seed
¼ cup red wine vinegar
2 teaspoons green peppercorns,
  drained
All-purpose flour

1. In large mixing bowl, combine veal, pork, and pork fat. Add salt, pepper, coriander seed, and vinegar and mix together. Cover and refrigerate 2 days to allow seasonings to penetrate meat. Stir several times.

2. Using STEEL BLADE, with on/off turns, coarsely grind mixture 1 cup at a time and return to mixing bowl. Add green peppercorns and combine thoroughly. In small skillet, cook a small piece of sausage and correct seasoning to taste. Shape mixture into 10 or 12 sausages. Roll lightly in flour and refrigerate overnight.

3. Broil about 20 minutes, turning to brown on all sides. (May also be sautéed, over low flame, for about 15 minutes, browning on all sides.)

4. Serve with mustards and/or relish.

TO PREPARE IN ADVANCE: Through step 2.
TO FREEZE: Through step 2. Defrost 2 or 3 hours in refrigerator. To reheat, sauté or broil approximately 20 minutes.

VARIATION: Completely cool the lightly browned sausage and wrap in Puff Pastry (page 257). (You may enclose completely or wrap, leaving both ends exposed.) Brush pastry with egg wash and bake in preheated 425°F. oven for 20 to 25 minutes, until pastry is golden brown. Serve as above.

No need to order these out anymore. Just watch your kids devour them. For an informal dinner party, serve all ingredients in separate bowls and let your guests make their own tostadas.

TOSTADAS

Serves 6

8 ounces Cheddar cheese, chilled
1 head iceberg lettuce, quartered
1 medium onion, quartered
2 medium tomatoes, quartered
1 cup cooked beef, pork, or chicken
Vegetable oil

6 corn tortillas
1½ cups Refried Beans (page 154)
Avocado Dip (page 32)
Sour cream
Salsa Fresca (page 199)

1. Using MEDIUM SHREDDING BLADE, grate cheese. Reserve.

2. Using MEDIUM SLICING BLADE, slice lettuce. Reserve.

3. Using STEEL BLADE, with on/off turns, coarsely chop onion and tomatoes, separately. Drain onion as necessary. Reserve separately. Clean work bowl.

4. Using STEEL BLADE, with on/off turns, coarsely chop meat or chicken. Reserve.

5. In small skillet, over moderate flame, heat ½ inch oil. Crisp tortillas, one at a time, turning with tongs, until lightly browned, 40 to 50 seconds. Drain on paper towels.

6. To assemble tostadas, place crisp tortillas on serving plate and layer, in order, with hot Refried Beans, meat or chicken, onions, tomatoes, Avocado Dip, and a dollop of sour cream. Pour sauce over all and serve.

TO PREPARE IN ADVANCE: Through step 5.
TO FREEZE: Do not freeze.

This appeals to young and old alike. The trick is to double the recipe and freeze.

PIZZA

Yield: 1 twelve-inch pizza

DOUGH:

1 package active dry yeast
½ teaspoon sugar
½ cup warm water (105°-115°F.)
1¼ cups all-purpose flour
1 teaspoon salt
1½ teaspoons vegetable oil

FILLING:

½ cup fresh parsley leaves
2 medium onions, quartered
4 tablespoons (½ stick) unsalted
    butter
3 medium tomatoes, peeled,
    seeded, and quartered
3 tablespoons tomato paste
Salt and freshly ground pepper
2 teaspoons fresh basil (or ½
    teaspoon dried basil)
½ teaspoon dried oregano
10 large pitted black olives
8 ounces salami
6 ounces Swiss cheese, chilled

1. To prepare dough: Dissolve yeast and sugar in warm water.

2. Using STEEL BLADE, combine flour and salt with 1 or 2 on/off turns. Add yeast mixture and combine with on/off turns. Pour oil through feed tube and process just until ball begins to form and dough leaves sides of work bowl. Clean work bowl.

3. Turn dough out of work bowl and lightly knead as you form into ball. Set in small oiled bowl, turning dough to grease all sides. Cover bowl with towel and place in warm spot until dough doubles in size, about 1 hour.

4. Turn dough out on lightly floured board and roll to fit pizza pan. Arrange in pan, turning edges under.

5. Preheat oven to 400°F.

6. To prepare filling: Using STEEL BLADE, chop parsley fine. Reserve.

7. Using STEEL BLADE, chop onions fine, one at a time (4 quarters), with on/off turns. Drain as necessary. Heat butter in large skillet over moderate flame. Add onions and cook until translucent, about 10 minutes. Spread over pizza dough.

8. Using STEEL BLADE, purée tomatoes with tomato paste, salt, pepper, basil, and oregano. Pour over onions. Clean work bowl.

9. Using MEDIUM SLICING BLADE, with light pressure, slice olives. Distribute evenly over tomato mixture.

10. Using MEDIUM SLICING BLADE, with firm pressure, slice salami. Arrange on pizza.

11. Using MEDIUM SHREDDING BLADE, grate cheese. Sprinkle over entire surface of pizza and top with parsley.

12. Bake 30 to 35 minutes, or until crust browns lightly.

TO PREPARE IN ADVANCE: Through step 11.
TO FREEZE: Through step 12 (I like to slice pizza into individual portions and then freeze so that single slices as well as the entire pizza may be taken out as needed). Place pizza on baking tray. To reheat individual slices, place in preheated oven and bake 8 to 10 minutes. The whole pizza should bake 20 minutes.

VARIATIONS: 1. A vegetarian pizza can be made, eliminating salami and substituting cooked vegetables (artichokes, zucchini, etc.).
2. Anchovies or sausages or meatballs may be used.
3. Mozzarella may be substituted for Swiss cheese.

Plain, with fish or poultry, this dish plus salad makes a filling meal.

Baked Spaghetti

6 ounces Tillamook or Cheddar
    cheese, chilled
2 slices day-old bread, torn into
    pieces
2 medium onions, quartered
½ pound mushrooms
¼ cup vegetable oil

¼ pound (1 stick) plus 2
    tablespoons unsalted butter
1 can (28 ounces) plum tomatoes,
    drained and juice reserved
1 teaspoon salt
¼ teaspoon dried basil
1 pound spaghetti

1. Preheat oven to 350°F. Butter a 13½ x 8½ x 1½-inch baking dish.

2. Using MEDIUM SHREDDING BLADE, grate cheese. Reserve.

3. Using STEEL BLADE, process bread to make fine crumbs. Reserve.

4. Using STEEL BLADE, with on/off turns, coarsely chop onions, one at a time (4 quarters), scraping down sides of work bowl as necessary. Drain.

5. Using MEDIUM SLICING BLADE, slice mushrooms. Reserve.

6. In a large skillet, melt oil and ¼ pound butter over moderate flame. Sauté onions until lightly browned, 12 to 15 minutes. Add mushrooms and cook 3 or 4 minutes longer.

7. Using STEEL BLADE, with on/off turns, coarsely chop plum tomatoes.

8. Add tomatoes, juice from tomatoes, salt, and basil to skillet and cook, uncovered, 20 minutes. Stir in two-thirds of the cheese.

9. Meanwhile, cook spaghetti according to package directions, al dente. Drain and arrange in buttered baking dish. Stir in sauce and sprinkle with remaining cheese and bread crumbs. Dot with the 2 tablespoons butter. Bake 1 hour, or until top is brown and crusty. Serve immediately.

TO PREPARE IN ADVANCE: Through step 9, unbaked.
TO FREEZE: Through step 9, unbaked. To reheat, place in preheated oven and bake 1½ hours.

VARIATIONS: 1. Cooked shrimp or lobster pieces may be added with sauce (step 9).
2. Shredded, cooked chicken may be added with sauce (step 9).

LASAGNE

½ cup fresh parsley leaves
1¼ pounds lean beef, cut in 1-inch pieces
1 tablespoon vegetable oil
1 medium onion, quartered
2 cloves garlic
1 stalk celery, strings removed, cut in 1-inch pieces
1 recipe Tomato Sauce (page 201)
½ teaspoon salt

Freshly ground pepper
Pinch of dried oregano
1 one-inch piece Parmesan cheese, cut in half
1 pound ricotta cheese
1 egg
4 ounces mozzarella cheese, chilled
9 packaged lasagne noodles, cooked, or 1 recipe Pasta Dough (page 248)

1. Using STEEL BLADE, chop parsley fine. Reserve.

2. Using STEEL BLADE, with on/off turns, grind meat fine, 1 cup at a time.

3. In large skillet over moderate flame, heat oil and lightly brown meat, stirring occasionally, 5 to 8 minutes. Drain fat from pan.

4. Using STEEL BLADE, with on/off turns, coarsely chop onion, garlic, and celery, separately. Drain onion and add to skillet with other vegetables. Cook 10 minutes. Add 2 cups of the tomato sauce, salt, pepper, oregano, and chopped parsley and simmer 5 minutes longer. Correct seasoning to taste. Clean work bowl.

5. Preheat oven to 350°F. Butter a 13½ x 8½ x 1½-inch baking dish.

6. Using STEEL BLADE, grate Parmesan cheese fine, dropping through feed tube with motor running. Reserve.

7. Using MEDIUM SHREDDING BLADE, grate mozzarella. Reserve.

8. Using STEEL BLADE, process ricotta cheese, with egg, until smooth. Reserve.

9. Spread small amount of tomato sauce on bottom of buttered baking dish and top with 3 lasagne noodles (or 2 strips of homemade Pasta Dough). Spoon half the ricotta mixture over noodles and cover with one-third of the beef mixture. Continue layering with sauce, 3 noodles (or 2 strips), remaining ricotta mixture, half the remaining meat, sauce, remaining 3 noodles (or 2 strips), and remaining meat. Sprinkle with mozzarella cheese, Parmesan cheese, and pour remaining tomato sauce over all.

10. Bake 35 to 40 minutes and serve with additional grated Parmesan cheese in a separate bowl.

TO PREPARE IN ADVANCE: Through step 9.
TO FREEZE: Through step 10. Defrost overnight in refrigerator. To reheat, place in preheated oven and bake 20 to 25 minutes.

VARIATION: To prepare spinach lasagne, using STEEL BLADE, chop 1 cup cooked, drained spinach and combine with ricotta mixture.

From Alan Hooker's Ranch House restaurant in Ojai, California. This is served as a main dish.

PECAN LOAF

Serves 8

6 tablespoons fresh parsley leaves
3 slices white bread, torn into
   pieces
6 ounces shelled pecans
2 stalks celery, strings removed,
   cut in 1-inch pieces
¼ small onion, cut in half

3 large eggs
2½ cups milk
1 teaspoon herb salt
3 tablespoons melted unsalted
   butter
Sauce Zoia (page 200)

1. Preheat oven to 375°F. Butter a 9 x 4½ x 2½-inch baking pan.

2. Using STEEL BLADE, chop parsley fine. Remove to large mixing bowl.

3. Using STEEL BLADE, separately chop fine bread, pecans, celery, and onion, draining onion if necessary. Add all to mixing bowl.

4. Using STEEL BLADE, beat eggs until frothy. Add to mixing bowl with milk, herb salt, and melted butter. Combine all ingredients thoroughly and let stand for 20 minutes.

5. Pour into prepared pan and bake 45 to 50 minutes, until nicely browned.

6. Serve with Sauce Zoia.

TO PREPARE IN ADVANCE: Through step 4.
TO FREEZE: Through step 5. To reheat, place in preheated oven and bake 30 minutes.

Marvelous for brunch. I like it cold the next day.

VEGETABLE FRITTATA

Serves 6 to 8

4 or 5 sprigs fresh parsley leaves
4 ounces sharp Cheddar cheese,
    chilled
4 shallots
1 medium zucchini, cut in half
    lengthwise
½ green pepper, seeded
½ sweet red pepper, seeded

8 medium mushrooms
4 tablespoons (½ stick) unsalted
    butter
¼ teaspoon dried oregano
Salt and freshly ground pepper
10 eggs
2 or 3 dashes of Tabasco

1. Using STEEL BLADE, chop parsley fine. Reserve.

2. Using MEDIUM SHREDDING BLADE, grate cheese. Reserve.

3. Using STEEL BLADE, with motor running, drop shallots through feed tube. Chop fine. Reserve.

4. Using MEDIUM SLICING BLADE, slice zucchini, green and red peppers, and mushrooms, separately. Reserve each separately.

5. Preheat oven to 500°F.

6. Melt butter in 10-inch ovenproof skillet. Over moderate flame, sauté shallots and peppers until shallots are transparent, about 5 minutes. Add zucchini and mushrooms and continue to cook until vegetables are tender but still crisp, about 5 minutes longer. Season with oregano and salt and freshly ground pepper.

7. Meanwhile, using STEEL BLADE, beat eggs until foamy, about 10 seconds. Season with Tabasco. Pour eggs over vegetables in skillet and lower flame. Allow eggs to cook until set, 8 to 10 minutes. Sprinkle with cheese.

8. Place skillet in oven, directly under broiler, and cook until top puffs and browns and frittata is firm to the touch. Do not overcook (frittata must still be moist inside).

9. Remove from oven, sprinkle with reserved parsley, and serve directly from skillet.

TO PREPARE IN ADVANCE: Through step 4.
TO FREEZE: Do not freeze.

VARIATION: Sliced cooked meat or sausage can be added to skillet just before eggs are poured in.

VEGETABLES

This is a master vegetable purée recipe. Use a vegetable of your choice and combine with ingredients listed, according to taste and texture desired.

Vegetable Puree

2 pounds vegetables (broccoli, cauliflower, stringbeans, spinach, mushrooms, etc.), cooked
½ to ⅔ cup Crème Fraîche *(page 205)*

Salt and freshly ground pepper to taste
Dash of nutmeg *(optional)*
1½ to 2 tablespoons freshly grated Parmesan cheese *(optional)*

1. Using STEEL BLADE, purée vegetables (see Table of Foods, page 2–15). Transfer to medium mixing bowl.

2. Add remaining ingredients, as desired, and stir through.

3. Use as a vegetable side dish, as is, or fill Tartlet Shells (page 252).

TO PREPARE IN ADVANCE: Through step 2.
TO FREEZE: Do not freeze.

Turnip and Potato Puree

Serves 6 to 8

Fresh parsley leaves
1 bunch turnips, peeled
4 medium boiling potatoes, peeled
½ cup Crème Fraîche *(page 205)*
1½ teaspoons salt

½ teaspoon white pepper
½ bunch chives, snipped
6 or 8 Tartlet Shells *(page 252, optional)*

1. Using STEEL BLADE, chop parsley fine. Reserve. Clean work bowl.

2. Using WIDE SLICING BLADE, slice turnips. Steam 20 minutes, or until just barely cooked (al dente).

3. Using WIDE SLICING BLADE, slice potatoes. Steam 10 to 12 minutes, or until al dente.

4. Using STEEL BLADE, purée turnips and potatoes until smooth,

scraping down sides of work bowl as necessary. Add *Crème Fraîche*, salt, pepper, and chives and process 10 seconds longer. Correct seasoning to taste.

5. Serve hot as is or spoon into baked Tartlet Shells and sprinkle with reserved parsley.

TO PREPARE IN ADVANCE: Through step 4. Reheat as necessary.
TO FREEZE: Do not freeze.

VARIATIONS: 1. Sprinkle top with crisp, chopped bacon.
2. Peeled celery root can be substituted for turnips.

ZUCCHINI SOUFFLE

Serves 4

½ slice day-old bread, crusts
   removed
1 tablespoon snipped fresh chives
   or tops of green onions
½ teaspoon fresh thyme or pinch
   of dried thyme
2 small shallots
2 medium zucchini

2 tablespoons unsalted butter
2 tablespoons Crème Fraîche
   (page 205) or heavy cream
4 egg yolks
¼ teaspoon salt
¼ teaspoon white pepper
7 egg whites

1. Preheat oven to 400°F.

2. Using STEEL BLADE, process bread into fine crumbs. Butter 1-quart soufflé dish and sprinkle with crumbs, shaking out excess.

3. Using STEEL BLADE, chop chives and thyme fine. Reserve.

4. Using MEDIUM SHREDDING BLADE, grate shallots and zucchini. In medium skillet, melt butter and sauté shallots and zucchini until zucchini is tender but still crisp, 3 to 4 minutes. Clean work bowl.

5. Using STEEL BLADE, purée zucchini mixture. Add *Crème Fraîche*, chopped herbs, egg yolks, salt, and pepper and process until smooth, scraping down sides of work bowl as necessary. Remove to large mixing bowl.

6. Using wire whisk or rotary beater, beat egg whites until stiff but not dry. Stir one-quarter of beaten whites into purée and then fold in remaining whites as quickly as possible.

7. Pour into prepared soufflé dish and bake 20 minutes. Top will be lightly browned but center will still be creamy. Serve immediately.

TO PREPARE IN ADVANCE: Through step 5.
TO FREEZE: Do not freeze.

TIMBALES OF VEGETABLES

Serves 6

1 pound carrots, peeled
6 tablespoons unsalted butter
2 pounds spinach, washed and
    stemmed
1 pound cauliflower, in small
    flowerettes

6 eggs
Salt and white pepper
Pinch of sugar (optional)

1. Preheat oven to 400°F. Butter 6 one-half-cup timbales or custard cups.

2. Using MEDIUM SLICING BLADE, slice carrots. In a medium saucepan, over high flame, cook carrots in salted boiling water to cover until tender, about 10 minutes. Drain, add 2 tablespoons of the butter, and reserve.

3. In medium saucepan, over moderate flame, melt 2 tablespoons of the butter. Add spinach and cook until wilted, 2 to 3 minutes. Drain and reserve.

4. In medium saucepan, over high flame, cook cauliflower in salted water to cover until tender, 8 to 10 minutes. Drain, add remaining 2 tablespoons butter, and reserve.

5. Using STEEL BLADE, purée carrots, spinach, and cauliflower, separately, adding 2 eggs to each vegetable. Season each vegetable with salt and pepper to taste and add sugar to carrots, if desired.

6. Into buttered timbales layer vegetables—first carrots, then cauliflower, and last of all, spinach.

7. Place timbales in bain-marie on top of stove and bring water just to boil. Transfer to oven and bake 20 to 25 minutes, until barely firm.

8. Unmold timbales on plates and serve as is or with Julienne of Vegetables (page 153).

TO PREPARE IN ADVANCE: Through step 6.
TO FREEZE: Do not freeze.

VARIATION: Substitute turnips for cauliflower and zucchini for spinach.

Julienne of Vegetables

Serves 6

2 medium carrots, peeled
3 stalks celery, strings removed
3 medium tomatoes, peeled and seeded
4 tablespoons (½ stick) unsalted butter

2 cups Chicken Stock (page 83)
1 cup heavy cream
Salt and freshly ground pepper

1. Cut carrots and celery width of pusher. Using MEDIUM SHREDDING BLADE, shred carrots and celery. In a medium saucepan, over high flame, cook vegetables in boiling water to cover until tender but still crisp, 3 or 4 minutes.* Drain and reserve.

2. Using STEEL BLADE, with on/off turns, coarsely chop tomatoes. In medium skillet, over moderate flame, melt 1 tablespoon of the butter. Add tomatoes and cook until most of juices have disappeared. Season with salt and pepper to taste. Reserve.

3. In medium saucepan, over moderate flame, reduce stock to 1 cup. Pour in cream and continue to reduce until 1½ cups liquid remain.

4. Remove pan from heat, slowly stir in remaining 3 tablespoons butter, a small amount at a time. Add vegetables and heat through. Do not boil.

5. Serve with timbales, broiled fish, etc. Top with tomatoes and nap with sauce.

TO PREPARE IN ADVANCE: Through step 3.
TO FREEZE: Do not freeze.

*I find the easiest way to cook the vegetables is to place them in a French-fry basket and set the basket in the boiling water.

REFRIED BEANS

Make 2½ cups

½ pound dried pinto or red kidney
   beans, rinsed
1 large onion, quartered
½ teaspoon salt

Freshly ground pepper
¼ to ½ cup vegetable oil
Sour cream for garnish

1. In 2-quart saucepan, combine beans with 5 cups water and, over moderate flame, bring to boil. Lower heat and simmer 30 minutes.

2. Using STEEL BLADE, with on/off turns, coarsely chop onion. Add to beans with the salt and pepper to taste and continue to simmer until tender, about 1½ hours. Stir occasionally, adding boiling water as necessary. Mixture should be thick, but you must be careful that beans do not stick to pan.

3. Drain whatever water still remains and remove beans to work bowl. Using STEEL BLADE, with on/off turns, mash beans.

4. In medium skillet, over moderate flame, heat ¼ cup oil. Add beans and cook, stirring occasionally, until quite thick, adding more oil as necessary. Correct seasoning to taste.

5. Serve hot, topped with a dollop of sour cream.

TO PREPARE IN ADVANCE: Through step 4.
TO FREEZE: Do not freeze.

Aunt Ruth's Cabbage-Noodle Casserole

1 medium onion, quartered
¼ pound (1 stick) unsalted butter
1 large head cabbage, cored and
   quartered

1½ teaspoons salt
12 ounces packaged wide noodles
½ teaspoon freshly ground pepper

1. Using STEEL BLADE, with on/off turns, chop onion fine. Drain. In large skillet, over low flame, melt butter. Sauté onion until translucent, about 15 minutes.

2. Using MEDIUM SLICING BLADE, grate cabbage. Place 2 or 3 layers of grated cabbage on paper towels and sprinkle with the salt. After 15 or 20 minutes, squeeze out water and add cabbage to onion. Sauté until cabbage is tender, about 40 minutes.

3. Boil noodles according to package directions. Drain and add to skillet. Stir to combine. Add pepper and correct seasoning to taste.

4. Serve hot.

TO PREPARE IN ADVANCE: Through step 2.
TO FREEZE: Do not freeze.

VARIATION: Caraway seeds may be added to skillet with noodles.

A favorite at Ma Maison restaurant in Los Angeles.

Gateau de Carottes
(Carrot Loaf)

2 pounds carrots, peeled
¼ pound (1 stick) unsalted butter
¼ pound mushrooms
1 pound spinach, washed and
   stemmed

4 ounces Swiss cheese, chilled
4 eggs
1 teaspoon salt
½ teaspoon freshly ground pepper

1. Preheat oven to 400°F. Line a 9 x 4 x 3-inch loaf pan with aluminum foil. Butter foil generously.

2. Using MEDIUM SLICING BLADE, with firm pressure, slice carrots. In a medium skillet, on moderate flame, slowly sauté carrots in half the butter until tender, 10 to 15 minutes. Return to work bowl and, using STEEL BLADE, chop coarsely. (This must be done in 2 or 3 batches with on/off turns for an even chop.) Remove carrots to mixing bowl, as chopped.

3. Using MEDIUM SLICING BLADE, with medium pressure, slice mushrooms. In a small skillet, on moderate flame, sauté mushrooms in half the remaining butter until tender, 3 to 5 minutes. Drain and return to work bowl. Using STEEL BLADE, chop coarsely, with 3 to 4 on/off turns. Add to carrots. Clean work bowl.

4. Heat remaining butter in medium saucepan and sauté spinach over moderate flame, about 5 minutes. Drain and reserve.

5. Using MEDIUM SHREDDING BLADE, grate Swiss cheese. Reserve.

6. Using PLASTIC BLADE, beat eggs until frothy. Add cheese and beat 2 or 3 seconds longer. Add to carrots and mushrooms and combine thoroughly. Season with salt and pepper. Correct seasoning to taste.

7. Fill prepared loaf pan with half the carrot mixture. Spread drained spinach over mixture and fill with remaining carrot mixture.

8. Place loaf pan into a slightly larger pan. Pour hot water into larger pan, bring just to boil on stove top, and then remove to the oven. Bake 45 minutes, or until knife plunged into center comes out clean.

9. Invert onto warm serving platter and let rest 10 minutes. Carefully remove foil. Slice and serve.

TO PREPARE IN ADVANCE: Through step 7.
TO FREEZE: Do not freeze.

This is very rich, but oh so good!

TIMBALES OF LEEKS

Serves 6

3 medium leeks, white part only | Half-and-half
3 tablespoons unsalted butter | ½ teaspoon salt
3 eggs | ¼ teaspoon white pepper

1. Preheat oven to 350°F. Thoroughly butter insides of 6 one-half cup timbales or custard cups.

2. Clean leeks and trim to fit upright in feed tube. Using THIN SLICING BLADE, slice leeks. Melt butter in medium skillet and sauté leeks, partially covered, over low flame until they are limp, about 10 minutes.

3. Using PLASTIC BLADE, beat eggs until frothy. Combine eggs and cooked leeks in 2-cup measure. Add enough half-and-half to fill measure. Season with salt and pepper and gently stir through mixture. Correct seasoning to taste. Divide mixture into prepared timbales.

4. Place timbales in bain-marie, bring just to boil on stove top, remove to oven, and bake 25 minutes, or until barely firm. Timbales will stay warm in bain-marie for up to 20 minutes.

5. To serve, run knife around edges and invert on plates.

TO PREPARE IN ADVANCE: Through step 3.
TO FREEZE: Do not freeze.

Duxelles may be used to stuff croustades, mushroom caps, and as a flavoring for many kinds of stuffings.

DUXELLES

Makes about 1½ cups

4 sprigs fresh parsley, leaves only
2 large shallots, cut in half
3 tablespoons unsalted butter
1 pound fresh mushrooms
  (if large, cut in half)

¼ teaspoon salt
Few grinds fresh pepper
Dash of Tabasco

1. Using STEEL BLADE, chop parsley fine. Reserve.

2. Using STEEL BLADE, with motor running, drop shallots through feed tube and chop fine.

3. In large skillet, over low flame, melt butter. Add shallots to skillet and sauté until translucent.

4. Meanwhile, using STEEL BLADE, with on/off turns, chop mushrooms fine, 1 cup at a time, scraping down sides of work bowl as necessary. Wrap chopped mushrooms in a clean linen or tea towel and wring to remove as much liquid as possible.

5. Add mushrooms to skillet and sauté until all liquid has evaporated, about 10 minutes, stirring occasionally. Add remaining ingredients and correct seasoning to taste.

6. Refrigerate and use as needed.

TO PREPARE IN ADVANCE: Through step 5.
TO FREEZE: Through step 5. Defrost overnight in refrigerator. To reheat, place in skillet and heat through over low flame.

MUSHROOM RATATOUILLE

Serves 10 to 12

½ cup fresh parsley leaves
¼ cup fresh basil leaves
1 tablespoon fresh tarragon leaves
2 pounds medium tomatoes, peeled and quartered
3 cloves garlic
1 medium onion
1 pound mushrooms
8 tablespoons olive oil

3 medium zucchini
1 medium green pepper, halved, cored, and seeded
1 large eggplant (1¾ pounds) cut to fit feed tube
2 teaspoons salt
20 grinds fresh pepper
Lemon wedges for garnish (optional)

1. Using STEEL BLADE, chop parsley, basil, and tarragon fine. Reserve.

2. Using STEEL BLADE, with on/off turns, coarsely chop tomatoes and garlic. Reserve. Clean work bowl.

3. Using MEDIUM SLICING BLADE, slice mushrooms. Reserve.

4. Using MEDIUM SLICING BLADE, slice onion. In large skillet, over low flame, heat 6 tablespoons of the olive oil. Sauté onion until translucent, about 10 minutes.

5. Using WIDE SLICING BLADE, slice zucchini, green pepper, and eggplant. Add to skillet.

6. In medium skillet, over moderate flame, heat remaining 2 tablespoons oil and sauté mushrooms until juices evaporate, about 10 minutes. Add to vegetables, along with reserved parsley and herbs, salt, and pepper. Bring to boil, over low heat, then cover and continue cooking over *very* low heat 2½ to 3 hours.* Liquid will evaporate but vegetables will still be slightly crunchy. Correct seasoning to taste.

7. Serve hot or cold. If cold, serve with lemon wedges and correct seasoning to taste.

TO PREPARE IN ADVANCE: Through step 6. This will keep refrigerated up to one week.
TO FREEZE: Do not freeze.

*It may be advisable to set skillet on asbestos pad while cooking over low heat so vegetables do not cook too rapidly.

To fill potato baskets . . . or to use as a side dish.

PUREE OF PEAS

Serves 6

2 boxes (8 or 10 ounces each)   *Pinch of sugar (optional),*
  frozen peas   *2 or 3 dashes of nutmeg*
¼ *pound (1 stick) unsalted butter,*   *Salt and freshly ground pepper*
  at room temperature, cut in 6   *Potato Baskets (page 160; optional)*
  pieces

1. Cook peas according to package directions. Drain.

2. Using STEEL BLADE, add all ingredients to work bowl. Purée until smooth, about 60 seconds. Correct seasoning to taste.

3. When ready to serve, reheat peas and fill Potato Baskets.

TO PREPARE IN ADVANCE: Through step 2.
TO FREEZE: Do not freeze.

If you want to impress friends, try these potato baskets.

POTATO BASKETS

Serves 6

2 *pounds baking potatoes,*   *Wire baskets, 1 large, 1 small*
  scrubbed but unpeeled   *(see note below)*
Vegetable oil for deep frying

1. Using MEDIUM SHREDDING BLADE, grate potatoes. Remove to cold water. (This will keep potatoes white and also remove excess starch.) Drain and dry potatoes well before using.

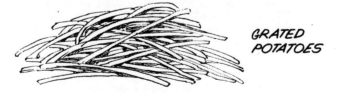

GRATED
POTATOES

2. In wok or pot used for deep frying, heat oil to 360°F. (If you do not have a thermometer, test with piece of green onion. When onion dropped into oil turns very brown, oil is ready.) Dip larger basket into oil, remove, and then fill with potatoes, using about ⅔ cup grated potato for each basket. Dip smaller basket into oil, remove, and then press into potato-lined larger basket. Secure.

GRATED POTATOES IN BASKET

3. Plunge 2 baskets into hot oil and fry until lightly browned, about 10 to 12 minutes.

4. Separate 2 wire baskets and gently remove potato basket, using a knife if necessary. Drain baskets on paper towels. Repeat this procedure to make 6 baskets. As oil gets hoter, it may take a shorter time for potatoes to cook.

5. When ready to serve, reheat oil and set baskets into hot oil until brown and crisp. Fill with Purée of Peas (page 160), sliced sautéed mushrooms, or creamed vegetables.

POTATO BASKET

TO PREPARE IN ADVANCE: Through step 4.
TO FREEZE: Through step 4. To reheat, plunge potato baskets into hot oil for 2 or 3 minutes, until brown and crisp.

NOTE: Special wire baskets may be purchased in shops selling gourmet equipment.

It will be difficult to eat a packaged potato chip after you taste these. At parties they are an overwhelming success.

POTATO CHIPS

Serves 4

*4 large Idaho potatoes, well   Vegetable oil for deep frying
   scrubbed   Salt*

1. Cut potatoes to fit feed tube and, using MEDIUM SLICING BLADE, slice. Immediately remove to bowl of cold water for at least 1 hour. (This removes excess starch, makes potatoes crisp rather than soggy, and keeps them white.)

2. In a wok or deep-fryer, over medium flame, heat oil to 360°F. Drain and dry potato slices. Drop, a few at a time, into hot oil and fry until golden brown. Remove with slotted spoon to paper towels to drain. Season with salt to taste.

3. Store in airtight container in cool place.

TO PREPARE IN ADVANCE: Through step 3.
TO FREEZE: Through step 2. To reheat, place potatoes on baking tray in very hot oven (450°F.) until golden brown, turning occasionally. Or drop in hot oil until golden. Drain as above.

VARIATIONS: 1. Sprinkle cooked potatoes with grated Parmesan cheese.
2. Slice sweet potatoes, following above directions, and sprinkle with sugar and a dash of nutmeg.

Small potato pancakes make a marvelous hors d'oeuvre, but they are delicious, large or small. This recipe is from The World Famous Ratner's Meatless Cookbook.

POTATO PANCAKES

Serves 6 to 8

6 medium potatoes, peeled and
    quartered
1 medium onion, quartered
2 eggs
1½ teaspoons salt

¼ teaspoon freshly ground pepper
½ cup all-purpose flour
Vegetable oil for frying
Applesauce (page 284; optional)
Sour cream (optional)

1. Using STEEL BLADE, process one potato at a time until finely grated. Remove to large bowl of cold water as processed.

2. Using STEEL BLADE, with on/off turns, chop onion fine. Drain if necessary and return to work bowl. Add eggs, salt, pepper, and flour and process with on/off turns until just combined.

3. Drain potatoes, pressing out all liquid. Add onion-egg mixture to potatoes and combine thoroughly.

4. In large skillet, over moderate flame, heat ½ inch oil. Drop batter by tablespoons into hot oil. Flatten out to 4-inch pancakes and fry slowly until brown and crisp. Turn and brown on other side.

5. Remove to heated platter and keep warm until ready to serve.

6. Serve with Applesauce (page 284) or sour cream.

TO PREPARE IN ADVANCE: Through step 4, lightly browned.
TO FREEZE: Through step 4, lightly browned. To reheat, drop pancakes into hot oil and fry until brown and crisp.

VARIATION: Cut lightly browned potato pancakes into strips. Drop a few at a time into deep oil heated to 360°F. and fry until brown and crisp.

This simple, tasty preparation of potatoes will enhance any meal.

Scalloped Potatoes

Serves 4 to 6

3 tablespoons fresh parsley leaves
3 medium boiling potatoes, peeled
1½ teaspoons salt

¼ teaspoon white pepper
2½ to 3 cups heavy cream

1. Preheat oven to 375°F. Butter a 9 x 13-inch baking dish.

2. Using STEEL BLADE, chop parsley fine. Reserve.

3. Using THIN SLICING BLADE, slice potatoes. Arrange in baking dish, making only 2 layers.

4. Season with salt and pepper and pour in enough cream to cover.

5. Bake about 25 minutes, or until potatoes are fork tender.

6. Sprinkle with reserved parsley and serve immediately.

TO PREPARE IN ADVANCE: Through step 4. Refrigerate until 30 minutes before baking time.
TO FREEZE: Do not freeze.

VARIATIONS: 1. One-half cup grated Swiss cheese may be sprinkled over potatoes before baking.
2. A layer of thinly sliced cooked ham, lightly sautéed onions, or chopped cooked bacon can be put between the two layers of potatoes.

Use your imagination to fill this shell. A quiche filling (see page 59) or eggs combined with a variety of meats or vegetables make a marvelous filling.

Potato Shell

Makes one 9-inch crust

1 medium onion, quartered
3 medium potatoes, peeled

1 teaspoon salt
Freshly ground pepper

1. Preheat oven to 375°F. Generously butter 9-inch pie pan.

2. Using STEEL BLADE, with on/off turns, chop onion fine. Drain well and transfer to medium mixing bowl.

3. Using MEDIUM SHREDDING BLADE, grate potatoes. Remove to cold water. Drain and dry well and combine with onion. Season with salt and pepper.

4. Press potato mixture over bottom and up sides of buttered pie pan.

5. Bake 10 to 12 minutes. Cool, fill as desired, and bake until firm and lightly brown on top.

TO PREPARE IN ADVANCE: Through step 5.
TO FREEZE: Through step 5. Shell may be filled directly from freezer.

VARIATION: Add 1 cup grated Cheddar or Swiss cheese to potato mixture and proceed as above.

SCALLOPED TOMATOES

Serves 4 to 6

3 tablespoons unsalted butter, melted
3 slices day-old bread, torn in pieces*
½ medium green pepper, cored, seeded, and cut in 1-inch pieces
1 large stalk celery, strings removed, cut in 1-inch pieces
1 clove garlic

1 medium onion, quartered
1 pound tomatoes, quartered
3 or 4 fresh basil leaves or pinch of dried basil
1 teaspoon salt
Freshly ground pepper
Pinch of dried thyme
2 tablespoons unsalted butter, cut in small pieces

1. Preheat oven to 350°F. Generously butter 2-quart casserole, using the melted butter.

2. Using STEEL BLADE, process bread into fine crumbs. Reserve.

3. Using STEEL BLADE, with on/off turns, coarsely chop pepper, celery, garlic, and onion separately. Drain onion as necessary. Remove vegetables to casserole as chopped.

4. Using STEEL BLADE, with on/off turns, coarsely chop tomatoes and basil. Add to vegetables in casserole and season with salt, pepper, and thyme.

5. Sprinkle with reserved bread crumbs and dot with the 2 tablespoons butter.

6. Bake, uncovered, 25 minutes, or until crumbs are lightly browned.

TO PREPARE IN ADVANCE: Through step 5.
TO FREEZE: Do not freeze.

*Substitute 1½ cups Seasoned Bread Crumbs (page 245).

SALADS

Spinach Salad

8 ounces Swiss cheese
½ pound bacon, crisply cooked,
   cut in 1-inch pieces
3 hard-cooked eggs, peeled and cut
   in half
¾ pound fresh mushrooms

2 pounds spinach, washed,
   stemmed, and dried
Mustard-Vinaigrette Dressing
   (pages 186 and 187)
Tomato wedges

1. Using MEDIUM SHREDDING BLADE, grate Swiss cheese. Reserve.

2. Using STEEL BLADE, coarsely chop bacon. Reserve. Clean work bowl.

3. Using STEEL BLADE, with on/off turns, chop eggs until fluffy. Do not overprocess. Reserve.

4. Using MEDIUM SLICING BLADE, slice mushrooms. Reserve.

5. In large salad bowl, arrange spinach leaves. Add mushrooms, eggs, bacon, and cheese and toss with dressing. Garnish with tomato wedges.

TO PREPARE IN ADVANCE: Through step 4. Refrigerate until needed.
TO FREEZE: Do not freeze.

Middle Eastern Cabbage Salad

¼ cup fresh parsley leaves
2 green onions, white part only,
   chilled
½ medium head cabbage, cut in
   half and cored
½ cup cooked green peas

½ to ¾ cup Classic Mayonnaise
   (page 182)
1 to 2 teaspoons curry powder
½ cup peanuts
Salt and freshly ground pepper

1. Using STEEL BLADE, chop parsley and green onions. Transfer to medium mixing bowl.

2. Using THIN SLICING BLADE, slice cabbage. Add to mixing bowl. Add peas.

3. Flavor mayonnaise with curry powder to taste. Add to mixing bowl and toss everything together. Refrigerate 1 hour, to blend flavors.

4. Garnish with peanuts and season with salt and pepper to taste.

TO PREPARE IN ADVANCE: Through step 3.
TO FREEZE: Do not freeze.

This can be served with beef, veal, or fowl. I like to freeze packages of cranberries so my family can have relish a good part of the year.

CRANBERRY RELISH

Yield: About 5 cups

½ cup walnut halves
1 medium orange, unpeeled,
   quartered and seeded
2 ripe medium pears, peeled,
   quartered, and cored

1 cup water
1 cup sugar
1 pound cranberries, washed and
   drained
1 cup raisins

1. Using STEEL BLADE, with 2 or 3 on/off turns, coarsely chop walnuts. Reserve.

2. Using STEEL BLADE, with on/off turns, coarsely chop oranges and pears, separately, 4 quarters at a time.

3. In 4-quart saucepan, over high flame, bring water and sugar to boil and cook until sugar dissolves completely and water is clear, about 5 minutes.

4. Add cranberries, oranges, and pears to saucepan, bring water back to a boil, and boil, stirring occasionally, until cranberries pop open, about 5 minutes. Remove from heat and stir in raisins and walnuts. Cool.

5. Refrigerate in covered container and use as desired.

TO PREPARE IN ADVANCE: Through step 5.
TO FREEZE: Do not freeze.

VARIATION: Use any combination of fruits, adding apples, pineapple, etc., as desired.

CARROT SALAD

Serves 4 to 6

1 bunch fresh dill, leaves only
1 pound carrots, peeled
Juice of ½ lemon
1 teaspoon sugar

1 teaspoon salt
Freshly ground pepper
3 tablespoons olive oil

1. Using STEEL BLADE, chop dill. Remove to mixing bowl.

2. Using FINE SHREDDING BLADE, shred carrots. Add to mixing bowl and toss lightly until well mixed.

3. Combine remaining ingredients and stir until sugar is dissolved. Toss lightly with carrots.

4. Serve at room temperature.

TO PREPARE IN ADVANCE: Through step 4.
TO FREEZE: Do not freeze.

RED ONION SALAD

Serves 4

1 large red onion, cut in half
2 cups water
4 tablespoons red wine vinegar

¼ teaspoon salt
¼ cup vegetable oil
½ teaspoon whole mustard seed

1. Using THIN SLICING BLADE, slice onion.

2. In medium saucepan, bring water to boil. Add 2 tablespoons of

the vinegar and sliced onions and return to boil. Drain thoroughly.

3. Using PLASTIC BLADE, combine remaining 2 tablespoons vinegar and the salt with 1 or 2 on/off turns. With motor running, pour oil through feed tube. Remove to medium mixing bowl and combine with mustard seed. Add onion slices and mix thoroughly. Correct seasoning to taste.

TO PREPARE IN ADVANCE: Through step 3.
TO FREEZE: Do not freeze.

Mushrooms a la Grecque

Serves 6

Juice of 1 lemon
2 pounds button or slightly larger
  mushrooms, cut in half
1 medium onion, quartered
2 cloves garlic
¼ cup olive oil
4 medium tomatoes, peeled,
  seeded, and quartered

1 medium green pepper, seeded
  and cut in 1-inch pieces
Pinch of dried thyme
1 bay leaf
1 cup white wine
4 cups Chicken Stock (page 83)
½ teaspoon salt
Freshly ground pepper

1. In large mixing bowl, squeeze lemon juice over mushrooms to prevent discoloration. Stir to combine.

2. Using STEEL BLADE, with on/off turns, chop onion and garlic fine. Drain as necessary.

3. In large stainless-steel or enameled saucepan, heat oil over moderate flame. Add onion and garlic and sauté until translucent.

4. Using STEEL BLADE, with on/off turns, coarsely chop tomatoes and green pepper separately. Add to onion with thyme and bay leaf and deglaze pan with white wine.

5. Pour stock into pan and bring to a boil. Season with salt and at least 20 grinds of fresh pepper (this should be on the peppery side).

6. Add mushrooms to pan and cook just until tender, about 5 minutes. Return mushrooms to mixing bowl and reduce liquid in pan until absorbed by vegetables. Pour vegetables over mushrooms and combine thoroughly. Remove bay leaf.

7. Mushrooms can be served hot, at room temperature, or cold. If served cold, refrigerate 2 to 3 hours.

TO PREPARE IN ADVANCE: Through step 6.
TO FREEZE: Do not freeze.

VARIATION: Artichoke bottoms may be substituted for mushrooms. Cut bottoms into bite-size pieces and cook 20 minutes, or until barely tender.

GERMAN POTATO SALAD

Serves 6 to 8

3 pounds small new potatoes,
    unpeeled
¼ cup fresh parsley leaves
½ pound thick-sliced bacon
1 large onion, quartered
2 tablespoons unsalted butter

½ cup red wine vinegar
2 tablespoons water
2 tablespoons sugar
1 teaspoon salt
Freshly ground pepper

1. In water to cover, boil potatoes until tender, about 20 minutes. Drain, peel, and cut in half (or if too large, cut accordingly). Return potatoes to pan to dry, then transfer to salad bowl.

2. Using STEEL BLADE, chop parsley leaves fine. Reserve.

3. Sauté bacon until crisp. Drain and dry on paper towels. Cut each slice into 3 pieces. Using STEEL BLADE, with on/off turns, coarsely chop bacon. Add to potatoes. Clean work bowl.

4. Using STEEL BLADE, with on/off turns, coarsely chop onion. Drain as necessary. In small skillet, melt butter and sauté onion until lightly browned. Add to potatoes.

5. In small saucepan, combine vinegar, water, sugar, salt, and pepper and simmer 2 minutes. Pour over salad, sprinkle with parsley, and gently toss. Correct seasoning to taste.

6. Serve hot or cold.

TO PREPARE IN ADVANCE: Through step 5.
TO FREEZE: Do not freeze.

TOMATO A L'ANTIBOISE

Serves 4

¼ cup fresh parsley leaves
4 medium tomatoes
1½ teaspoons salt
1 can (7 ounces) tuna, drained
*6 tablespoons unsalted butter, in 6
   pieces*
*1 hard-cooked egg, peeled and cut
   in half*

2 tablespoons olive oil
2 tablespoons safflower oil
Freshly ground pepper
Juice of ½ lemon
Lettuce leaves

1. Using STEEL BLADE, chop parsley fine. Reserve.

2. Cut slice off top of each tomato. Scoop out pulp to use another time. Sprinkle insides of tomatoes with 1 teaspoon of the salt and invert to drain, about 10 minutes.

3. Using STEEL BLADE, combine tuna, butter, egg, olive oil, safflower oil, remaining ½ teaspoon salt, the pepper, and lemon juice. Process until smooth, scraping down sides of work bowl as necessary. Correct seasoning to taste, adding more oil if necessary.

4. Stuff tomatoes with tuna mixture and sprinkle with reserved chopped parsley.

5. Serve on a bed of lettuce.

TO PREPARE IN ADVANCE: Through step 4.
TO FREEZE: Do not freeze.

TOMATO SALAD

Serves 6

1 or 2 cloves garlic
6 medium tomatoes, ripe but still
  firm
2 onions, chilled

2 green peppers, halved, cored,
  and seeded
2 to 4 tablespoons olive oil
2 to 4 teaspoons salt

1. Using STEEL BLADE, with motor running, drop garlic through feed tube to mince. Remove to large mixing bowl.

2. Cut tomatoes and onions to fit feed tube if necessary. Using FINE SLICING BLADE, slice tomatoes, onions, and green peppers, separately, adding them to garlic in mixing bowl.

3. Add olive oil and salt to taste to vegetables and combine thoroughly. Allow salad to stay at room temperature, covered, at least 2 hours.

4. Refrigerate and use as desired.

TO PREPARE IN ADVANCE: Through step 3. This salad will keep, refrigerated, 5 to 7 days.
TO FREEZE: Do not freeze.

CHOPPED SALAD

Serves 6 to 8

½ head iceberg lettuce, cut in
  1-inch pieces
1 small head chicory, cut in 1-inch
  pieces
½ head romaine lettuce, cut in
  1-inch pieces
½ bunch watercress
2 tomatoes, peeled, seeded, and
  quartered
6 slices bacon, cooked crisp and cut
  in 1-inch pieces
3 hard-cooked eggs, peeled and cut
  in half

2 ounces Roquefort cheese, cut in
  1-inch pieces
2 whole chicken breasts, skinned,
  boned, and poached, then chilled
  and cut in 1-inch pieces
1 avocado, peeled and cut in
  1-inch pieces
Juice of ½ lemon
Spicy Salad Dressing (page 186)
Snipped chives (optional)

1. Using STEEL BLADE, coarsely chop iceberg lettuce, chicory, romaine, and watercress separately, with on/off turns. Reserve separately, refrigerated.

2. Using STEEL BLADE, coarsely chop tomatoes with on/off turns, 1 tomato (4 quarters) at a time. Reserve, refrigerated. Clean work bowl.

3. Using STEEL BLADE, chop bacon fine. Start with on/off turns, then allow to run to desired texture. Reserve.

4. Using STEEL BLADE, with on/off turns, chop eggs. Reserve, refrigerated.

5. Using STEEL BLADE, with on/off turns, coarsely chop Roquefort cheese. Reserve, refrigerated. Clean work bowl.

6. Using STEEL BLADE, with on/off turns, coarsely chop chicken, chopping 1 cup at a time. Reserve, refrigerated.

7. Using STEEL BLADE, with 2 or 3 on/off turns, coarsely chop avocado. Sprinkle with lemon juice and reserve, refrigerated.

8. To serve, spread lettuce greens on bottom of a large serving bowl. Arrange tomatoes, bacon, eggs, Roquefort cheese, chicken, and avocado in rows atop lettuce. Pour dressing over salad and toss at table. Sprinkle with chives, as desired.

TO PREPARE IN ADVANCE: Through step 7.
TO FREEZE: Do not freeze.

VARIATION: Ham may be substituted for or used in addition to chicken.

My family enjoys this with knockwurst and potato salad.

SPANISH SALAD ANA

5 medium carrots, peeled
1 cup vegetable oil
3 bay leaves
10 whole cloves
3 medium onions, cut in half
2 green peppers, cut in half, cored, and seeded

1 medium head cabbage, green or red, quartered and cored
2 dashes hot pepper sauce
½ cup white vinegar
½ teaspoon salt
Freshly ground pepper

1. Using FINE SLICING BLADE, slice carrots. In large saucepan, over moderate flame, heat oil. Add carrots, bay leaves, and cloves and cook for about 5 minutes.

2. Using FINE SLICING BLADE, slice onions, green peppers, and cabbage, separately. Reserve separately.

3. Add onions and green peppers to carrots and cook 2 to 3 minutes.

4. Add cabbage to vegetables and cook 5 minutes longer. Vegetables should all be cooked al dente. Transfer to large mixing bowl, add remaining ingredients, and mix thoroughly. Correct seasoning to taste.

5. Serve hot or cold.

TO PREPARE IN ADVANCE: Through step 4.
TO FREEZE: Do not freeze.

NOTE: For a more piquant taste, add chopped chili pepper to vegetables.

The vegetables need not be peeled, only thoroughly washed. The result is a healthful salad with great eye appeal.

RAW VEGETABLE SALAD

Serves 6 to 8

3 *medium carrots*
3 *medium turnips*
1 *small bunch red radishes*
3 *medium beets*
1 *bunch watercress*

2 *cups sour cream*
5 *ounces cream cheese, cut in*
   1-inch pieces
1 *tablespoon seasoned salt*
6 *Bibb lettuce leaves*

1. Thoroughly wash and trim carrots, turnips, radishes, and beets. Using MEDIUM SHREDDING BLADE, grate vegetables separately. Refrigerate in individual bowls while preparing dressing. Clean work bowl.

2. Using STEEL BLADE, chop watercress fine. Place in cloth napkin or towel and squeeze out juice into small bowl. Discard watercress and reserve juice. Clean work bowl.

3. Using STEEL BLADE, process sour cream, cream cheese, and salt until smooth. Add enough watercress juice to give dressing a pleasing green color and process with 2 or 3 on/off turns.

4. To serve, place 1 lettuce leaf on each plate and top with individual mounds of vegetables. Pass dressing in separate bowl.

TO PREPARE IN ADVANCE: Through step 3.
TO FREEZE: Do not freeze.

NOTE: For a buffet, heap vegetables in individual mounds on serving platter around bowl of dressing.

The food processor gives chopped hard-cooked eggs a fluffy consistency that is otherwise difficult to obtain.

EGG SALAD WITH MUSTARD SEED

Serves 4

6 large hard-cooked eggs, peeled
    and cut in half
2 tablespoons Dijon mustard
1 tablespoon whole mustard seed

½ teaspoon whole cumin seed
¾ cup sour cream, or as needed
Salt and freshly ground pepper

1. Using STEEL BLADE, with on/off turns, chop eggs until fluffy. Do not overprocess or eggs will become pasty. Remove to medium mixing bowl.

2. Using STEEL BLADE, add remaining ingredients to work bowl and process just until blended. If a creamier dressing is desired, add more sour cream. Gently stir into eggs and season with salt and pepper.

3. For a light luncheon, serve Egg Salad piled in center of serving plate and surround with Cucumber Salad (page 179) and Red Onion Salad (page 170). Toasted buttered muffins are a delicious accompaniment.

TO PREPARE IN ADVANCE: Through step 2.
TO FREEZE: Do not freeze.

VARIATION: Add 1 teaspoon curry powder to dressing and stir through.

These cucumbers are called Japanese or European, depending on the market selling them. They are the long, slender ones.

CUCUMBER SALAD

1 large European or Japanese
  cucumber, unpeeled
1 cup rice wine vinegar
4 teaspoons sugar

1 tablespoon soy sauce
2 teaspoons lemon juice
2 teaspoons white or black sesame
  seeds, toasted

1. Using THIN SLICING BLADE, slice cucumber. Sprinkle with salt and let drain, about 30 minutes. Rinse and pat dry.

2. In small saucepan, combine vinegar, sugar, soy sauce, and lemon juice. Bring to boil, then lower flame and simmer 2 minutes. Correct seasoning to taste and cool.

3. To serve, pour dressing over cucumbers and sprinkle with toasted sesame seeds.

TO PREPARE IN ADVANCE: Through step 3.
TO FREEZE: Do not freeze.

VARIATION: Bean sprouts, chunks of fresh crabmeat, and *saifun* noodles,* softened in boiling water, may be combined with cucumbers.

*Saifun noodles may be purchased in markets that sell oriental foods. When soft, they become translucent.

TARAMASALATA

¼ cup fresh parsley leaves
½ medium onion, cut in half
4 ounces tarama (see note below)
2 slices day-old bread, crusts
  removed, torn in pieces

Juice of 1 medium lemon
1 cup olive or safflower oil

1. Using STEEL BLADE, chop parsley fine. Reserve.

2. Using STEEL BLADE, with 3 or 4 on/off turns, chop onion. Drain as necessary. Add tarama, bread, lemon juice, and half the parsley. Combine with 4 or 5 on/off turns, scraping down sides of work bowl as necessary.

3. With motor running, slowly pour oil through feed tube until mixture thickens and is smooth. Refrigerate until needed.

4. To serve, pack in serving bowl and sprinkle with remaining chopped parsley. Serve with crackers, pita, or thin-sliced bread.

TO PREPARE IN ADVANCE: Through step 3. This will keep up to 1 week refrigerated.
TO FREEZE: Do not freeze.

NOTE: Tarama is fish roe from the Middle East and is available in specialty food markets.

MAYONNAISE
AND
SALAD
DRESSINGS

Once you have tried homemade mayonnaise, you will never again buy a commercial product. This recipe makes a thin sauce with the consistency of heavy cream.

WHOLE-EGG MAYONNAISE

Makes 1 cup

1 egg
½ teaspoon salt
½ teaspoon dry mustard
1 tablespoon vinegar

1 tablespoon lemon juice
1 cup oil (vegetable, olive, walnut, or safflower), at room temperature

1. Using PLASTIC or STEEL BLADE, add egg, salt, mustard, vinegar, lemon juice, and a few drops of oil to work bowl. Process until combined.

2. With machine running, slowly pour remaining oil through feed tube in steady stream. Refrigerate until ready to use.

TO PREPARE IN ADVANCE: Through step 2. May be prepared and refrigerated, tightly covered, 7 to 10 days.
TO FREEZE: Do not freeze.

NOTE: For thicker mayonnaise, add ¼ cup more oil.

The texture of this is much thicker than Whole-Egg Mayonnaise.

CLASSIC MAYONNAISE

Makes about 2½ cups

2 egg yolks
¼ teaspoon salt
Freshly ground pepper
1 tablespoon Dijon mustard
2 tablespoons lemon juice or wine vinegar

2 cups oil (vegetable, safflower, almond, etc.), at room temperature

1. Using STEEL BLADE, combine all ingredients except oil in the work bowl with on/off turns.

2. With motor running, slowly add oil through feed tube. (As volume increases, oil may be added at a faster speed.) Refrigerate and use as needed.

TO PREPARE IN ADVANCE: Through step 2. May be prepared and refrigerated, tightly covered, 7 to 10 days.
TO FREEZE: Do not freeze.

NOTE: To lighten mayonnaise, add a few drops of heavy cream.

GREEN MAYONNAISE

Makes about 1 cup

1½ cups loosely packed
   combination of watercress,
   tarragon, chives, or parsley

1 cup Classic Mayonnaise
   (page 182)

1. Using STEEL BLADE, place combination of herbs, stems and all, in work bowl. Process until finely chopped. Remove to cloth napkin or towel and squeeze out juice into small mixing bowl.

2. Combine mayonnaise with juice for taste and eye appeal.

3. Serve with cold fish, fish pâté, asparagus, artichokes, or fried or grilled fish.

TO PREPARE IN ADVANCE: Through step 2.
TO FREEZE: Do not freeze.

The addition of whipped cream gives a more delicate texture and flavor to Classic Mayonnaise.

SAUCE MAYONNAISE LEGERE

Makes about 1 cup

2 tablespoons whipped cream
1 cup Classic Mayonnaise (page
   182)

1. Fold whipped cream into mayonnaise.

2. Serve with cold fish, fish pâté, asparagus, artichokes, or fried or grilled fish.

TO PREPARE IN ADVANCE: Through step 1.
TO FREEZE: Do not freeze.

Sauce Tartare

Makes about 1½ cups

1 teaspoon capers
1 hard-cooked egg, peeled and
   halved
2 sprigs tarragon, leaves only
3 stems chives

3 cornichon pickles
3 anchovies, patted dry
1 cup Mayonnaise Légère (page
   183)

1. Using STEEL BLADE, combine capers, egg, tarragon, chives, cornichons, and anchovies and process with on/off turns until chopped fine.

2. Fold chopped ingredients into mayonnaise.

3. Serve with roast beef, cold meats, grilled or fried fish, or fried mushrooms.

TO PREPARE IN ADVANCE: Through step 2.
TO FREEZE: Do not freeze.

Mustard Mayonnaise

Makes about 1 cup

1 cup Mayonnaise Légère (page
   183)

3 to 4 tablespoons Dijon mustard

1. Combine mayonnaise with Dijon mustard to taste.

2. Serve with roast beef, cold meats, grilled or fried fish, or fried mushrooms.

TO PREPARE IN ADVANCE: Through step 1.
TO FREEZE: Do not freeze.

W̲ATERCRESS MAYONNAISE

Makes about 1 cup

1 bunch watercress

1 cup Mayonnaise Légère (page 183)

1. Using STEEL BLADE, place watercress in work bowl, stems and all. Process until finely chopped. Remove to napkin or towel and squeeze out juice into small bowl.

2. Combine mayonnaise with watercress juice for taste and eye appeal.

3. Serve with cold fish, fish pâté, asparagus, artichokes, or fried or grilled fish.

TO PREPARE IN ADVANCE: Through step 2.
TO FREEZE: Do not freeze.

M̲AYONNAISE CONCASSEE

Makes about 1 cup

2 sprigs tarragon, leaves only
3 tablespoons Concassée
(page 191)

1 cup Mayonnaise Légère (page 183)

1. Using STEEL BLADE, chop tarragon leaves fine.

2. In medium mixing bowl, fold *Concassée* and tarragon into mayonnaise.

3. Serve with cold fish, fish pâtés, aspics, or grilled fish.

TO PREPARE IN ADVANCE: Through step 2.
TO FREEZE: Do not freeze.

Spicy salad dressing

Makes 3 cups

½ cup water
½ cup red wine vinegar
½ teaspoon sugar
Juice of ½ lemon
1 tablespoon salt

1 teaspoon white pepper
1 teaspoon Worcestershire sauce
1 teaspoon dry English mustard
1 clove garlic
2 cups olive or safflower oil

1. Using STEEL BLADE, combine all ingredients except oil.

2. Through feed tube, with motor running, slowly add oil. (When oil is partially incorporated, it can be poured more quickly through feed tube.)

3. Refrigerate and use as needed.

TO PREPARE IN ADVANCE: Through step 3.
TO FREEZE: Do not freeze.

A very special dressing. Walnut oil gives it a delicate flavor.

Mustard-vinaigrette dressing I

Makes about 1½ cups

1 egg
2 tablespoons Dijon mustard
2 tablespoons wine vinegar

Salt and freshly ground pepper
¾ cup walnut oil
¼ cup olive or safflower oil

1. Using STEEL BLADE, combine egg, mustard, vinegar, salt, and pepper to taste. Process until combined and then allow to rest, about 5 minutes.

2. Through feed tube, and with the motor running, slowly add oil. (If dressing is too thick, dilute with drops of lemon juice or white wine.)

3. Use dressing as needed.

TO PREPARE IN ADVANCE: Through step 2. Dressing may be refrigerated up to one week.
TO FREEZE: Do not freeze.

VARIATION: Chopped tarragon leaves may be added to dressing.

MUSTARD-VINAIGRETTE DRESSING II

Makes about 2 cups

2 teaspoons Dijon mustard
2 teaspoons fresh tarragon leaves
2 tablespoons sherry wine vinegar
2 egg yolks

¼ teaspoon salt
Large pinch of freshly ground
  pepper
2 cups vegetable oil

1. Using STEEL BLADE, process mustard, tarragon, vinegar, egg yolks, salt, and pepper until combined, scraping down sides of work bowl as necessary.

2. With motor running, slowly pour oil through feed tube until completely blended.

3. Use dressing as needed.

TO PREPARE IN ADVANCE: Through step 2. Dressing may be refrigerated up to 1 week.
TO FREEZE: Do not freeze.

SAUCES
AND
COMPOUND
BUTTERS

This is a low-calorie sauce prepared with nonfat dry milk.

ASPARAGUS SAUCE

Makes about 1½ cups

12 large asparagus, scraped with
    peeler to remove rough spots
2 tablespoons nonfat dry milk
1 cup water

1 tablespoon heavy cream
1 teaspoon lemon juice
Salt and freshly ground pepper

1. To cook asparagus, bring 3 quarts heavily salted water to boil in large saucepan. Add asparagus and, over high flame, cook until tender, about 10 minutes. Drain asparagus and immediately refresh under cold running water to halt cooking.

2. Dissolve nonfat dry milk in water. Reserve.

3. Reserve asparagus tips for garnish and cut remaining stalks into 1-inch pieces. Remove to work bowl fitted with STEEL BLADE.

4. Add milk and heavy cream and process until puréed, scraping down sides of work bowl as necessary.

5. Pour asparagus purée into small saucepan and heat through. Add lemon juice and season to taste with salt and pepper.

6. Serve with steamed or broiled fish.

TO PREPARE IN ADVANCE: Through step 4.
TO FREEZE: Through step 4. To reheat, place in saucepan and heat through over low flame, then continue with recipe.

This is a spicy sauce that can be used with grilled meat as well as with Mexican specialties.

GREEN CHILE SAUCE

Makes 2 cups

12 fresh long green jalapeño chiles,
    or 2 cans (7 ounches each) green
    chiles, drained
1 medium onion, quartered
1 clove garlic

1 medium tomato, peeled, seeded,
    and quartered
½ teaspoon salt
1 tablespoon olive oil

1. Either on baking sheet in hot (450°F.) oven or over gas flame, roast fresh chiles until skin begins to blister. Cool slightly, then peel and remove stems, seeds, and veins.

2. Using STEEL BLADE, with on/off turns, chop onion fine, dropping garlic through feed tube in the process. Drain as necessary and transfer to medium mixing bowl.

3. Using STEEL BLADE, chop chiles fine, scraping down sides of work bowl as necessary. Add to onion.

4. Using STEEL BLADE, purée tomato. Add to chile mixture with remaining ingredients and combine. Correct seasoning to taste.

5. Refrigerate in tightly covered container and use as needed.

TO PREPARE IN ADVANCE: Through step 5. This will keep up to 5 days.
TO FREEZE: Do not freeze.

This can be served with vegetables, fish, or chicken, or it can be added to mayonnaise to serve with fish pâté. It stores well, refrigerated.

CONCASSEE

Makes about 2 cups

1 small celery stalk, strings
  removed, cut in 1-inch pieces
2 cloves garlic or 1 tablespoon
  Garlic Purée (page 242)
3 large shallots
2 tablespoons unsalted butter or
  vegetable oil
3 pounds fresh tomatoes or 1 can
  (16 ounces) peeled tomatoes,
  drained

1 tablespoon tomato paste
1 teaspoon salt
2 tablespoons chopped fresh basil
  or tarragon
Freshly ground pepper

1. Using STEEL BLADE, mince celery, garlic, and shallots, dropping garlic cloves and shallots through feed tube, with motor running. Heat butter in medium skillet and sauté vegetables 2 to 3 minutes, stirring occasionally.

2. Peel, seed, and quarter fresh tomatoes.* Using STEEL BLADE, and in 2 batches, coarsely chop tomatoes. Add to skillet and bring to boil. Lower flame and simmer mixture until liquid has evaporated, about 20 or 25 minutes.

3. Add remaining ingredients, stir through, and correct seasoning to taste. Cool, refrigerate, and use as needed.

TO PREPARE IN ADVANCE: Through step 3.
TO FREEZE: Through step 3. Defrost overnight in refrigerator.

*To peel tomatoes, remove core from one end and with the sharp point of a knife, lightly score an X on the other end. Plunge tomato into boiling water for 8 seconds, then under cold water. Peel will slip right off. To seed, cut tomato in half and squeeze out seeds.

This is a spicy sauce, excellent with roast beef or brisket.

Horseradish Sauce

Makes 1 cup

2 one-inch pieces horseradish
   root*

1 cup sour cream
¼ teaspoon salt

1. Using STEEL BLADE, drop horseradish root through feed tube with motor running and grate fine. Remove to medium mixing bowl.

2. Stir in sour cream and season with salt. Taste and correct seasoning. Refrigerate until needed.

TO PREPARE IN ADVANCE: Through step 2.
TO FREEZE: Do not freeze.

*Adjust amount of horseradish to taste.

This and the next three sauces are important as an accompaniment to many recipes in this book, even though they are not necessarily made in the food processor.

BECHAMEL SAUCE

Makes 2 cups

4 tablespoons (½ stick) unsalted
    butter
¼ cup all-purpose flour
2¼ cups milk, brought to a boil

¼ teaspoon salt
White pepper
Pinch nutmeg
Tabasco (optional)

1. In large heavy-duty skillet, over low flame, melt butter. Add flour and cook 3 to 4 minutes, stirring occasionally. Do not allow to brown.

2. Gradually whisk in heated milk, raise flame to moderate, and bring to boil. Cook, stirring, until sauce thickens.

3. Remove from flame and add remaining ingredients. Correct seasoning to taste.

4. Use as needed.

TO PREPARE IN ADVANCE: Through step 3.
TO FREEZE: Through step 3.

VARIATION: To enhance flavor of sauce, sauté ½ small onion, ½ small carrot, ½ small celery stalk, all coarsely chopped, in 4 table-spoons butter. Stir in flour and continue with recipe as above. Strain.

BEURRE BLANC

Makes about 2 cups

2 large shallots
⅔ cup dry white wine
2 teaspoons fresh tarragon leaves
½ teaspoon salt

½ teaspoon white pepper
¼ cup heavy cream
¾ pound (3 sticks) chilled unsalted
    butter, cut in 12 pieces

1. Using STEEL BLADE, with motor running, drop shallots through feed tube and chop fine. In medium saucepan, combine shallots, wine, tarragon leaves, salt, and pepper. Over high flame, bring to boil and boil until liquid is reduced to 5 teaspoons.

2. Add cream, lower flame to moderate, and continue to cook 2 minutes longer.

3. Remove saucepan from flame and, with a wire whip, whisk in 1 or 2 pieces of butter. As each piece of butter is incorporated, add another piece. Set pan on *very* low flame and slowly add remaining butter, whisking constantly. *Do not permit mixture to boil.* (If mixture gets too hot, remove from flame and continue adding butter.) Strain and serve.

TO PREPARE IN ADVANCE: Through step 2, heating mixture before adding butter. (You may also prepare through step 3, keeping warm in a bain-marie or in a warmed Thermos; see page 19.)
TO FREEZE: Do not freeze.

Madeira Sauce

Makes about 1½ cups

2 shallots
1 cup Madeira
1 cup heavy cream
½ cup Beef Stock (page 84)

2 tablespoons unsalted butter, cut
   in small pieces
Salt and freshly ground pepper

1. Using STEEL BLADE, with motor running, drop shallots through feed tube and chop fine. Remove to medium saucepan.

2. Pour Madeira into pan and cook, over high flame, until about 3 tablespoons remain. Add cream and reduce by about one-third.

3. Add stock and bring back to boil.

4. Remove from heat, strain, and gradually whisk in butter. Season with salt and pepper to taste.

TO PREPARE IN ADVANCE: Through step 4. Keep warm in

bain-marie or fill wide-mouth Thermos with boiling water, empty, and then pour in sauce. This will keep warm at least 2 hours.
TO FREEZE: Do not freeze.

VARIATION: Dry red wine may be used instead of Madeira.

To serve with chicken or fish.

MUSTARD SAUCE

Makes about 1 cup

3 shallots
Leaves from 3 sprigs fresh
   tarragon or pinch of dried
   tarragon
1 cup dry white wine
¼ cup heavy cream

½ pound (2 sticks) unsalted
   butter, cut into small pieces
Juice of ½ lemon
2 tablespoons snipped chives
1 tablespoon Dijon mustard*

1. Using STEEL BLADE, chop shallots and tarragon, dropping shallots through feed tube with motor running.

2. In medium saucepan, over high flame, combine white wine, shallots, and tarragon. Reduce until 2 tablespoons remain.

3. Add cream and reduce, cooking 1 minute.

4. Remove pan from flame and slowly add butter, using wire whip and whisking all the while. Return to heat if sauce cools and continue to add butter. Do not boil.

5. Strain sauce and stir in lemon juice, chives, and mustard. Keep warm in bain-marie or pour into wide-mouthed Thermos (see page 19).

TO PREPARE IN ADVANCE: Through step 5 (do not prepare more than 1 or 2 hours in advance).
TO FREEZE: Do not freeze.

*Use combination of Dijon and Pommery mustard if desired.

This is a simple mushroom sauce that can be prepared at the last minute.

Mushroom Sauce

Makes about 2½ cups

½ pound mushrooms
3 tablespoons unsalted butter

3 tablespoons Madeira
Salt and freshly ground pepper

1. Using FINE SLICING BLADE, slice mushrooms.

2. In medium skillet, over moderate flame, melt butter and sauté mushrooms just until tender, about 3 minutes.

3. Add Madeira, then bring to boil. Lower flame and simmer 1 minute. Season to taste with salt and pepper.

4. Serve with broiled meat, chicken, or fish.

TO PREPARE IN ADVANCE: Through step 3, reheating when needed.
TO FREEZE: Do not freeze.

This is an unusual sauce that goes well with lamb.

Peanut Butter Sauce

Makes about 1½ cups

1 cup Peanut Butter (page 213)
½ cup heavy cream
1 tablespoon Worcestershire sauce
2 dashes Tabasco

2 tablespoons soy sauce
Juice of ½ medium lemon
1 teaspoon brown sugar

1. Using STEEL BLADE, combine all ingredients in work bowl and process until creamy, scraping down sides of bowl as necessary.

2. Refrigerate in covered container 1 to 2 hours before using, in order to thicken.

3. Serve with barbecued lamb or lamb chops.

TO PREPARE IN ADVANCE: Through step 2. This will keep up to 2 weeks.
TO FREEZE: Do not freeze.

If you like garlic, you'll love this sauce. It is not the classic pesto, but you'll find that the addition of cream cheese gives the sauce less bite and a richer texture.

PESTO

Makes 3 cups

2 ounces Parmesan cheese, cut in 1-inch pieces
4 cups tightly packed fresh basil leaves
½ cup pignolia (pine nuts)
1 small head garlic,* separated into cloves and peeled

4 ounces cream cheese, cut in 6 pieces
½ teaspoon salt
Freshly ground pepper to taste
1 cup olive oil

1. Using STEEL BLADE, with motor running, drop Parmesan cheese through feed tube and process until finely grated. Reserve.

2. Using STEEL BLADE, combine basil leaves, pignolia, garlic, cream cheese, salt, and pepper in work bowl and process to a fine paste. Through feed tube, with motor running, slowly add oil. Add reserved Parmesan cheese and continue to process until well blended.

3. Serve hot over pasta or julienned zucchini.

TO PREPARE IN ADVANCE: Through step 2.
TO FREEZE: Through step 2. To reheat, place in saucepan and heat through over low flame.

VARIATIONS: 1. Walnuts may be substituted for pignolia.
2. In winter, when fresh basil is not available, a combination of raw spinach and Italian parsley leaves makes an admirable substitution.

*If you are not a garlic lover, use half this amount.

Ragu

2 stalks celery, strings removed,
  cut in 1-inch pieces
1 small carrot, peeled and cut in
  1-inch pieces
½ medium onion, cut in half
1 clove garlic
¼ cup oil
1½ pounds beef, cut in 1-inch
  pieces
2 teaspoons dried rosemary

2 teaspoons dried sage
2 bay leaves
1¼ cups dry red wine
1 can (6 ounces) tomato paste
1¼ cups brown sauce or Beef
  Stock (page 84), or as needed
1 tablespoon salt
1 teaspoon freshly ground pepper
Dash of nutmeg

1. Using STEEL BLADE, with on/off turns, coarsely chop celery, carrot, onion, and garlic separately. Drain onion as necessary.

2. In large saucepan, over moderate flame, heat oil. Add vegetables and sauté lightly.

3. Using STEEL BLADE, with on/off turns, coarsely chop meat, 1 cup at a time. Add to saucepan, along with rosemary, sage, and bay leaves. Cook until particles of meat separate, about 10 minutes, stirring occasionally.

4. Add wine and cook until reduced by half.

5. Stir in tomato paste and enough brown sauce to cover meat. Simmer 20 to 25 minutes, stirring occasionally. Remove bay leaves.

6. Season with salt, pepper, and nutmeg. Correct seasoning to taste.

7. To serve, pour over cooked pasta and sprinkle with freshly grated Parmesan cheese and chopped parsley.

TO PREPARE IN ADVANCE: Through step 6.
TO FREEZE: Through step 6. To reheat, place in saucepan and heat through over low flame, then continue with recipe.

Can be used on tostadas or to liven up a plain hamburger.

Salsa Fresca

1 small onion, quartered
2 fresh or canned jalapeño chiles,
   cored, seeded, and quartered
3 medium tomatoes, peeled and
   seeded
1 medium cucumber, peeled,
   seeded, and cut in 1-inch
   pieces

Salt
Freshly ground pepper
1 tablespoon snipped fresh
   coriander
½ teaspoon sugar
¼ cup red wine vinegar
2 tablespoons vegetable oil

1. Using STEEL BLADE, with on/off turns, chop onion fine. Drain as necessary and remove to medium mixing bowl.

2. Using STEEL BLADE, with on/off turns, coarsely chop chiles, tomatoes, and cucumber, separately. Add to onion in mixing bowl. Add remaining ingredients and mix thoroughly. Correct seasoning to taste.

3. Refrigerate and use as needed.

TO PREPARE IN ADVANCE: Through step 3.
TO FREEZE: Do not freeze.

Can be used as a Bar B Que sauce to brush over chicken, fish, or meat.

Sizzle Sauce

½ cup ketchup
2 tablespoons vinegar
1 tablespoon brown sugar

1 teaspoon Worcestershire sauce
2 teaspoons Dijon mustard
Dash of Tabasco

1. In small saucepan, combine all ingredients and cook, over moderate flame, until sugar dissolves and sauce is heated, stirring occasionally.

2. Serve in heated bowl.

TO PREPARE IN ADVANCE: Through step 1.
TO FREEZE: Through step 1.

Sauce Zoia

3 large onions, cut in half
¼ pound (1 stick) unsalted butter
1 pound mushrooms
1 tablespoon Marmite*
½ teaspoon herb salt

½ cup milk
1 cup Béchamel Sauce (page 193)
1½ cups sour cream
¼ teaspoon Kitchen Bouquet

1. Using FINE SLICING BLADE, slice onions. In large skillet, over moderate flame, melt butter and lightly brown onions, about 10 minutes.

2. Using FINE SLICING BLADE, slice mushrooms. Add to lightly browned onions and sauté 2 to 3 minutes. Stir in Marmite and herb salt.

3. Combine milk, Béchamel Sauce, sour cream, and Kitchen Bouquet and add to skillet. Heat through but do not boil.

4. Serve over Pecan Loaf (page 145) or meat loaf.

TO PREPARE IN ADVANCE: Through step 3, but do not heat.
TO FREEZE: Do not freeze.

*Can be obtained in most health-food shops or gourmet sections of supermarkets.

An all-purpose sauce that can be used on meat, fish, or pasta.

TOMATO SAUCE

Makes about 5 cups

1 medium onion, quartered
5 cloves garlic
½ cup plus 2 tablespoons olive oil
6 to 8 fresh basil leaves or ¼
   teaspoon dried

2 cans (16 ounces each) plum
   tomatoes, undrained
Freshly ground pepper
2 tablespoons salt
Pinch of dried oregano

1. Using STEEL BLADE, chop onion with on/off turns. Drop garlic through feed tube while motor is running. Drain onion as necessary.

2. In large skillet, on moderate flame, heat oil. Sauté onion and garlic until golden.

3. Using STEEL BLADE, chop basil leaves and tomatoes, one can at a time, with 2 or 3 on/off turns, until just coarsely chopped. Add to skillet with juice.

4. Add pepper to taste and the salt and bring to a boil. Reduce heat and simmer 15 to 20 minutes, or until sauce thickens. Add oregano and correct seasoning to taste.

TO PREPARE IN ADVANCE: Through step 4.
TO FREEZE: Through step 4. To reheat, place in saucepan and heat through over low flame.

VARIATIONS: 1. Grated cheese may be added to taste.
2. Fresh oregano may be substituted for basil.

The food processor takes the mystery out of many sauces, like this hollandaise, and simplifies the procedure.

Hollandaise Sauce

Makes 2 cups

½ pound (2 sticks) unsalted butter
4 egg yolks
¼ cup water

Juice of ½ lemon
Pinch of white pepper
Pinch of salt

1. Clarify butter (page 205) and keep hot in bain-marie.

2. Pour hot water in work bowl containing STEEL BLADE and then empty. Immediately attach work bowl to base and add egg yolks, water, lemon juice, salt, and pepper. Process with 2 or 3 on/off turns until combined.

3. With motor running, slowly pour clarified butter, in steady stream, through feed tube. When mixture thickens, stop motor. Correct seasoning to taste.

4. Serve with asparagus, broccoli, or poached fish.

TO PREPARE IN ADVANCE: Through step 3. Hollandaise can be prepared earlier and kept warm in a bain-marie or poured directly into a wide-mouthed Thermos that has been rinsed well with hot water.
TO FREEZE: Do not freeze.

Bearnaise Sauce

Makes about 1¼ cups

1 large shallot
2 sprigs fresh tarragon, leaves only
2 tablespoons red wine vinegar

Pinch of white pepper
1 cup Hollandaise Sauce
(page 202)

1. Using STEEL BLADE, and with motor running, drop shallot and tarragon leaves through feed tube and process until finely minced.

2. In small saucepan, combine shallot, tarragon, red wine vinegar, and white pepper. Cook over moderate flame, allowing to reduce until liquid has evaporated, being careful not to burn herbs.

3. Combine saucepan ingredients in with Hollandaise Sauce and fold together. Keep warm in bain-marie.

4. Serve with grilled meat, grilled fish, or fish *en croûte*.

TO PREPARE IN ADVANCE: Through step 3, keeping warm in bain-marie.
TO FREEZE: Do not freeze.

Makes about 1¼ cups

1 cup *Béarnaise Sauce* (*page 202*)   1 to 2 tablespoons Concassée (*page 191*)

1. Combine béarnaise with *Concassée*. Correct seasoning to taste.

2. Serve with grilled meat, grilled fish, or fish *en croûte*.

TO PREPARE IN ADVANCE: Through step 1, keeping warm in bain-marie.
TO FREEZE: Do not freeze.

Makes about 1¼ cups

¼ cup *whipped cream*   1 cup Hollandaise Sauce (*page 202*)

1. Fold whipped cream into hollandaise for a lighter texture. Correct seasoning to taste.

---

2. Serve with asparagus, poached chicken, poached fish, or boiled shellfish.

TO PREPARE IN ADVANCE: Through step 1, keeping warm in bain-marie.
TO FREEZE: Do not freeze.

MUSTARD MOUSSELINE

Makes about 1¼ cups

1 cup Mousseline (page 203)   2 tablespoons Dijon mustard

1. Combine Mousseline with Dijon mustard. Correct seasoning to taste, adding more mustard if desired.
2. Serve with grilled and poached fish or grilled chicken.

TO PREPARE IN ADVANCE: Through step 1, keeping warm in bain-marie.
TO FREEZE: Do not freeze.

SAUCE MOSCOVITE

Makes about 1¼ cups

1 cup Mousseline (page 203)   Caviar

1. Combine Mousseline with caviar to taste.
2. Serve with poached fish or boiled or broiled shellfish.

TO PREPARE IN ADVANCE: Through step 1, keeping warm in bain-marie.
TO FREEZE: Do not freeze.

Crème fraîche may be substituted for heavy cream in many recipes for added richness and texture. It is also wonderful on fresh fruit like strawberries or raspberries.

CREME FRAICHE

Makes about 3½ cups

8 ounces Neufchâtel cheese   2½ to 3 cups heavy cream

1. Using PLASTIC BLADE, process cheese until smooth.

2. Through feed tube, with motor running, slowly add cream and process to desired texture. To test, stop motor and stick spoon into mixture. If spoon stands up, *Crème Fraîche* is ready.*

3. Refrigerate and use as needed.

TO PREPARE IN ADVANCE: Through step 3, will keep refrigerated up to 2 weeks.
TO FREEZE: Do not freeze.

*Crème Fraîche prepared with buttermilk or sour cream has to ripen at room temperature; this can be used immediately.

CLARIFIED BUTTER

Makes 1⅔ cups

1 pound unsalted butter

1. In medium saucepan, over low flame, melt butter. Remove from heat and let stand 2 minutes.

2. Skim foam from top and pour clear oily liquid (butter) into container. Stop pouring when you reach the milky residue in bottom of pan. Refrigerate and use as needed.

TO PREPARE IN ADVANCE: Through step 2.
TO FREEZE: Through step 2. Defrost in refrigerator and use as needed.

ANCHOVY BUTTER

Makes about ½ cup

5 anchovy fillets, drained
¼ pound (1 stick) unsalted butter,
   chilled, cut in 8 pieces

1 clove garlic (optional)

1. Using STEEL BLADE, combine all ingredients in work bowl and process until smooth, scraping down sides of bowl as necessary.

2. Refrigerate, covered, until needed.

3. Serve with broiled or sautéed meats and fish.

TO PREPARE IN ADVANCE: Through step 2.
TO FREEZE: Through step 2. Defrost 1 hour in refrigerator, slice, and use as needed.

AVOCADO BUTTER

Makes about 1½ cups

2 tablespoons fresh parsley leaves
½ pound (2 sticks) unsalted
   butter, chilled, cut in 16 pieces
½ medium avocado, peeled and cut
   in 1-inch pieces

1 clove garlic
4 teaspoons lemon juice
Dash of Tabasco
½ teaspoon Worcestershire sauce
Salt and freshly ground pepper

1. Using STEEL BLADE, chop parsley leaves fine. Add remaining ingredients and process until smooth. Correct seasoning to taste.

2. Refrigerate, covered, until needed.

3. Serve on grilled fish.

TO PREPARE IN ADVANCE: Through step 2.
TO FREEZE: Through step 1. Defrost 1 hour in refrigerator, slice, and use as needed.

BERCY BUTTER

1 cup dry white wine
4 shallots, cut in thirds
2 tablespoons fresh parsley leaves
¼ pound (1 stick) unsalted butter,
  chilled, cut in 8 pieces

4 ounces poached beef marrow, in
  1-inch pieces
Salt and freshly ground pepper

1. In small saucepan, over high flame, cook wine and shallots until ¼ cup liquid remains. Cool.

2. Using STEEL BLADE, chop parsley leaves fine. Add contents of saucepan, butter, and beef marrow and process until smooth. Season with salt and pepper to taste.

3. Refrigerate, covered, until needed.

4. Serve with broiled or grilled steak or chops.

TO PREPARE IN ADVANCE: Through step 3.
TO FREEZE: Through step 3. Defrost 1 hour in refrigerator, slice, and use as needed.

NOTE: To poach bone marrow, remove marrow from bone and soak in running cold water until all traces of blood are removed. Drain. Place in saucepan with cold water to cover. Bring to boil, lower flame, and gently poach, about 5 minutes.

GARLIC BUTTER

4 cloves garlic
¼ pound (1 stick) unsalted butter,
  chilled, cut in 8 pieces

2 tablespoons snipped chives
Salt

1. Using STEEL BLADE, combine garlic, butter, and chives in work bowl and process until smooth. Season with salt to taste.

2. Refrigerate, covered, until needed.

3. Serve with broiled or grilled fish or meat. Use to prepare garlic bread.

TO PREPARE IN ADVANCE: Through step 2.
TO FREEZE: Through step 2. Defrost 1 hour in refrigerator, slice, and use as needed.

GORGONZOLA BUTTER

Makes about 1 cup

6 ounces Gorgonzola Dolce cheese, cut in 1-inch pieces

3 ounces (¾ stick) unsalted butter, chilled, cut in 8 pieces

1. Using STEEL BLADE, combine Gorgonzola and butter in work bowl and process until smooth, scraping down sides of bowl as necessary.

2. Refrigerate, covered, until needed.

3. Serve with pasta, slicing butter into small bits and combining with pasta. Top with freshly ground pepper.

TO PREPARE IN ADVANCE: Through step 2.
TO FREEZE: Through step 2. Defrost 1 hour in refrigerator, slice, and use as needed.

GREEN BUTTER

1 cup spinach leaves, washed and
    stemmed
2 small shallots, cut in thirds
1 tablespoon parsley leaves

2 teaspoons fresh tarragon leaves
¼ pound (1 stick) unsalted butter,
    chilled, cut in 8 pieces

1. In small saucepan, over moderate flame, blanch spinach, shallots, parsley, and tarragon in salted water to cover for 5 minutes. Drain well.

2. Using STEEL BLADE, chop fine drained contents of saucepan. Add butter and process until smooth, scraping down sides of work bowl as necessary.

3. Refrigerate, covered, until needed.

4. Serve with broiled or sautéed fish or chicken.

TO PREPARE IN ADVANCE: Through step 3.
TO FREEZE: Through step 3. Defrost 1 hour in refrigerator, slice, and use as needed.

HERB BUTTER

1 tablespoon fresh chervil
¼ cup fresh parsley leaves
2 tablespoons fresh tarragon
    leaves

1 pound (4 sticks) unsalted butter,
    chilled, cut in 16 pieces
1 teaspoon Dijon mustard
Salt and freshly ground pepper

1. Using STEEL BLADE, chop chervil, parsley, and tarragon fine. Add remaining ingredients and process until smooth, scraping down sides of work bowl as necessary.

2. Refrigerate, covered, until needed.

3. Serve with broiled chicken or fish; use to stuff chicken Kiev.

TO PREPARE IN ADVANCE: Through step 2.
TO FREEZE: Through step 2. Defrost 1 hour in refrigerator, slice, and use as needed.

NOTE: It is best to use fresh herbs, but you can substitute dried. The combination can be varied to taste.

*H*ORSERADISH BUTTER

Makes about ½ cup

3 tablespoons horseradish root, peeled and cut in small pieces, or 1½ tablespoons prepared horseradish, drained

¼ pound (1 stick) unsalted butter, chilled, cut in 8 pieces

1. Using STEEL BLADE, grate horseradish fine. Add butter and process until smooth, scraping down sides of work bowl as necessary.

2. Refrigerate, covered, until needed.

3. Serve with broiled or grilled meat or fish.

TO PREPARE IN ADVANCE: Through step 2.
TO FREEZE: Through step 2. Defrost 1 hour in refrigerator, slice, and use as needed.

*M*AITRE D'HOTEL BUTTER

Makes about ½ cup

2 tablespoons fresh parsley leaves
Juice of ½ lemon
Salt and freshly ground pepper

¼ pound (1 stick) unsalted butter, chilled, cut in 8 pieces

1. Using STEEL BLADE, chop parsley fine. Add remaining ingredients and process until smooth, scraping down sides of work bowl as necessary.

2. Refrigerate, covered, until needed.

3. Serve with broiled meat, chicken, or vegetables.

TO PREPARE IN ADVANCE: Through step 2.
TO FREEZE: Through step 2. Defrost 1 hour in refrigerator, slice, and use as needed.

MARCHAND DE VINS BUTTER Makes about ¾ cup

---

1 cup dry red wine
6 shallots, cut in thirds
1 tablespoon fresh parsley leaves

¼ pound (1 stick) unsalted butter,
*   chilled, cut in 8 pieces*
Salt and freshly ground pepper

1. In small saucepan, over high flame, cook wine and shallots until reduced to about ¼ cup. Cool.

2. Using STEEL BLADE, chop parsley fine. Add remaining ingredients and process until smooth. Correct seasoning to taste.

3. Refrigerate, covered, until needed.

4. Serve with broiled steaks or chops.

TO PREPARE IN ADVANCE: Through step 3.
TO FREEZE: Through step 3. Defrost 1 hour in refrigerator, slice, and use as needed.

Mustard Butter

¼ pound (1 stick) unsalted butter, chilled, cut in 8 pieces

1 tablespoon Dijon mustard, or to taste
1 teaspoon lemon juice

1. Using STEEL BLADE, combine all ingredients in work bowl and process until smooth, scraping down sides of bowl as necessary.
2. Refrigerate, covered, until needed.
3. Serve on broiled fish or on sandwiches.

TO PREPARE IN ADVANCE: Through step 2.
TO FREEZE: Through step 2. Defrost 1 hour in refrigerator, slice, and use as needed.

Nut Butter

4 ounces nuts (walnuts, pecans, or blanched almonds)

¼ pound (1 stick) unsalted butter, chilled, cut in 8 pieces

1. Using STEEL BLADE, combine all ingredients in work bowl and process until smooth.
2. Refrigerate, covered, until needed.
3. Serve with hamburgers or broiled lamb.

TO PREPARE IN ADVANCE: Through step 2.
TO FREEZE: Through step 2. Defrost 1 hour in refrigerator, slice, and use as needed.

ORANGE BUTTER

Rind and juice of 1 medium
   orange
Pinch of nutmeg

Pinch of ground cinnamon
¼ pound (1 stick) unsalted butter,
   chilled, cut in 6 or 8 pieces

1. With a vegetable peeler, remove strips of rind from orange. Using STEEL BLADE, chop orange rind fine with nutmeg and cinnamon.

2. Add orange juice and butter and process until well blended.

3. Refrigerate, covered, and use as needed.

4. Serve on toast, pancakes, or waffles.

TO PREPARE IN ADVANCE: Through step 3.
TO FREEZE: Through step 3. Defrost 1 hour in refrigerator, slice, and use as needed.

I like the flavoring of walnut oil, but peanut oil is generally used.

PEANUT BUTTER

Makes about 1½ cups

2 cups shelled peanuts (raw or
   roasted)

4 to 5 teaspoons peanut or walnut
   oil
½ teaspoon salt

1. Using STEEL BLADE, process peanuts and 4 teaspoons oil until creamy, scraping down sides of work bowl as necessary. Add more oil if creamier texture is desired.

2. Refrigerate in covered container.

TO PREPARE IN ADVANCE: Through step 2. This will keep up to 2 weeks.
TO FREEZE: Do not freeze.

VARIATIONS: 1. Hazelnuts, cashews, pignolia (pine nuts) all make delicious nut butter, too.
2. To prepare almond butter, use blanched almonds and almond oil.

Tomato Butter

Makes about 1½ cups

½ pound (2 sticks) unsalted
  butter, at room temperature, cut
  in 16 pieces
2 tomatoes, peeled, seeded, and
  quartered

⅛ teaspoon dry basil or 2 to 3
  fresh basil leaves
Salt
Freshly ground pepper

1. Using STEEL BLADE, combine butter, tomatoes, and basil and process until smooth, scraping down sides of work bowl as necessary.

2. Season with salt and pepper to taste. Refrigerate until needed.

3. Use on grilled or baked fish.

TO PREPARE IN ADVANCE: Through step 1.
TO FREEZE: Through step 2. Defrost 1 hour in refrigerator, slice, and use as needed.

Roquefort Butter

Makes about 1½ cups

6 ounces Roquefort cheese, cut in
  1-inch pieces

6 ounces (1½ sticks) unsalted
  butter, chilled, cut in 8 pieces

1. Using STEEL BLADE, combine Roquefort cheese and butter. Process until smooth, scraping down sides of work bowl as necessary.

2. Refrigerate, covered, until needed.

3. Serve with hamburgers or broiled steaks and chops.

TO PREPARE IN ADVANCE: Through step 2.
TO FREEZE: Through step 2. Defrost 1 hour in refrigerator, slice, and use as needed.

BREADS

Prepare 2 or 3 batches of bread and allow them to rise at the same time. This is a good rule of thumb for all your bread making. It is not necessary for the yeast to dissolve completely.

Basic Bread

1 package active dry yeast	2 tablespoons unsalted butter
1 tablespoon sugar	3 cups all-purpose flour
¼ cup warm milk	1 teaspoon salt
1 cup cold milk	

1. Butter an 8½ x 4½ x 2½-inch loaf pan.

2. Using STEEL BLADE, without processing, dissolve yeast and sugar in warm milk.

3. In small saucepan, over low flame, combine cold milk and butter and heat just until butter melts.

4. Add flour and salt to work bowl and, with motor running, pour ingredients from saucepan through feed tube. Process just until dough begins to form a ball and leaves sides of work bowl, about 10 to 15 seconds. Turn dough out onto lightly floured board and knead a few times while shaping into a ball.

5. Place dough into buttered or oiled mixing bowl, turning to grease all sides. Cover bowl with plastic wrap and set in warm spot to let rise until doubled in bulk, about 1 hour.

6. Punch dough down, turn out of bowl, and form into a smooth ball. Cover with bowl and let rest 15 to 20 minutes.

7. On lightly floured board, roll out dough into rectangle the length of your loaf pan. Starting at one end, roll dough like a jelly roll, tucking in edges as it is being rolled. Set in buttered loaf pan, seam side down, then cover and allow to rise in a warm spot until doubled in bulk, 45 minutes to 1 hour.

8. Preheat oven to 375°F.

9. Bake 50 to 60 minutes, until top of loaf is lightly colored and sounds hollow when tapped. Transfer to rack to cool.

TO PREPARE IN ADVANCE: Through step 9.
TO FREEZE: Through step 9. To reheat, place in preheated oven and bake 30 minutes.

VARIATIONS: 1. *Cinnamon-Raisin Bread:* Combine 2 tablespoons sugar, 2 teaspoons cinnamon, and ¼ cup raisins. When dough is rolled into rectangle, sprinkle with mixture and then roll as directed in recipe.
2. *Onion Bread:* Sprinkle with 1 small chopped onion, 1 teaspoon caraway seeds, and 1 teaspoon poppy seeds when bread is rolled into a rectangle and then continue with recipe.
3. *Dinner Rolls:* Divide dough into 20 to 24 pieces and shape into balls. Place on greased pastry sheet. Let rise, then bake in preheated 400°F. oven about 15 minutes, brushing with melted butter first.

Dill Bread

Makes 1 loaf

½ medium onion, cut in half
2 tablespoons unsalted butter
1 package active dry yeast
¼ cup lukewarm water
1 cup creamed cottage cheese
2 tablespoons sugar

3 tablespoons dill weed, or 2
   teaspoons dill seed
1 teaspoon salt
¼ teaspoon baking soda
1 egg
2½ cups all-purpose flour

1. Using STEEL BLADE, with on/off turns, coarsely chop onion. Drain as necessary. Clean work bowl.

2. In small skillet, over moderate flame, melt 1 tablespoon of the butter and sauté onion until soft, 1 or 2 minutes. Do not allow to color.

3. Using STEEL BLADE, without processing, soften yeast in warm water.

4. In small skillet, over moderate flame, melt remaining 1 tablespoon butter and heat cottage cheese, about 30 seconds.

5. Add onions and cottage cheese to work bowl with sugar, dill, salt, baking soda, egg, and 1 cup of the flour. Process just to combine.

6. Add remaining 1½ cups flour and process until a mass forms on blade. Dough will be sticky. Turn out on lightly floured board and knead, shaping into a ball.

7. Place in greased bowl, turning to grease all sides. Let rise, covered, in warm spot until doubled in bulk, about 1½ hours.

8. Punch down and shape into smooth ball. Place in greased 2-quart casserole or soufflé dish and let rise, covered, in warm spot 30 to 40 minutes.

9. Preheat oven to 350°F.

10. Bake 45 to 55 minutes, until golden brown.

11. Serve directly from casserole, cutting into pie-shaped wedges.

TO PREPARE IN ADVANCE: Through step 10.
TO FREEZE: Through step 10. Defrost, wrapped, in refrigerator overnight. To reheat, place in preheated oven and bake approximately 25 minutes.

VARIATION: Remove bread from oven through step 10 and brush with melted butter. Sprinkle with coarse salt.

A deliciously wholesome bread that can be sliced thin for spreads and dips.

WHOLE-WHEAT BREAD

Makes 1 loaf

1 package active dry yeast
¼ cup lukewarm water
1 tablespoon sugar
1 teaspoon salt
½ to 1 teaspoon anise, seeds or ground

1 tablespoon safflower oil
¾ cup lukewarm milk
1¼ cups all-purpose flour
1½ cups whole-wheat flour

1. Using PLASTIC BLADE, without processing, soften yeast in lukewarm water.

2. Add sugar, salt, anise, oil, and milk and process until combined.

3. Pour flour into work bowl and process until dough begins to form a ball on blade.

4. Turn out dough on lightly floured board and knead lightly while

forming into a ball. Place in greased bowl, turning to grease all sides, and let rise, covered, in warm place until doubled in bulk, 1½ to 2 hours.

5. Punch down, knead lightly, and roll out into 9-inch square.

6. Roll up like a jelly roll and place, seam side down, in greased 9 x 5 x 3-inch loaf pan. Let rise, covered, in warm place until doubled in bulk, about 30 minutes.

7. Preheat oven to 400°F.

8. Brush top of loaf with egg wash and, with sharp knife or STEEL BLADE, make 3 or 4 slashes.

9. Bake 40 to 45 minutes, or until loaf sounds hollow when tapped.

10. Cool thoroughly on a rack and slice.

TO PREPARE IN ADVANCE: Through step 10.
TO FREEZE: Through step 10. To reheat, place in preheated oven and bake 30 minutes. Individual slices can be toasted directly from freezer.

I like to cut Challah into thick slices. It is delicious toasted and especially good when used for making French toast.

CHALLAH

Makes 1 loaf or 8 rolls

1 package active dry yeast
1 cup lukewarm water
1 egg
¼ cup vegetable oil

2 teaspoons salt
¾ tablespoon sugar
2½ to 3 cups all-purpose flour
1 egg, lightly beaten, for egg wash

1. Using PLASTIC BLADE, without processing, soften yeast in water.

2. Add egg, oil, salt, and sugar and process until combined.

3. Add flour and process until dough begins to leave sides of work bowl. Dough will be sticky.

4. Turn out dough on lightly floured board and knead while forming smooth, elastic ball. Dust with flour as necessary.

5. Place dough into greased bowl, turning to grease all sides. Let rise, covered, in warm spot until tripled in bulk, 2½ to 3 hours.

6. Punch down, knead slightly, and divide into 3 pieces.

7. Roll out each piece into a rope 12 inches long. Braid the 3 ropes together, pinching ends to seal.

8. Place on greased baking sheet, brush with egg wash, and let rise, loosely covered, in warm spot until doubled in bulk, about 30 minutes.

9. Preheat oven to 375°F.

10. Brush loaf again with egg wash and bake 35 to 40 minutes, until golden brown and loaf sounds hollow when tapped.

TO PREPARE IN ADVANCE: Through step 10.
TO FREEZE: Through step 10. To reheat, place in preheated oven and bake 30 minutes.

VARIATIONS: 1. In step 6, knead in 1 cup raisins and continue with recipe.
2. In step 6, divide dough into 8 pieces. Roll each piece into a rope 8 inches long and coil each rope into a spiral. Place on greased cookie sheet, brush with egg wash, and let rise in warm spot until doubled in bulk, about 25 minutes. Brush again with egg wash and bake in preheated 375°F. oven 25 to 30 minutes, until golden brown.
3. In step 10, after brushing with egg wash, sprinkle top with poppy seeds and bake as directed.

*F*RENCH BREAD

Makes 1 large loaf

1 package active dry yeast	1 teaspoon salt
¼ cup lukewarm water	¾ to 1 cup warm water
3 cups all-purpose flour	Cornmeal
1 teaspoon sugar	1 egg, lightly beaten, for egg wash

1. Using STEEL BLADE, without processing, dissolve yeast in lukewarm water.

2. Add ½ cup of the flour, the sugar, and salt and process about 10 seconds.

3. Add remaining 2½ cups flour all at once and, with motor running, pour just enough warm water through feed tube so that dough forms a ball on blade.

4. Turn out dough on lightly floured board and knead a few minutes. Clean work bowl.

5. Place dough in greased bowl, turning to grease all sides. Let rise, covered, in warm place until doubled in bulk, 1 to 1½ hours. Punch down and form into a long or round loaf.

6. Sprinkle greased cookie sheet with cornmeal and set loaf on sheet. Cover loosely and let rise in a warm spot until doubled in bulk, about 40 minutes.

7. Preheat oven to 425°F.

8. Brush egg wash over loaf. Slash top of loaf with sharp knife or STEEL BLADE, making 3 or 4 cuts.

9. Bake 25 to 30 minutes, or until loaf is nicely browned and sounds hollow when tapped. Cool on rack.

TO PREPARE IN ADVANCE: Through step 9.
TO FREEZE: Through step 9. To reheat, place in preheated oven and bake approximately 20 minutes.

VARIATIONS: 1. After first rise, shape dough into 12 to 14 individual rolls. Cover and let rise 20 minutes. Brush with egg wash and bake 20 to 30 minutes.
2. After first rise, shape dough into 32 to 36 breadsticks, 8 to 10 inches long. Cover and let rise 15 minutes. Brush with egg wash and bake 15 minutes.
3. After brushing with egg wash, sprinkle rolls or breadsticks with caraway seeds, poppy seeds, coarse salt, sesame seeds, or garlic salt.

MONKEY BREAD WITH GREEN ONIONS AND POPPY SEEDS

Makes 1 loaf

1 package active dry yeast
1 teaspoon sugar
1 cup warm water
3 cups all-purpose flour
1 teaspoon salt
¼ cup melted unsalted butter, plus
    additional melted butter for
    brushing bread

1 large egg
6 medium green onions, cut in
    1-inch pieces
¼ pound (1 stick) unsalted butter
1 tablespoon poppy seeds

1. Using PLASTIC BLADE, without processing, dissolve yeast and sugar in ¼ cup of the warm water.

2. Pour flour and salt into work bowl. With motor running, add remaining ¾ cup warm water, ¼ cup melted butter, and then egg through feed tube. Process until dough begins to form a ball and leaves sides of work bowl.

3. Turn dough out onto lightly floured board and cut in half. Return each half to work bowl, separately, and knead for about 15 seconds with PLASTIC BLADE. On lightly floured board, combine both halves into smooth ball. Dough will be very sticky at first, but will become easier to handle as you work with it.

4. Place dough in greased bowl, turning to grease all sides. Cover with plastic wrap, set in warm spot, and let rise until doubled in bulk, about 1½ hours. Clean work bowl.

5. Punch dough down and refrigerate, covered, until ready to use.

6. Using STEEL BLADE, chop green onions fine, starting with on/off turns. In small skillet, over moderate flame, melt ¼ pound butter. Add green onions and immediately remove skillet from flame.

7. On lightly floured board, roll dough out into an 8 x 10-inch rectangle about ½ inch thick. Cut dough into 2-inch squares. Dip each square into the onion butter and form into a ball.

8. Butter a 6-cup soufflé dish and layer bottom of dish with balls of dough (balls should be loosely placed in dish). Sprinkle with half the poppy seeds. Repeat with second layer and sprinkle with remaining

poppy seeds. Cover lightly and let rise in warm spot until doubled in bulk, about 45 minutes.

9. Preheat oven to 350°F.

10. Bake bread 1 hour, or until it sounds hollow when tapped.

11. Cool on rack. Serve warm, brushing top with small amount of melted butter.

TO PREPARE IN ADVANCE: Through step 5 or 10.
TO FREEZE: Through step 10. To reheat, place in preheated oven and bake 30 minutes.

VARIATION: *Country Bread with Rosemary and Muscat Raisins:* Prepare Monkey Bread through step 5. Combine ¼ cup olive oil with ¼ cup melted butter. On lightly floured board, roll dough out into an 8- or 9-inch circle. Brush generously with olive oil mixture and sprinkle with 2 tablespoons rosemary and ¼ cup raisins. Roll dough like a jelly roll. Pour half the remaining oil mixture into a loaf or tart pan. Place dough into pan, seam side down. Pour remaining oil mixture over and sprinkle with 2 tablespoons sugar. Bake in preheated 350°F. oven 50 minutes. Serve hot.

---

*B*RIOCHE

Makes 1 standard loaf
or large round

---

1 package active dry yeast
2 teaspoons sugar
¼ cup warm water
2¼ cups all-purpose flour

1½ teaspoons salt
7 ounces (1¾ sticks) unsalted
*   butter, very cold, cut in 8 pieces*
5 eggs

1. Using STEEL BLADE, without processing, dissolve yeast and sugar in warm water.

2. Add flour and salt. Distribute butter evenly over flour and process with on/off turns until flour resembles coarse meal.

3. With motor running, add 4 of the eggs, one at a time, through feed tube. Process until dough begins to form a ball and is smooth.

4. Remove dough to greased bowl, turning to grease all sides.

Cover with plastic wrap and set in warm place to rise until doubled in bulk, about 45 minutes.

5. Punch down dough, shape into a ball, and place in a large greased brioche mold. Or form into a standard loaf and place in greased 9 x 5 x 3-inch loaf pan. Let rise, covered, in warm spot until doubled in bulk, about 45 minutes.

6. Preheat oven to 350°F.

7. Lightly beat remaining egg for egg wash.

8. Brush loaf with egg wash and bake 45 minutes, or until golden brown.

9. Cool on rack, slice, and serve.

TO PREPARE IN ADVANCE: Through step 8. Or refrigerate dough overnight, bring back to room temperature, and bake as above.
TO FREEZE: Through step 8. To reheat, place in preheated oven and bake 30 minutes.

---

*P*OPPY SEED ROLLS

Makes 1 dozen rolls

1 package active dry yeast
1 cup lukewarm water
½ cup whole eggs (about 2)
¼ cup melted unsalted butter
¼ cup sugar

¾ tablespoon salt
2½ to 3¼ cups all-purpose flour
1 egg, lightly beaten, for egg wash
1 tablespoon poppy seeds

1. Using STEEL BLADE, without processing, dissolve yeast in warm water.

2. Add eggs, melted butter, sugar, and salt and process just until combined.

3. Add flour, starting with 2½ cups, and process just until ball begins to form on blade. Turn out on floured board, knead lightly, and place in greased bowl, turning to grease all sides. Let rise, covered, in warm place until doubled in bulk, about 1 hour.

4. Punch dough down and knead slightly on lightly floured board. Cut dough into 12 pieces.

5. Shape each piece into smooth ball and set on greased cookie sheet. Flatten each piece into rounds ½ inch thick. With sharp knife or STEEL BLADE, slash tops of rounds in crisscross design.

6. Brush rounds with egg wash and sprinkle with poppy seeds. Let rise, covered, in warm place until doubled in bulk, about 30 minutes.

7. Preheat oven to 400°F.

8. Bake rolls 15 to 20 minutes, until golden brown.

9. Serve warm.

TO PREPARE IN ADVANCE: Through step 8.
TO FREEZE: Through step 6, after sprinkling with poppy seeds. When ready to bake, place frozen rolls on greased cookie sheet and let rise in warm place until doubled in bulk, about 1 hour. Bake as above. To reheat, place rolls in preheated oven and bake 10 to 15 minutes.

NOTE: Caraway seeds may be substituted for poppy seeds.

Prepare 2 batches of this bread. It freezes very well.

CHEDDAR CHEESE LOAF

Makes 1 loaf

4 ounces sharp Cheddar cheese,
   chilled
1 package active dry yeast
2 tablespoons lukewarm water
1 cup milk

1 tablespoon sugar
1 tablespoon unsalted butter
1 teaspoon salt
2½ to 2¾ cups all-purpose flour

1. Butter an 8½ x 4½ x 2½-inch loaf pan.

2. Using MEDIUM SHREDDING BLADE, grate Cheddar cheese.

3. Dissolve yeast in 2 tablespoons water.

4. In small saucepan, combine cheese, milk, sugar, butter, and salt.

Cook, stirring over low heat, until lukewarm. Remove from heat and add dissolved yeast.

5. Using STEEL BLADE, combine flour with cheese mixture and process just until ball begins to form on blade. Turn dough out on lightly floured board and lightly knead into a smooth ball.

6. Place in greased bowl, turning to grease all sides. Let rise, covered, in warm place until doubled in bulk, about 1 hour. Punch down and knead slightly.

7. Roll out on lightly floured board into a 9-inch square. Roll up like a jelly roll and place, seam side down, into prepared pan. Let rise, covered, in warm place until doubled in bulk, 30 to 40 minutes.

8. Preheat oven to 375°F.

9. Bake bread 30 to 35 minutes, or until richly browned. Cool thoroughly on rack before slicing.

TO PREPARE IN ADVANCE: Through step 9.
TO FREEZE: Through step 9. I recommend slicing and then freezing so you can take out as many slices as desired. To reheat, place bread in preheated oven and bake 30 minutes. Slices can be toasted directly from freezer.

Because these freeze so well, you can always have corn muffins at a moment's notice.

CORN MUFFINS

Makes 12 muffins

Peel of ½ medium lemon
¼ cup sugar
1 cup yellow cornmeal
1 cup all-purpose flour
½ teaspoon salt

4 teaspoons baking powder
1 egg
1 cup milk
¼ cup safflower oil
½ teaspoon vanilla extract

1. Preheat oven to 400°F.

2. Line muffin tins with cupcake papers.

3. Using STEEL BLADE, combine lemon peel and sugar and let machine run until peel is finely chopped. Add cornmeal, flour, salt, and baking powder and process just until flour disappears.

4. Add egg, milk, oil, and vanilla and process until smooth.

5. Pour batter into prepared tin, three-fourths up sides of papers.

6. Bake 15 to 20 minutes, until lightly golden. Muffins will not be brown.

7. Transfer to rack to cool.

TO PREPARE IN ADVANCE: Through step 7.
TO FREEZE: Through step 7. To reheat, place in preheated oven and bake 10 to 15 minutes.

POPOVERS

Makes 8 six-ounce popovers or
12 four-ounce popovers

2 cups all-purpose flour
1 teaspoon salt
4 eggs, at room temperature

2 cups milk, taken out of
refrigerator 20 minutes before
needed
2 teaspoons vegetable oil

1. Sift together flour and salt.

2. Using STEEL BLADE, combine flour, salt, and eggs.

3. With motor running, pour milk through feed tube and process until blended. Transfer to spouted pitcher and let rest 15 to 20 minutes.

4. Preheat oven to 450°F.

5. Oil each popover cup. If using individual cups, set on baking tray for easier handling. Place in oven to heat.

6. Pour in batter to fill two-thirds of each cup and return to oven. Bake 15 minutes, then lower oven temperature to 375°F. and continue baking 20 minutes longer, until brown and crusty.

7. Serve immediately with butter and/or preserves.

TO PREPARE IN ADVANCE: Through step 3 or step 6, reheating before serving.
TO FREEZE: Do not freeze.

VARIATION: Using STEEL BLADE, grate 2 ounces Cheddar or Parmesan cheese. Add to work bowl with flour and continue with recipe as above.

NOTE: Popovers fall slightly on standing. Reheated popovers are good to eat but not as full and puffed as when first baked.

---

*B*ACON BISCUITS

1 cup heavy cream
1 tablespoon vinegar
½ pound bacon, cooked until crisp
    and cut in 1-inch pieces
2 cups all-purpose flour
½ teaspoon baking soda

½ teaspoon salt
4 tablespoons (½ stick) unsalted
    butter, chilled, cut in 4 pieces
1 egg, lightly beaten, for egg wash
1 teaspoon freshly ground pepper

1. Preheat oven to 325°F. Lightly butter a baking sheet.

2. To make soured cream, combine heavy cream and vinegar. Reserve.

3. Using STEEL BLADE, chop bacon fine. Reserve.

4. Using STEEL BLADE, with on/off turns, combine flour, baking soda, and salt. Add butter and, with on/off turns, process until mixture resembles coarse meal.

5. Add bacon and process 2 or 3 seconds. Add soured cream and process just until combined.

6. Turn out on lightly floured board and roll into ½-inch thick circle approximately 10 inches in diameter. Using cookie cutter, cut into 1½-inch circles and place on buttered baking sheet. Gather together scraps of dough and repeat procedure.

7. Brush tops of biscuits with egg wash and sprinkle with pepper.

8. Bake 15 to 20 minutes, until golden brown.

9. Serve warm.

TO PREPARE IN ADVANCE: Through step 8.

TO FREEZE: Through step 8. To reheat, place in preheated oven and bake 10 to 15 minutes.

In this recipe I combine yeast and biscuit mix with marvelous results.

*R*AISED ONION BISCUITS

Makes about 2 dozen biscuits

1 medium onion, cut in half	¼ cup warm water
5 tablespoons unsalted butter	2½ cups biscuit mix
1 package dry yeast	⅓ cup milk
1 tablespoon sugar	3 tablespoons melted butter

1. Using MEDIUM SHREDDING BLADE, grate onion. Drain as necessary. In small skillet, over moderate flame, melt 2 tablespoons of the butter and sauté onion just until it begins to brown, 5 to 7 minutes. Remove from heat and cool. Clean work bowl.

2. Using PLASTIC BLADE, without processing, dissolve yeast and sugar in warm water.

3. Add biscuit mix to work bowl and, with motor running, pour milk through feed tube. Process until dough begins to form a ball and leaves sides of work bowl.

4. Remove dough from work bowl and divide into 3 parts. Processing one part at a time, using STEEL BLADE, knead until smooth, about 15 seconds. Repeat with remaining 2 pieces of dough.

5. On lightly floured board, combine all 3 pieces and form smooth ball. Place in greased bowl, turning to grease all sides. Cover and let rise in warm spot until doubled in bulk, about 45 minutes.

6. On lightly floured board, gently roll out dough to an 8 x 16-inch rectangle. Brush with melted butter and spread onion evenly over half the dough, along one long side. From the long side, fold dough over onion and press edges together. (You now have a 4 x 16-inch rectangle.) Brush with melted butter and, with cookie cutter, cut into 1½-inch circles, using scraps as necessary. Place on greased baking tray, edges barely touching. Cover and let rise in warm spot 40 minutes.

7. Preheat oven to 400°F.

8. Bake biscuits 15 to 18 minutes, until golden brown.

9. Serve warm, with unsalted butter.

TO PREPARE IN ADVANCE: Through step 8.
TO FREEZE: Through step 8. To reheat, place in preheated oven and bake 10 to 15 minutes.

NOTE: If desired, 1 teaspoon caraway seeds may be sprinkled over biscuits just before baking or added to onions before folding dough.

BANANA BREAD WITH PEAR GLAZE

Makes 1 loaf

2 large, ripe bananas, peeled, cut in 1-inch pieces
6 tablespoons unsalted butter, cut in 6 pieces
⅔ cup sugar
2 eggs

1⅓ cups all-purpose flour
¼ teaspoon salt
1 teaspoon baking soda
¾ teaspoon baking powder
1 cup walnuts, plus 6 perfect halves
½ cup pear preserves

1. Preheat oven to 325°F.

2. Butter an 8½ x 4½ x 2½-inch loaf pan. Line bottom only with waxed paper. Butter waxed paper.

3. Using STEEL BLADE, mash bananas. Add butter, sugar, and eggs and process with on/off turns until combined.

4. Add flour, salt, baking soda, baking powder, and 1 cup walnuts and process with on/off turns until flour is incorporated, scraping down sides of work bowl as necessary. Do not overprocess. Clean work bowl.

5. Pour batter into prepared pan, smooth out top, and bake 50 to 60 minutes, or until tester inserted into center of bread comes out clean. Turn out onto rack to cool. Glaze while warm.

6. To prepare glaze: Using STEEL BLADE, process pear preserves

until smooth. Brush on top of warm bread. Arrange nuts on glaze, adding more glaze as bread cools.

TO PREPARE IN ADVANCE: Through step 6.
TO FREEZE: Through step 6. Place bread in freezer unwrapped until glaze freezes. Then wrap and freeze. Defrost, wrapped. Slice and serve as needed.

---

*B*ASIC CREPES

Makes 12 to 14 six-inch crêpes

2 eggs
1½ cups milk
½ teaspoon salt
2 tablespoons melted unsalted
  butter

1 cup all-purpose flour
Butter for crêpe pan

1. Using STEEL BLADE, combine eggs, milk, salt, melted butter, and flour and process until smooth. Transfer to medium mixing bowl and let rest at least 1 hour.

2. Heat 7-inch crêpe pan and butter thoroughly.*

3. Pour in scant ¼ cup batter and tilt pan immediately to cover entire bottom surface. Cook until underside of crêpe is lightly browned, about 1 minute. Turn and lightly brown other side, 2 to 3 seconds. Remove to platter and cover with foil or towel, stacking crêpes until all the batter is used.

4. Use as needed.

TO PREPARE IN ADVANCE: Through step 3.
TO FREEZE: Through step 3, placing waxed paper between crêpes so that each may be removed as needed. Wrap in aluminum foil and place in low oven until crêpes are heated through. Or defrost, wrapped, in refrigerator.

VARIATION: *Dessert Crêpes:* Add 2 tablespoons Cognac, 2 egg yolks, and 1 tablespoon powdered sugar in step 1 and proceed with recipe.

*If using a Teflon-coated or Calphalon crêpe pan, use very little butter.

Simple pancakes made simpler with the food processor.

BLUEBERRY–SOUR CREAM PANCAKES

Makes about 20 pancakes

¾ cup all-purpose flour
1 teaspoon salt
½ teaspoon baking soda
½ cup cottage cheese
2 eggs

¾ cup sour cream
1 cup blueberries, plus additional,
   if desired
Melted butter (optional)
Syrup (optional)

1. In medium mixing bowl, sift together flour, salt, and baking soda. Reserve.

2. Using STEEL BLADE, combine cottage cheese, eggs, and sour cream, starting with on/off turns and then allowing motor to run until mixture is smooth. Scrape down sides of work bowl as necessary.

3. Add sifted dry ingredients and process, with on/off turns, just until incorporated.

4. Return mixture to mixing bowl and fold in 1 cup blueberries.

5. Using a tablespoon, spoon batter onto heated, lightly greased griddle, spreading lightly with spoon. Bake pancakes until brown on both sides. Serve with butter and warm syrup. (Additional berries may be sprinkled over pancakes when served, if desired.)

TO PREPARE IN ADVANCE: Through step 4.
TO FREEZE: Do not freeze.

I have served this with goose, roast beef, and turkey. It goes well with all of them.

YORKSHIRE PUDDING

1¾ cups all-purpose flour
1 teaspoon salt
4 eggs, at room temperature
1 cup milk, taken out of
  refrigerator 20 minutes before
  needed

1 cup water
¼ cup melted unsalted butter, or
  beef drippings

1. Sift together flour and salt.

2. Using STEEL BLADE, combine flour, salt, and eggs. With motor running, pour milk and water through feed tube. Transfer to pitcher or bowl and let stand, unrefrigerated, 1 hour.

3. Preheat oven to 400°F.

4. Pour butter into 11 x 7-inch baking dish and heat until smoking.

5. Using STEEL BLADE, return batter to work bowl and process for 2 seconds. Pour into prepared pan and bake 20 minutes. Lower oven temperature to 350°F. and continue baking 35 minutes longer.

6. Serve immediately as accompaniment to main dish.

TO PREPARE IN ADVANCE: Through step 2.
TO FREEZE: Do not freeze.

CONDIMENTS
AND
PRESERVES

A deliciously tart marmalade that can be varied with different combinations of fruits.

CITRUS MARMALADE

Makes 4 pints

3 medium oranges
1 medium lemon
1 medium grapefruit

1 cup water
5 cups sugar

1. Have ready sterilized pint or half-pint jars.

2. Cut oranges, lemon, and grapefruit to fit feed tube, removing seeds.

3. Using MEDIUM SLICING BLADE, with firm pressure, slice fruits. Transfer to 4-quart heavy saucepan.

4. Add water to saucepan and, over high flame, bring to boil. Lower flame and simmer until fruit is tender, 20 to 25 minutes.

5. Add sugar and cook, uncovered, over medium flame, until mixture thickens, about 25 minutes, stirring frequently. Skim foam as it accumulates.

6. Remove from heat, cover saucepan, and keep at room temperature 24 hours.

7. Divide marmalade into sterilized jars and seal, following manufacturers' directions. Store in cool area.

TO PREPARE IN ADVANCE: Through step 7.
TO FREEZE: Do not freeze.

PEACH CHUTNEY

4 pounds very ripe peaches, peeled, halved, and pitted
²⁄₃ cup preserved (candied) ginger, cut in 1-inch pieces
1 medium onion, chilled, cut in 1-inch pieces
2 cloves garlic
1 quart cider vinegar

½ pound white raisins
1 teaspoon red chili powder
2 tablespoons whole mustard seed
1 tablespoon salt
1½ pounds brown sugar (3¼ cups firmly packed)

1. Have ready sterilized pint or half-pint jars.

2. Using MEDIUM SLICING BLADE, slice peaches. Transfer to 5- or 6-quart enameled or Calphalon saucepan.

3. Using STEEL BLADE, process ginger, onion, and garlic until puréed, using ¼ cup vinegar if necessary. Add to peaches.

4. Stir in remaining vinegar, raisins, chili powder, mustard seed, salt, and brown sugar.

5. Over moderate flame, bring to boil, then lower flame and simmer, uncovered, 1 hour, stirring frequently.

6. Pour into sterilized jars and seal, following manufacturers' instructions.

7. Store in cool place at least 6 months before using.

TO PREPARE IN ADVANCE: Through step 6.
TO FREEZE: Do not freeze.

APRICOT JAM

3½ pounds apricots, halved, pitted, but unpeeled
¼ cup lemon juice

1 package pectin, 2 ounces
3 pounds sugar

1. Have ready sterilized half-pint jars.

2. Using STEEL BLADE, with on/off turns, chop apricots coarsely, 1 cup at a time. Remove to 8-quart saucepan and add lemon juice and pectin.

3. Over high flame, bring to hard boil and add sugar. Return to hard, rolling boil for 1 minute, stirring constantly. Remove from heat, stir, and skim foam from top for 5 minutes. Ladle into sterilized jars.

VARIATION: Slivered almonds may be added to hot apricots just before ladling into jars.

*B*READ-AND-BUTTER PICKLES   Makes about 4 quarts

4 cups sugar	1½ teaspoons mustard seed
4 cups white vinegar	1¼ teaspoons turmeric
¼ cup salt	3 medium onions, cut in half
1½ teaspoons celery seed	16 medium cucumbers, unpeeled

1. Have ready hot, sterilized pint or quart jars.

2. In large saucepan, combine sugar, vinegar, salt, celery seed, mustard seed, and turmeric. Bring to boil and boil 1 minute.

3. Using FINE SLICING BLADE, with firm pressure, slice onions. Reserve.

4. Using FINE SLICING BLADE, with firm pressure, slice cucumbers. Reserve.

5. In the bottom of hot, sterilized jars, place equal amounts of sliced onions. Divide cucumbers in jars and fill with hot liquid to ¼ inch of rim. Cover. Cool.

6. Refrigerate and allow to ripen for 2 weeks. Pickles will keep up to 3 months.

7. Serve as accompaniment to cold meat and poultry.

TO PREPARE IN ADVANCE: Through step 6.
TO FREEZE: Do not freeze.

Caponata is delicious as an accompaniment to grilled fish, or served as a relish on thick slices of French bread.

Makes about 2 quarts

1 cup fresh parsley leaves
½ cup fresh basil leaves
2½ pounds eggplant, stemmed
3 medium zucchini, ends removed
1 medium sweet red pepper, cored,
  seeded, and cut in half
1 medium onion, quartered
1 large stalk celery, strings
  removed, cut in 1-inch pieces

½ cup vegetable oil
1 can (28 ounces) plum tomatoes
¼ cup red wine vinegar
2 tablespoons tomato paste
1½ tablespoons salt
Freshly ground pepper
Pinch of dried thyme
3 tablespoons drained capers

1. Using STEEL BLADE, chop parsley fine. Reserve.

2. Using STEEL BLADE, chop basil fine. Reserve.

3. Using MEDIUM SLICING BLADE, cut eggplant to fit feed tube and slice, using firm pressure. Salt liberally and let drain for 30 minutes. Pat dry.

4. Using MEDIUM SLICING BLADE, slice zucchini and red pepper. Reserve.

5. Using STEEL BLADE, with on/off turns, chop onion coarsely. Drain if necessary and reserve.

6. Using STEEL BLADE with on/off turns, chop celery coarsely. Reserve.

7. In large saucepan, heat oil and sauté eggplant, zucchini, red pepper, onion, and celery until tender, about 20 minutes, stirring occasionally. Add tomatoes, vinegar, tomato paste, salt, pepper, thyme, and reserved basil and bring to boil. Cover, reduce heat, and simmer 30 minutes.

8. Remove cover and simmer until mixture thickens, about 10 minutes longer. Stir in reserved parsley and the capers and cool.

9. Refrigerate and use as needed.

TO PREPARE IN ADVANCE: Through step 7. *Caponata* will keep, refrigerated, up to 3 weeks.
TO FREEZE: Do not freeze.

This can be used instead of raw garlic for a more delicate flavor.

Garlic Puree

Makes about 1½ cups

1 *pound garlic, peeled*
2 *tablespoons water or vegetable*
  stock

1. In a small covered saucepan, over moderate flame, combine garlic and water and steam about 10 minutes.

2. Using STEEL BLADE, purée garlic until smooth, scraping down sides of work bowl as necessary.

3. Refrigerate in tightly covered container. Use as needed.

TO PREPARE IN ADVANCE: Through step 3. This will keep for weeks.
TO FREEZE: Do not freeze.

SPICED LEMON PICKLES

1 pound small lemons, ends
   removed
3 tablespoons salt
4 tablespoons crushed hot red
   pepper

2 garlic cloves
3 cups vegetable oil

1. Select lemons that will fit feed tube. If lemon is too large for feed tube, cut to fit. Try loading from bottom if necessary. Using MEDIUM SLICING BLADE, with firm pressure, slice lemons. Remove to large mixing bowl and sprinkle with salt. Cover and let stand 3 or 4 days at room temperature.

2. Using STEEL BLADE, process red pepper and garlic to a paste. Add to lemons in mixing bowl.

3. In medium saucepan, warm oil. Pour over lemons and let cool. Cover and keep at room temperature 3 or 4 days, then refrigerate and use as needed.

4. Serve as a condiment with meat or poultry.

TO PREPARE IN ADVANCE: Through step 3. This will keep 4 weeks or longer.
TO FREEZE: Do not freeze.

CRISP ONION RELISH

Makes 1 quart

4 large onions, cut in half
3 tablespoons pickling spice
¾ cup cider vinegar
1½ cups dry white wine

5 tablespoons brown sugar
1 stick cinnamon
1 teaspoon fresh dill
3 teaspoons salt

1. Have ready sterilized quart jar.

2. Using THIN SLICING BLADE, with firm pressure, slice onions. Remove to large mixing bowl and cover with boiling water. Let stand 2 to 3 minutes, then drain and cover with ice cubes. (This process will make ordinary yellow onions nearly as sweet and mild as Hawaiian Maui onions.)

3. To prepare marinade: Tie pickling spice into a cheesecloth package. In medium saucepan, over moderate flame, place spice package and remaining ingredients and bring to boil. Lower flame and simmer 10 minutes.

4. Thoroughly drain onions and pack into sterilized jar. Pour marinade over onions, being careful to cover all slices. Seal jar and refrigerate 24 hours before using.

TO PREPARE IN ADVANCE: Through step 4. This will keep refrigerated 2 to 3 weeks.
TO FREEZE: Do not freeze.

NOTE: Adding a few pieces of dried chili to the marinade will make it hot and spicy.

PEAR CHUTNEY

Makes 6 pints

12 firm medium pears, peeled,
  cored, and cut in 1-inch pieces
2 medium apples, peeled, cored,
  and cut in 1-inch pieces
2 medium green peppers, cored,
  seeded, and cut in 1-inch pieces
6 medium onions, quartered
1-inch piece fresh ginger, peeled
4 firm medium tomatoes, peeled,
  seeded, and quartered

2 cups raisins
4 teaspoons pickling spice,
  wrapped in cheesecloth
4 cups cider vinegar
1 teaspoon salt
2 cups granulated sugar
2 cups light brown sugar, firmly
  packed

1. Have ready hot, sterilized pint or half-pint jars.

2. Using STEEL BLADE, with on/off turns, coarsely chop pears, apples, peppers, and onions, separately. Drain onion as necessary. Chop no more than 2 cups at a time. As chopped, remove to large enamel or stainless steel saucepan.

3. Using STEEL BLADE, with motor running, drop ginger through feed tube and chop coarsely. Add tomatoes and chop coarsely. Remove to saucepan.

4. Add remaining ingredients to saucepan and bring to boil over moderate flame. Lower flame and simmer, covered, about 2 hours, stirring often to prevent sticking.

5. Remove bag of pickling spice and ladle chutney into hot, sterilized jars to within ¼ inch of rim. Cover and process in hot waterbath for 10 minutes.

6. Serve with curries or Chicken Barcelona (page 114).

TO PREPARE IN ADVANCE: Through step 5.
TO FREEZE: Do not freeze.

NOTE: If you want to eliminate waterbath process, cool chutney and refrigerate. Will keep up to 2 months.

VARIATION: Use any combination of fruit: peaches, pears, apricots, apples, for example.

You will never buy commercial bread crumbs again once you have sampled the good taste of these seasoned bread crumbs and realize the ease with which they can be prepared and stored. They can be used in stuffings, as breading, sprinkled on cooked vegetables and casseroles, among other things.

SEASONED BREAD CRUMBS   Makes about 1½ cups

¼ cup fresh parsley leaves
2 cups day-old white bread, crusts
   removed, torn in small pieces
1 ounce Parmesan cheese, cut in
   1-inch pieces

¼ teaspoon salt
¼ teaspoon white pepper
¼ teaspoon garlic powder

1. Using STEEL BLADE, chop parsley fine. Remove to large mixing bowl.

2. Using STEEL BLADE, chop bread to desired texture. Add to parsley.

3. Using STEEL BLADE, with motor running, drop cheese through feed tube and process until finely grated. Combine with parsley and bread. Add remaining ingredients and correct seasoning to taste.

4. Refrigerate in covered container and use as needed.

TO PREPARE IN ADVANCE: Through step 4.
TO FREEZE: Through step 3.

QUATRE-EPICES

Makes about ¾ cup

7 tablespoons whole peppercorns	*1 tablespoon ground ginger*
1 tablespoon whole cloves	*1 tablespoon ground nutmeg*

1. Using STEEL BLADE, combine all ingredients in work bowl. Process until finely ground, about 2 minutes. (This is a very noisy procedure, but worth it.)

2. Store in covered jar as you would any spice.

3. Use to season roasts, stews, ham, pâtés, etc.

TO PREPARE IN ADVANCE: Through step 2.
TO FREEZE: Do not freeze.

DOUGHS
AND
CRUSTS

If you've never tasted homemade pasta, you're in for a treat. Once you taste it, you will find it difficult to eat packaged pasta.

Pasta DOUGH

Makes 1½ pounds
(or serves 6 to 8)

3 cups all-purpose flour, plus
   additional for dusting
Large pinch of salt

4 eggs
2 tablespoons water
2 tablespoons vegetable oil

1. Using STEEL BLADE, combine 3 cups flour and the salt with 1 or 2 turns. Add remaining ingredients and process until dough begins to form a ball. Divide dough into 3 pieces, wrap each piece in plastic wrap, and allow to rest 30 to 40 minutes. Or refrigerate, wrapped in plastic wrap, until ready to roll out.

2. If you use a pasta machine, set rollers at widest opening. Flatten first ball of dough slightly, and make sure it is no wider than your machine. Dust with flour and run through the machine. Fold in thirds, dust with flour, and run through the machine again. Repeat this procedure 3 more times.

3. Set machine to next smaller opening and run dough through rollers. Continue stretching dough, using smaller opening each time, until the lowest opening is used.* Adjust cutting mechanism to desired width and cut dough into strips. Dry at least 30 minutes and then store in air-tight container until needed. Repeat with remaining dough.

4. To make pasta by hand, roll out each piece of dough as thin as possible on a lightly floured board, to form a rectangle. Lightly sprinkle with flour and roll up rectangle loosely, like a jelly roll. Using a sharp knife, cut into strips ⅛ inch, ¼ inch, or ½ inch wide, as desired. Dry and store as above until needed.

5. To cook pasta, bring at least 4 quarts of salted water to a full boil, add pasta, and bring water back to a boil, about 3 or 4 minutes. Pasta should be tender but firm to the bite. Drain in colander and refresh with running cold water (to stop cooking process and to prevent pasta from sticking together). Reserve until needed.

6. When ready to serve, using a wire basket, plunge pasta into boiling water, just to heat. Serve with favorite sauce (see Index).

TO PREPARE IN ADVANCE: Through step 3, or step 5.
TO FREEZE: Through step 3.

NOTE: To make lasagne noodles, proceed through step 2. Set machine to smaller opening and run dough through roller. Continue stretching dough, using smaller opening each time, to next to the smallest opening. Cut each strip into 2 pieces, 4 x 9 inches, making 6 strips.

VARIATION: To prepare spinach pasta, sauté 1 cup spinach leaves that have been washed and stemmed in 1 tablespoon vegetable oil. Drain well. Using STEEL BLADE, purée spinach, add pasta ingredients, and proceed as above.

*If you prefer a slightly thicker pasta noodle, stretch dough until you reach next to the smallest opening.

This is the classic recipe. Puffs can be used for many things—as a sweet or as an hors d'oeuvre, depending on the filling.

PATE A CHOUX

Makes 1 dozen eclairs or large cream puffs or approximately 2 dozen profiteroles

---

¼ *pound (1 stick) unsalted butter,*
  cut in 6 pieces
¼ *teaspoon salt*
1 *cup water*

1 *cup all-purpose flour*
4 *large eggs*
1 *egg, lightly beaten, for egg wash*

---

1. Preheat oven to 400°F. Butter large baking sheet and sprinkle with cold water, pouring off excess.

2. In medium saucepan, over moderate flame, combine butter, salt, and water and bring to rolling boil. When butter is completely melted, remove pan from flame and add the flour, all at once. Stir vigorously with wooden spoon until flour is absorbed. Return to low flame and cook for 1 or 2 minutes, stirring all the while, until dough comes away from the sides of the pan and forms a ball. Dump into work bowl fitted with STEEL BLADE.

3. With motor running, add 4 eggs to work bowl all at once and process until dough is very smooth and shiny, scraping down sides of work bowl as necessary.

---

4. To make puffs, fill pastry bag fitted with plain tube—¼ inch (for profiteroles) or ½ inch (for larger puffs)—and pipe onto prepared baking sheet in rounded mounds 2 inches apart. (Or drop puffs off a rounded tablespoon onto prepared pastry sheet.) Brush with egg wash, taking care that egg does not drip down on pan, and smooth any peaks that may have formed. (For eclairs, pipe into strips 6 inches long and 1 inch wide, and brush with egg wash.)

5. Bake 45 to 50 minutes, then prick each puff with point of knife and return to oven 5 minutes longer. Cool on rack.

6. Slice off tops and remove any soft dough inside puffs. Fill with desired filling and serve.

TO PREPARE IN ADVANCE: Through step 5.
TO FREEZE: Through step 5. To reheat, place in preheated oven, bake 10 to 15 minutes, then continue with recipe.

VARIATION: You can prepare *beignets* with the *choux* recipe (classic or cheese, as in *Gougère* on (page 48). In deep frying pan, heat vegetable oil to 365°F. Drop *choux* dough into hot oil by the tablespoon, using second spoon as pusher. *Beignets* will brown on one side and then turn over and brown on the other side (you may have to aid in this process). When *beignets* are brown on both sides, remove to ovenproof dish lined with paper towels and keep warm in low oven. Repeat this procedure until you have made desired number, being careful that you do not overfill frying pan at any time. Sprinkle with powdered sugar, if sweet *beignets* are desired, and serve.

PATE BRISEE

Makes pastry for 1
eight-inch crust

1 cup all-purpose flour
1 tablespoon powdered sugar
Pinch of salt
½ pound (2 sticks) unsalted
    butter, chilled, cut in 6 pieces
1 egg

2 or 3 tablespoons ice water

1. Using STEEL BLADE, with 1 or 2 on/off turns, combine flour, sugar, and salt.

2. Add butter and process until mixture resembles very coarse meal.

3. In small mixing bowl, combine egg and 2 tablespoons water. With motor running, add to work bowl through feed tube and process just until dough begins to form ball on blade, using remaining 1 tablespoon water if necessary.

4. Turn dough out on lightly floured board and pat into 6-inch circle; wrap in plastic wrap. (Patting into circle at this stage simplifies rolling of dough when needed.) Refrigerate at least 2 hours, preferably overnight.

TO PREPARE IN ADVANCE: Through step 4.
TO FREEZE: Through step 4. Defrost overnight in refrigerator, then roll into desired shape and use as needed.

PATE SUCREE

Makes 1 eight- or nine-inch shell

Rind of ½ small lemon
2 tablespoons sugar
1 cup all-purpose flour
6 tablespoons unsalted butter,
    chilled, cut in 6 pieces

1 egg yolk
Pinch of salt
1 tablespoon ice water

1. Using STEEL BLADE, combine rind and sugar and chop fine.

2. Add remaining ingredients and process with on/off turns just until ball begins to form on blade and dough leaves sides of work bowl.

3. Turn dough out on lightly floured board and pat into 6-inch circle (to facilitate rolling out later). Wrap in plastic wrap, and refrigerate at least 2 hours. Use as needed.

TO PREPARE IN ADVANCE: Through step 3.
TO FREEZE: Through step 3. Defrost overnight in refrigerator, then roll into desired shape and use as needed.

All-American flaky pie crust. Can be doubled for 2-crust pie.

Single-CRUST PIE SHELL

Makes 1 nine- or ten-inch pie crust

1 cup all-purpose flour
½ teaspoon salt

⅓ cup unsalted butter, chilled, cut
  in 8 pieces
3 to 4 tablespoons ice water

1. Using STEEL BLADE, combine flour and salt with 1 or 2 on/off turns.

2. Add butter and process until consistency of coarse meal.

3. With motor running, slowly pour water through feed tube, using only enough water to form ball. Do not overprocess.

4. Turn dough out on lightly floured board and pat into small circle. Wrap in plastic wrap and refrigerate at least 30 minutes before using.

5. On lightly floured board, roll dough out into a circle 1 inch larger than size of pie plate. Roll pastry over rolling pin and unroll it over pie plate, leaving slight overhang. Gently press dough into plate and fold overhang under edge of crust and flute, using thumb of one hand and forefinger of other hand. Refrigerate until needed.

TO PREPARE IN ADVANCE: Through step 5.
TO FREEZE: Through step 4. Defrost overnight in refrigerator, then roll into desired shape and use as needed. Through step 5, shell can be filled directly from freezer.

Tartlet SHELLS

Makes 8 four-inch shells

1 cup all-purpose flour
½ teaspoon salt

¼ pound (1 stick) unsalted butter,
  chilled, cut in 8 pieces
1 to 2 tablespoons ice water

1. Using STEEL BLADE, combine flour, salt, and butter and process until mixture resembles coarse meal. With motor running, add water through feed tube, just until dough begins to form ball on blade.

2. Turn out dough on lightly floured board, divide in half, and pat each half into a 6-inch circle, to facilitate rolling out later. Wrap dough in plastic wrap and refrigerate at least 2 hours, preferably overnight. (This dough is very soft and needs to be well chilled.)

3. Preheat oven to 425°F.

4. Work with one circle at a time, refrigerating unused portion. On lightly floured board, roll out dough as thin as possible (⅛ inch). With cookie cutter, cut into 4-inch circles and fit into small tartlet pans. Line with aluminum foil and fill with beans, rice, or pie weights.

5. Bake 10 minutes, then remove weights and foil, return to oven, and bake 2 to 3 minutes longer, or until lightly browned. Transfer to rack and let cool.

6. Fill as desired.

TO PREPARE IN ADVANCE: Through step 6.
TO FREEZE: Through step 2 or 6. Shells can be filled directly from freezer.

CHEDDAR CHEESE PASTRY
Makes pastry for 1 eight-inch springform pan

1½ cups sifted all-purpose flour
1 teaspoon salt
¼ pound (1 stick) unsalted butter,
  chilled, cut in 6 pieces

4 ounces Cheddar cheese, chilled,
  cut in 6 pieces
2 to 2½ tablespoons ice water

1. Butter 8-inch springform pan.

2. Using STEEL BLADE, add flour and salt to work bowl and combine with 1 or 2 on/off turns. Add butter and cheese and process until mixture resembles coarse meal.

3. Through feed tube, and with motor running, gradually add ice water and process until pastry begins to form ball on blade. Turn out dough on very lightly floured board and gently roll out into a circle large enough to fit pan.

4. Carefully press down pastry so that it fits snugly on bottom and then up sides of prepared pan. Remove excess dough and shape pastry so it is slightly higher than pan. (Try to shape dough so height is the same all around.) Refrigerate until ready to fill.

TO PREPARE IN ADVANCE: Through step 4.
TO FREEZE: Through step 4. Shell may be filled directly from freezer.

VARIATION: Can be divided among small tart pans and filled as desired.

CREAM CHEESE PASTRY

Makes 1 nine- or ten-inch crust

4 ounces cream cheese, at room
    temperature, cut in 6 pieces
¼ pound (1 stick) unsalted butter,
    at room temperature, cut in 6
    pieces

2 tablespoons heavy cream
1¼ cups all-purpose flour
¼ teaspoon salt

1. Using STEEL BLADE, process cream cheese and butter until smooth, scraping down sides of work bowl as necessary.

2. Add cream and process with 1 or 2 on/off turns.

3. Add flour and salt and process just until dough begins to form ball on blade. Pat into flat 6-inch circle (to facilitate rolling out later), wrap in plastic wrap, and refrigerate at least 1 hour.

4. Roll out on lightly floured board and fit into pan.

TO PREPARE IN ADVANCE: Through step 3 or 4.
TO FREEZE: Through step 3. Defrost overnight in refrigerator and continue with recipe. Through step 4, shell may be filled directly from freezer.

CHOCOLATE-WAFER CRUMB CRUST

24 *chocolate wafers*
½ *teaspoon instant coffee*

6 *tablespoons melted, unsalted*
butter

1. Using STEEL BLADE, coarsely chop wafers.

2. Add remaining ingredients and process to desired texture, scraping down sides of work bowl as necessary.

3. Press firmly into lightly buttered pie plate, chill, and use as needed. Reserve 3 or 4 tablespoons of mixture to sprinkle over filling, if desired.

TO PREPARE IN ADVANCE: Through step 3.
TO FREEZE: Through step 3. Shell may be filled directly from freezer.

 GRAHAM-CRACKER CRUST

24 *graham crackers, broken in half*   ⅓ *cup melted, unsalted butter*
2 *tablespoons sugar*

1. Using STEEL BLADE, coarsely chop graham crackers.

2. Add remaining ingredients and process to desired texture, scraping down sides of work bowl as necessary.

3. Press firmly into lightly buttered pie plate, chill, and use as needed. Reserve 3 or 4 tablespoons of mixture to sprinkle over filling, if desired.

TO PREPARE IN ADVANCE: Through step 3.
TO FREEZE: Through step 3. Shell may be filled directly from freezer.

VARIATION: Flavor graham crackers with ¼ teaspoon ginger or ¼ teaspoon cinnamon in step 2.

Vanilla-Wafer Crumb Crust

Makes 1 eight- or nine-inch crust

30 small vanilla wafers
Rind of ½ small lemon

⅓ cup melted, unsalted butter

1. Using STEEL BLADE, coarsely chop wafers and lemon rind.

2. Add melted butter and process to desired texture, scraping down sides of work bowl as necessary.

3. Press firmly into lightly buttered pie plate, chill, and use as needed. Reserve 3 or 4 tablespoons of mixture to sprinkle over filling, if desired.

TO PREPARE IN ADVANCE: Through step 3.
TO FREEZE: Through step 3. Shell may be filled directly from freezer.

Zwieback Crumb Crust

Makes 1 nine-inch crust

1 box (6 ounces) zwieback, cut in
* 1-inch pieces*
¾ cup sugar
1 teaspoon ground cinnamon

¼ pound (1 stick) unsalted butter,
at room temperature, cut in 6
or 8 pieces

1. Using STEEL BLADE, process zwieback until coarsely crumbed. Start with on/off turns and then allow motor to run to desired texture.

2. Add remaining ingredients and process until thoroughly combined, scraping down sides of work bowl as necessary.

3. Press firmly into lightly buttered pan, chill, and use as needed. Reserve 3 or 4 tablespoons of mixture to sprinkle over filling, if desired.

TO PREPARE IN ADVANCE: Through step 3.
TO FREEZE: Through step 3. Shell may be filled directly from freezer.

Somehow even experienced cooks are bewildered by puff pastry. Following these simple directions, there should no longer be any mystery to this technique.

PUFF PASTRY

Makes 2¼ pounds

DÉTRÊMPE:*

1 cup pastry flour**
1½ cups all-purpose flour
4 tablespoons (½ stick) unsalted
    butter, chilled, cut in 4 pieces
1 teaspoon salt
¾ cup ice water

BUTTER BLOCK:

11 ounces (2¾ sticks) unsalted
    butter, removed from
    refrigerator 30 minutes before
    using and cut in 1-tablespoon
    pieces
½ cup all-purpose flour

1. To prepare *détrêmpe:* Using STEEL BLADE, combine pastry flour, all-purpose flour, butter, and salt and process until texture resembles coarse meal.

2. With motor running, slowly pour ice water through feed tube, until dough forms ball on blade (which happens almost immediately). Turn out on very lightly floured board and pat into a small square, which will make it easier to roll. Lightly score (see illustration on page 258) to take out elasticity in the pastry. Wrap securely in plastic wrap and refrigerate 1 hour. Clean work bowl.

3. To prepare butter block: Using STEEL BLADE, combine butter pieces and all-purpose flour and process just until bits of butter become one piece. Do not overprocess. Remove from work bowl, place between 2 pieces of waxed paper, and roll into 6-inch square. Wrap in plastic wrap and refrigerate about 30 minutes.

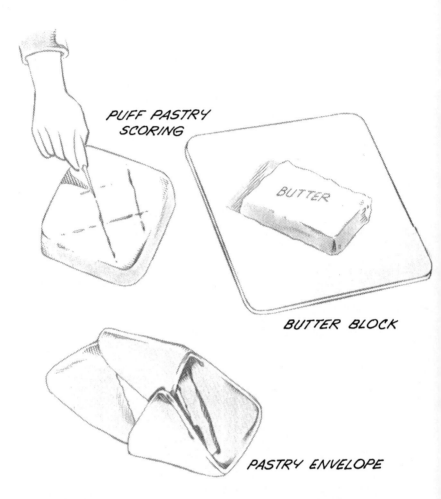

PUFF PASTRY
SCORING

BUTTER

BUTTER BLOCK

PASTRY ENVELOPE

4. On lightly floured board, roll out *détrêmpe* to 10-inch square. Place butter block in center of pastry, at an angle (see illustration), and poke indentations in butter with your finger to ensure puffier pastry. Cover butter completely with ends of pastry, meeting in center like an envelope, and pinch together any opening in pastry.

5. On lightly floured board, roll pastry out to rectangle approximately 8 x 18 inches. Do not press down on dough; you want to flatten butter between the layers of dough without allowing it to ooze through. Starting with 8-inch side in front of you, fold dough into thirds (see illustration).

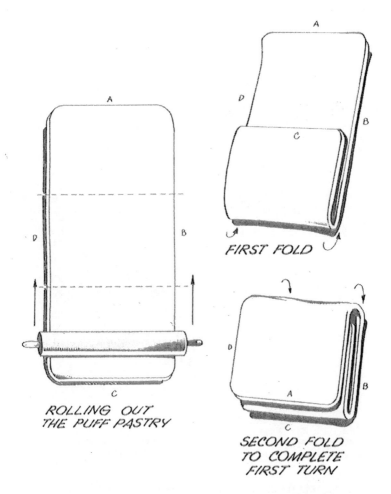

ROLLING OUT
THE PUFF PASTRY

FIRST FOLD

SECOND FOLD
TO COMPLETE
FIRST TURN

6. Turn dough so that seam is on your right and again roll out to same size rectangle, sprinkling board and pastry with flour as needed to prevent sticking. Using large, dry pastry brush, brush away excess flour *before* and *after* folding. With your rolling pin, "block" pastry as it is being rolled (see illustration) so that it keeps its shape. Again fold dough into thirds. You have just completed 2 turns on your pastry. Using your knuckle, lightly press 2 indentations in dough to remind you of number of turns you have made, and repeat as you continue your turns. Wrap securely in plastic wrap and refrigerate for 30 minutes between each set of turns.

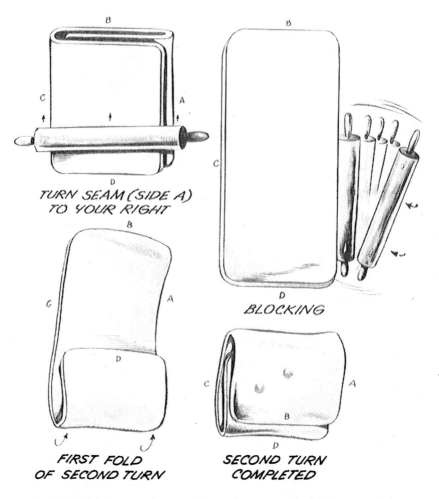

TURN SEAM (SIDE A)
TO YOUR RIGHT

BLOCKING

FIRST FOLD
OF SECOND TURN

SECOND TURN
COMPLETED

7. Repeat this procedure until you have completed 6 turns. Your Puff Pastry is now ready to be used in your favorite recipe.

TO PREPARE IN ADVANCE: Through step 7.
TO FREEZE: Through step 7. Defrost, wrapped, overnight in refrigerator, then roll into desired shape and use as needed.

*French for a mixture of flour and water to be used in the preparation of pastry.

**Pastry flour may be purchased in health food or specialty food stores.

DESSERTS

The texture is spongy and the taste delicately flavored.

AMARETTO MADELEINES

¼ teaspoon baking soda
½ teaspoon salt
1½ cups cake flour
¼ pound (1 stick) unsalted butter,
   chilled, cut in 1-inch pieces
1¼ cups sugar
3 eggs

½ cup sour cream
½ teaspoon vanilla extract
½ teaspoon orange extract
½ teaspoon lemon extract
1 teaspoon almond extract
¼ cup Amaretto

1. Preheat oven to 325°F.

2. Butter well madeleine forms.* Sprinkle with cold water and pour out any excess.

3. Sift together baking soda, salt, and cake flour. Reserve in mixing bowl.

4. Using STEEL BLADE, cream butter and sugar until smooth.

5. Through feed tube, add eggs, one at a time, and combine with 2 on/off turns for each egg. Add sour cream, vanilla, orange, lemon, and almond extracts, and Amaretto. Process until combined, scraping down sides of work bowl as necessary.

6. Sprinkle sifted dry ingredients on top of batter and process with on/off turns just until incorporated.

7. Spoon batter into prepared madeleine pans and bake 20 to 30 minutes, until golden brown and tops spring back when lightly touched.

8. Turn out on racks to cool.

TO PREPARE IN ADVANCE: Through step 8.
TO FREEZE: Through step 8. Defrost, wrapped, at room temperature.

NOTE: Madeleines can be made into crumbs and used as topping for cakes and pies (see Strawberry Amaretto Mousse, page 282).

*Madeleine forms may be purchased at gourmet kitchenware shops.

Make this only when apricots are fresh. Canned apricots are too watery for this recipe.

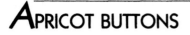APRICOT BUTTONS

Makes 24 pastries

SWEET PASTRY:

1 cup all-purpose flour
½ teaspoon salt
1 tablespoon sugar
5⅓ tablespoons unsalted butter,
   chilled, cut in 6 pieces
1 egg yolk
⅓ cup cold water

FILLING:

3 tablespoons all-purpose flour
½ cup brown sugar, firmly packed
1½ tablespoons unsalted butter,
   chilled
½ teaspoon ground cinnamon
12 fresh apricots, halved and pitted
1 egg white, lightly beaten, for
   wash

1. To prepare pastry: Using STEEL BLADE, with 2 or 3 on/off turns, blend flour, salt, and sugar.

2. Add butter and process until texture of coarse meal. Add egg yolk and process with 2 on/off turns.

3. With motor running, slowly add water through feed tube until dough begins to form ball on blade. Wrap in plastic wrap and refrigerate 30 minutes. Clean work bowl.

4. Preheat oven to 350°F.

5. To prepare filling: Using PLASTIC BLADE, process flour, brown sugar, butter, and cinnamon until combined. Reserve.

6. On lightly floured board, roll out pastry to 8 x 12-inch rectangle. Cut into 24 two-inch squares.

7. Arrange 1 apricot half, cut side up, in center of each square. Fill each apricot half with 1 teaspoon filling mixture. Reserve some of the filling for topping. Bring together all 4 corners of pastry square and form into a ball, rolling it in palms of your hands. Place on buttered cookie sheet as rolled.

8. Brush egg-white wash over buttons and sprinkle with remaining filling.

9. Bake 45 minutes, reversing position of cookie sheet after 25 minutes.

10. Cool on rack.

TO PREPARE IN ADVANCE: Through step 10.
TO FREEZE: Through step 3. Defrost, wrapped, overnight in re-frigerator, then continue with recipe.

This is one of Maida Heatter's unpublished recipes. She prepared these cookies in one of our classes at Ma Cuisine.

PRETZEL COOKIES

Makes 30 cookies

Rind of 2 medium lemons
2 large eggs, separated
1 large egg
2½ cups sifted all-purpose flour
½ teaspoon salt
Rounded ¼ teaspoon mace

1 cup confectioners sugar
6 ounces unsalted butter, chilled,
    cut in 1-inch pieces
1½ teaspoons vanilla extract
Crystallized sugar

1. Adjust 2 racks high in oven (with enough room between them for air to circulate). Preheat oven to 375°F. Line 2 cookie sheets with aluminum foil.

2. Using vegetable peeler, scrape strips of rind from lemons. Using STEEL BLADE, grate rind fine (you may want to add a little of the powdered sugar here).

3. Using STEEL BLADE, process yolks and whole egg with flour, salt, mace, powdered sugar, butter, vanilla, and grated rind, only until ingredients hold together.

4. Turn dough out onto smooth work surface and knead briefly, only until smooth. Form into ball and divide into 2 even pieces. (If dough is too sticky to handle, wrap in plastic wrap and refrigerate or freeze only until you can handle it.) Clean work bowl.

5. Lightly flour work surface and, with your hands, roll each piece of dough into a roll 15 inches long and about 1 inch in diameter. (Again, if dough is too sticky, refrigerate or freeze as necessary.) Cut each roll into 1-inch pieces. With your fingers, roll each piece into a pencil shape about 10 inches long. Transfer each piece to prepared cookie sheet and shape into a pretzel.

6. Using PLASTIC BLADE, beat egg whites until barely foamy. With soft pastry brush, brush white on pretzels, trying not to let it run down onto the foil. With your fingers, sprinkle each cookie generously with crystal sugar.

7. Bake 25 to 30 minutes, until cookies are golden brown. During baking, reverse sheets top to bottom and front to back as necessary to ensure even browning. Do not underbake—these must be very dry and crisp.

8. With wide metal spatula, transfer cookies to racks to cool. (If egg white has run down sides and made it difficult to remove the cookies, let stand on foil until completely cool and then peel foil away from the backs.)

9. Store in airtight containers. They are even better the next day. Do not eat while still warm.

TO PREPARE IN ADVANCE: Through step 8.
TO FREEZE: Through step 8. Defrost, wrapped, at room temperature. Store in airtight containers.

VANILLA BEAN COOKIES

Makes 30 two-inch cookies

4 ounces blanched almonds
½ pound (1 stick) unsalted butter, unrefrigerated for 30 minutes before using, cut in 1-inch pieces
½ cup granulated sugar

1½ cups sifted all-purpose flour
2 cups powdered sugar
1 vanilla bean, cut in ½-inch pieces

1. Using STEEL BLADE, grind almonds fine. Reserve.

2. Using STEEL BLADE, cream butter until light. Through feed tube, with motor running, slowly add granulated sugar.

3. Add almonds and flour and process until well combined, scraping down sides as necessary. Remove dough from work bowl and cover with plastic wrap. Refrigerate overnight. Clean work bowl.

4. To prepare vanilla sugar: Using STEEL BLADE, combine vanilla bean with 1 cup powdered sugar. Process until bean is pulverized. Allow the machine to run 60 seconds, then check. Remove to medium mixing bowl and stir in remaining sugar.

5. Preheat oven to 325°F.

6. Pinch off pieces of dough the size of walnuts. Using the bottom of a glass that has been dipped in flour, press pieces of dough into 2-inch rounds. Arrange on buttered cookie sheets and bake about 12 minutes, or until cookies are lightly colored. Remove to racks to cool just until crisp, but still warm. Dip in vanilla sugar to coat both sides.

7. Store in airtight container. Will keep 2 to 3 weeks.

TO PREPARE IN ADVANCE: Through step 6.
TO FREEZE: Through step 3. Defrost, wrapped, at room temperature.

From bowl to oven in 5 minutes . . . and if your family is like ours, it may not last long enough to "cool on rack."

*B*ANANA CAKE

Serves 8 to 12

¼ cup sour cream
1 teaspoon baking soda
1¾ cups all-purpose flour
1 teaspoon baking powder
¼ teaspoon salt
¼ pound (1 stick) unsalted butter,
   chilled, cut in 4 pieces

1¼ cups sugar
2 eggs
2 large, ripe bananas, peeled and
   cut in 1½-inch pieces
1 teaspoon vanilla extract
Powdered sugar

1. Preheat oven to 350°F. Butter a 9 x 4 x 13-inch loaf pan.

2. Combine sour cream and baking soda. Reserve.

3. Sift together flour, baking powder, and salt. Reserve.

4. Using STEEL BLADE, cream butter and sugar, scraping down sides of bowl as necessary.

5. Add eggs, sour cream, bananas, and vanilla. Process with on/off turns 4 or 5 times. Distribute flour mixture evenly around work bowl and process just until flour disappears.

6. Pour into prepared loaf pan. Bake 1 hour, or until tester inserted in center of cake comes out dry. Cool on rack.

7. To serve, invert on plate and dust with powdered sugar.

TO PREPARE IN ADVANCE: Through step 6.
TO FREEZE: Through step 6. Defrost, wrapped, at room temperature, then continue with recipe.

NOTE: One-half cup coarsely chopped walnuts may be folded in after step 5.

CARROT CAKE

Serves 10 to 12

2 cups sifted all-purpose flour
2 teaspoons baking powder
2 teaspoons baking soda
2 teaspoons ground cinnamon
1 teaspoon salt
1 cup walnuts or pecans

5 or 6 medium carrots
2 cups sugar
1½ cups vegetable oil
4 eggs
Cream Cheese Icing (page 294)

1. Preheat oven to 350°F. Butter 3 nine-inch round cake tins.

2. Sift together flour, baking powder, baking soda, cinnamon, and salt. Reserve.

3. Using STEEL BLADE, with on/off turns, coarsely chop nuts. Reserve.

4. Using FINE SHREDDING BLADE, shred enough carrots to make 3 cups. Reserve. Clean work bowl.

5. Using STEEL BLADE, cream together sugar and oil. Add eggs and process until well combined. Distribute sifted ingredients evenly around work bowl and process just until incorporated. Remove to large mixing bowl. Fold in carrots and nuts, reserving 1 or 2 tablespoons nuts to decorate cake.

6. Divide cake into prepared pans and bake 50 minutes, or until cake springs back when touched. Cool on rack.

7. Fill each layer and frost top with the icing. Sprinkle with reserved chopped nuts.

TO PREPARE IN ADVANCE: Through step 7.
TO FREEZE: Through step 6. Defrost, wrapped, at room temperature, then continue with recipe.

This is a very rich, very chocolate cheese cake.

CHOCOLATE CHEESE CAKE
Serves 10 to 12

Chocolate-Wafer Crumb Crust
   (page 255)
1 package (6 ounces) chocolate
   chips
6 tablespoons unsalted butter
1 teaspoon vanilla extract
2 tablespoons unsweetened cocoa

½ cup sugar
2 eggs
1 pound cream cheese, at room
   temperature, cut in 1-inch
   pieces
1½ cups sour cream

1. Preheat oven to 350°F. Butter bottom and sides of 8-inch spring-form pan.

2. Prepare crumb crust. Reserve ¼ cup of crumb mixture and press remaining crumbs into bottom and 2 inches up sides of prepared pan. Refrigerate until needed. Clean work bowl.

3. To prepare filling: In top of double boiler, combine chocolate chips, butter, vanilla, and cocoa and heat until chocolate melts, stirring occasionally. Cool slightly.

4. Using STEEL BLADE, thoroughly combine sugar and eggs. Through feed tube, with motor running, add cream cheese, a small amount at a time, and process until smooth, scraping down sides of work bowl as necessary. Add chocolate and sour cream to cheese mixture. Process until combined, scraping down sides of work bowl as necessary.

5. Pour into prepared crust and level top by briskly rotating pan from one side to the other. Sprinkle reserved crumbs decoratively over top. Bake 45 minutes (center will appear undone).

6. Remove to rack to cool completely. Refrigerate overnight.

TO PREPARE IN ADVANCE: Through step 6.
TO FREEZE: Through step 6. Defrost, wrapped, in refrigerator.

This is a very moist cake that will delight young and old alike. It is my son's favorite.

CHOCOLATE DATE CAKE

Serves 8 to 10

1¾ cups all-purpose flour
1 cup whole dates, pitted
1 teaspoon baking powder
1 cup boiling water
2 tablespoons unsweetened cocoa
¼ teaspoon salt
6 ounces (1½ sticks) butter, cut in
    10 pieces

1 cup sugar
2 large eggs
1 teaspoon vanilla extract
1 package (6 ounces) chocolate
    chips

1. Preheat oven to 350°F. Butter an 8-inch baking pan.

2. Using STEEL BLADE, with on/off turns, process ¼ cup of the flour, dates, and baking powder until dates are coarsely chopped. Transfer to small mixing bowl and pour boiling water into bowl. Reserve.

3. In medium mixing bowl, sift together remaining 1½ cups flour, the cocoa, and salt. Reserve.

4. Using STEEL BLADE, cream butter and sugar, scraping down sides of work bowl as necessary. Add eggs and vanilla and process just until combined.

5. Distribute flour mixture evenly around work bowl and process with on/off turns, scraping down sides of work bowl as necessary.

6. Add date mixture and process just until combined.

7. Pour batter into prepared pan and sprinkle chocolate chips over entire surface of cake.

8. Bake 40 to 45 minutes. Center will not be firm but will become firm while cooling.

9. Cool on rack.

TO PREPARE IN ADVANCE: Through step 9.
TO FREEZE: Through step 9, slicing into portions before freezing if desired. Defrost, wrapped, at room temperature.

This is my husband's favorite cake. A little goes a long way.

Serves 10 to 12

---

1 cup hazelnuts
1 cup sliced almonds
1¼ cups sugar
10 large egg whites

1½ cups heavy cream
1½ to 2 cups Ganache (page 294)
Unsweetened cocoa (optional)

---

1. Spread hazelnuts and almonds in single layer on separate baking sheets. Bake almonds 10 minutes and hazelnuts 20 to 25 minutes. Cool slightly, then place hazelnuts in clean tea towel. Fold towel to enclose nuts and rub between your hands to remove nut skins. (Some will not come off, but remove as many as possible.)

2. Preheat oven to 350°F. Line two 12 x 15-inch jelly roll pans with parchment or waxed paper and butter lightly over entire surface.

3. Using STEEL BLADE, process almonds, hazelnuts, and 1 cup of the sugar until chopped fine, scraping down sides of work bowl as necessary. Reserve. Clean work bowl.

4. Using a wire whisk or rotary beater, whip egg whites until they form soft peaks. Add remaining ¼ cup sugar and continue to whip until whites are stiff and shiny.

5. Gently fold 2 cups nut mixture into beaten egg whites, reserving ¾ cup. Divide mixture in half and spread as evenly as possible over prepared pans. Bake 20 to 25 minutes.

6. Cool on racks and carefully remove paper.

7. Cut each cake lengthwise into 2 rectangles approximately 6 x 15 inches. Stack layers and trim edges so that layers match. Then unstack so that cake can be filled.

8. Using STEEL BLADE, process heavy cream until softly whipped. Add reserved nut mixture and process until cream is stiff, scraping down sides of work bowl as necessary.

9. To assemble cake, place first layer on serving platter and spread with half the cream mixture. Top with second layer and spread with 1 cup softened *Ganache*. Top with third layer and spread with remaining cream. Top with last layer and glaze entire cake with remaining *Ganache*, which has been melted in a bain-marie. Smooth sides with spatula or palette knife.

10. Chill overnight before serving.

11. Before serving, dust with sifted, unsweetened cocoa if desired.

TO PREPARE IN ADVANCE: Through step 10.
TO FREEZE: Through step 10. Defrost, wrapped, in refrigerator. Dust with sifted powdered sugar or cocoa before serving.

NOTE: If you have leftover *Ganache*, pipe chilled *Ganache* around edges of cake, using a ⅜-inch star tip, to form a decorative border.

At Christmas time I bake a batch of honey cakes, slice them into fingers, and include with cookies as gifts.

*H*ONEY CAKE

Serves 8 to 12

⅔ cup honey
⅓ cup sugar
2 teaspoons baking soda
¼ cup whole eggs (1 or 2)
¼ cup vegetable oil

¼ cup water
1 teaspoon ground cinnamon
1 teaspoon ground allspice
½ teaspoon salt
2 cups rye flour

1. Preheat oven to 275°F. Line ungreased 9 x 5 x 3-inch loaf pan with aluminum foil.

2. Using STEEL BLADE, combine all ingredients in work bowl and process until smooth.

3. Pour batter into prepared pan. Bake 1½ hours, or until cake is golden brown and firm to the touch. Cool on rack.

4. Gently remove foil and slice.

TO PREPARE IN ADVANCE: Through step 3.
TO FREEZE: Through step 3 or 4. Defrost, wrapped, at room temperature.

VARIATIONS: 1. Fold 1 cup coarsely chopped walnuts into batter and bake as above.
2. Fold 1 cup mixed candied fruit into batter and bake as above.

A coffee cake is a coffee cake—until you taste this one. This is adapted from one of Maida Heatter's marvelous recipes in her Book of Great Desserts.

Sour Cream Coffee Cake

Serves 10 to 12

FILLING:

1 cup walnuts
½ cup dark brown sugar, firmly
   packed
1 teaspoon ground cinnamon
¼ cup chocolate chips

CAKE BATTER:

3 cups all-purpose flour
1½ teaspoons baking powder
1½ teaspoons baking soda
½ teaspoon salt
6 ounces (1½ sticks) unsalted
   butter, chilled, cut in 6 pieces
1¼ cups granulated sugar
3 eggs
1 teaspoon vanilla extract
2 cups sour cream

GLAZE:

2 cups powdered sugar
1 teaspoon vanilla extract
3 tablespoons milk

1. Preheat oven to 375°F. Butter a 10-inch Bundt pan.

2. To prepare filling: Using STEEL BLADE, combine all ingredients with on/off turns until nuts and chips are coarsely ground. Scrape down sides of work bowl as necessary. Reserve.

3. To prepare cake batter: In mixing bowl, combine flour, baking powder, baking soda, and salt. Reserve.

4. Using STEEL BLADE, process butter and granulated sugar. A ball will form. Add eggs, vanilla, and sour cream. Use 3 on/off turns and then allow machine to run until mixture is well blended. Scrape down sides as necessary.

5. Distribute flour mixture evenly around work bowl. Use on/off method just until flour is incorporated. Clean work bowl.

6. Spread one-fourth of batter in prepared pan. Sprinkle with one-third filling and continue layering with one-fourth batter, one-third filling, one-fourth batter, remaining filling, and the last layer will be the remaining batter. (If a marbled effect is desired, gently run spatula through batter.)

7. Bake 45 to 50 minutes, or until cake tester comes out dry. Remove from oven, let rest for 5 minutes, and invert on rack.

8. While cake is baking, prepare glaze. Using PLASTIC BLADE, place all ingredients for glaze in work bowl. Process 2 or 3 seconds. If mixture is still thick, add more drops of milk as needed. Reserve. Glaze cake while still hot. Drop by spoonfuls on cake and let drip down sides. (Place waxed paper under rack to catch drippings.)

TO PREPARE IN ADVANCE: Through step 8.
TO FREEZE: Through step 8. Freeze uncovered until glaze sets, then wrap carefully. (I like to slice cake and then freeze so that I can remove one slice or entire cake as needed.) Defrost, wrapped, at room temperature.

This recipe comes from Jerry Di Vecchio, Southwest editor of Sunset *magazine. It is a variation of a Swedish pastry called* mazarin, *using a brown-butter pastry.*

BROWN BUTTER MAZARIN

Serves 8 to 10

PASTRY:

¼ pound (1 stick) unsalted butter, chilled, cut in 8 pieces
1½ cups all-purpose flour
¼ cup sugar
1 egg yolk

FILLING:

¾ cup Almond Paste, homemade (page 288) or commercial, cut in 1-inch pieces
2 tablespoons sugar
2 tablespoons all-purpose flour
2 whole eggs plus 1 egg white

GLAZE:

1 cup powdered sugar, unsifted
2 tablespoons milk
Whole or slivered blanched almonds (optional)

1. Preheat oven to 325°F. Butter a 9-inch springform or cake pan.

2. To prepare pastry: In small skillet, over moderate flame, melt butter until it begins to brown and smell toasty, about 5 minutes, taking care that butter does not burn. Remove from heat and cool slightly.

3. Using STEEL BLADE, process flour, sugar, and melted butter just until combined, 5 to 6 seconds. Add egg yolk and process until dough begins to form ball on blade. Press dough evenly into prepared pan so that it covers bottom and 1 inch up sides of pan. Clean work bowl.

4. To prepare filling: Using STEEL BLADE, process almond paste, sugar, and flour until smooth. Add whole eggs and egg white and continue to process until well blended. Pour into prepared pastry shell. Clean work bowl.

5. Bake 1 hour 10 minutes, or until top is golden brown. Remove to rack to cool.

6. While *mazarin* is baking, prepare glaze. Using PLASTIC BLADE, combine powdered sugar and milk and process until smooth.

7. When *mazarin* has finished baking, spread glaze over *mazarin* while still warm. If desired, decorate with blanched almonds.

TO PREPARE IN ADVANCE: Through step 7.
TO FREEZE: Through step 7, freezing unwrapped just until glaze hardens and then wrap for freezer. Defrost, wrapped, at room temperature.

This is a wonderful cake to have in your freezer. It goes well with coffee as well as tea.

ALMOND TEA CAKE

Serves 10 to 12

Butter for cake pan
¼ cup sliced, blanched almonds
1 recipe Almond Paste (page 288)
    or 1 pound commercial almond
    paste
2 whole eggs plus 3 egg yolks
2 tablespoons Grand Marnier

2 tablespoons rum
5 tablespoons sifted cornstarch
4 egg whites
2 tablespoons sugar
½ cup plus 2 tablespoons melted
    unsalted butter, cooled
2 tablespoons Amaretto (optional)

1. Preheat oven to 350°F.

2. Heavily butter 10-inch round cake pan and sprinkle bottom and sides with sliced almonds, tapping pan so nuts are distributed evenly. Refrigerate pan until needed.

3. Using STEEL BLADE, process almond paste, whole eggs, and egg yolks until smooth. With motor running, pour Grand Marnier and rum through feed tube.

4. Transfer batter to large mixing bowl and gently stir in cornstarch.

5. Using wire whisk or rotary beater, whip egg whites until soft peaks form. Add sugar and continue to whip until stiff and shiny.

6. Carefully stir one-fourth of the whites into the batter. Gently fold in remaining whites. Do not overmix.

7. Stir 1 cup of batter into melted butter and then fold butter mixture into batter. Do not overmix.

8. Pour into prepared pan. Bake in upper third of oven 35 to 40 minutes, until cake is firm to touch and golden brown.

9. Let cool 10 minutes and invert onto serving plate. Brush with Amaretto, if desired.

TO PREPARE IN ADVANCE: Through step 9.
TO FREEZE: Through step 9. Defrost, wrapped, at room temperature.

NOTE: If using commercial almond paste, increase Grand Marnier and rum to 3 tablespoons each. Use 7 egg whites and increase sugar to ¼ cup.

Lemon Almond Tart

Serves 8 to 10

Pâte Sucrée *(page 251)*
1 cup blanched, sliced almonds
1 cup sugar
Peel of 4 medium lemons, cut into 1-inch pieces
¼ pound (1 stick) unsalted butter, unrefrigerated for 30 minutes before using, cut in 8 pieces

2 whole eggs plus 2 egg yolks
Pinch of salt
2 tablespoons kirsch or Cointreau
Juice of 1 medium lemon
Crème Chantilly *(page 289)*
   made with kirsch or Cointreau

1. On lightly floured surface, roll out *Pâte Sucrée* to an 11-inch round and fit into 9-inch tart pan. Trim and pinch edges. Refrigerate until ready to fill.

2. Preheat oven to 375°F.

3. Using STEEL BLADE, combine almonds and ½ cup of the sugar and process until powdery in texture, scraping down sides of work bowl as necessary. Reserve.

4. Using STEEL BLADE, combine lemon rind and remaining ½ cup sugar and process until rind is chopped fine. Arrange butter over sugar and process until well creamed.

5. Add eggs and egg yolks and process just until blended. Add reserved almond mixture, salt, kirsch, and lemon juice and process until combined, scraping down sides of work bowl as necessary.

6. Pour into prepared tart shell and bake 40 minutes, or until lightly browned. Cool and refrigerate.

7. Serve with the *Crème Chantilly*.

TO PREPARE IN ADVANCE: Through step 6.
TO FREEZE: Through step 1 or step 6. Defrost, wrapped, in refrigerator.

VARIATION: Prepare recipe through step 6. Top with meringue, made with 2 egg whites and 4 tablespoons sugar, and bake in preheated 425°F. oven until meringue is lightly browned.

TANGY LEMON TART

Serves 8 to 10

Pâte Sucrée *(page 251)*
Peel of 1 small lemon, cut in
   1-inch pieces
¾ cup sugar
3 eggs

½ cup melted, unsalted butter,
   cooled
¾ cup strained lemon juice
Crème Chantilly *(page 289)*

1. Preheat oven to 450°F.

2. On lightly floured board, roll out pastry to an 11-inch round and fit into 9-inch quiche pan. Trim and pinch edges. Line with aluminum foil and fill with beans, rice, or pie weights. Bake 5 to 7 minutes. Carefully remove weights and foil.

3. Lower oven heat to 350°F.

4. Using STEEL BLADE, process lemon peel and sugar until chopped fine. Add eggs and process, scraping down sides of work bowl as necessary.

5. With motor running, pour melted butter and lemon juice through feed tube and process until just combined.

6. Pour into prepared shell and carefully slide into oven (filling is very liquid). Bake 20 to 25 minutes, until custard sets. Place under broiler until golden brown, watching carefully that top does not burn.

7. Serve with the *Crème Chantilly*.

TO PREPARE IN ADVANCE: Through step 6.
TO FREEZE: Do not freeze.

All components of this recipe may be prepared earlier and assembled at serving time.

*H*OT STRAWBERRY PUFFS

Serves 8

1 pound Puff Pastry (page 257)
1 egg, lightly beaten, for egg wash
24 to 32 firm strawberries, hulled

Sauce Caramel (page 292)
Lemon Mousse Filling (page 281)

1. Preheat oven to 400°F.

2. Divide Puff Pastry into 2 halves and roll out one half to a 6-inch square about ¼ inch thick. Cut into 4 three-inch squares and place on ungreased pastry sheet. Repeat with second half and refrigerate 20 to 30 minutes.

3. Brush squares with egg wash and bake 20 to 24 minutes, or until golden brown.

4. Using MEDIUM SLICING BLADE, with light pressure, slice strawberries. Reserve.

5. Slice puffs in half horizontally. Place bottom half on serving plate and cover with Sauce Caramel. Layer with Lemon Mousse, sliced strawberries, a second layer of Lemon Mousse, and top with remaining pastry half. Glaze with Sauce Caramel.

TO PREPARE IN ADVANCE: Through step 4. Heat sliced puffs before layering.
TO FREEZE: Do not freeze.

VARIATION: Substitute blueberries, peeled and sliced peaches, or sliced bananas, as season permits.

This is delicate and light.

CREAMY CHEESE PIE

Serves 8 to 10

BUTTER CRUNCH CRUST:

4 tablespoons (½ stick) unsalted
   butter, chilled, cut in 4 pieces
2 tablespoons brown sugar, packed
½ cup sifted all-purpose flour
¼ cup pecans or walnuts

FILLING:

Peel from ½ small lemon
1 envelope (1 tablespoon)
   unflavored gelatin
⅓ cup plus 2 tablespoons
   granulated sugar
Dash of salt
1 egg, separated
½ cup milk
1 tablespoon lemon juice
1 teaspoon vanilla extract
12 ounces cream-style cottage
   cheese
1 cup heavy cream, whipped

1. Preheat oven to 400°F. Butter the bottom and sides of 7- or 8-inch pie plate.

2. To prepare butter crunch: Place butter, brown sugar, and flour in work bowl and combine, using STEEL BLADE, with 2 or 3 on/off turns. Add nuts and process 2 or 3 seconds longer.

3. Spread mixture in flat pan and bake approximately 10 minutes, watching carefully to prevent burning. Immediately remove from oven and stir. Reserve ¼ cup for topping. Press remaining mixture against bottom and sides of prepared pan. Refrigerate until ready to fill. Clean work bowl.

4. To prepare filling: Combine lemon peel, gelatin, the ⅓ cup sugar, and the salt in work bowl. Using STEEL BLADE, process until rind is grated, about 10 to 15 seconds. Empty into small saucepan.

5. Using STEEL BLADE, combine egg yolk and milk, allowing processor to run 3 or 4 seconds. Add to sugar mixture. Over moderate flame, bring just to boil, stirring constantly. Remove from heat and stir in lemon juice and vanilla. Cool.

6. Using STEEL BLADE, mix cottage cheese until smooth, about 7 or 8 seconds. Add gelatin mixture and blend with on/off turns, until

279

combined. Remove to large bowl and chill, stirring occasionally until mounds form when mixture is dropped from a spoon.

7. Using rotary beater or small wire whip, beat egg white until small peaks form. Add the 2 tablespoons sugar and beat until shiny. Fold into cheese mixture.

8. Fold whipped cream into cheese mixture. Pour into buttercrunch crust and sprinkle reserved butter crunch over top. Refrigerate overnight.

TO PREPARE IN ADVANCE: Through step 8.
TO FREEZE: Through step 3. Shell may be filled directly from freezer. Through step 8: Defrost, wrapped, in refrigerator.

A simple-to-prepare tart that is absolutely marvelous.

Pear Tart

Serves 8 to 10

---

6 large ripe pears, peeled, cored,
 and cut in half
½ cup sugar
1 cup water
Juice of ½ medium lemon
1 tablespoon pear brandy

Pâte Brisée (page 250)
2 tablespoons unsalted butter, in
 bits
Sauce Caramel (page 292;
 optional)
Whipped cream (optional)

1. Preheat oven to 400°F.

2. Using MEDIUM SLICING BLADE, slice 3 of the pears (see note below). Combine in medium saucepan with sugar, water, and lemon juice. Cook, over moderate flame, until soft and sugar begins to caramelize, 20 to 25 minutes, stirring occasionally.

3. Using STEEL BLADE, purée soft pears and transfer to small mixing bowl. Add brandy and cool.

4. Roll out pastry and fit into 9-inch tart pan, trimming and pinching edges. Refrigerate until ready to fill.

5. Using THIN SLICING BLADE, slice remaining 3 pears. Spread cooled purée on bottom of pastry shell, top with pears arranged in concentric circles, and dot with butter. Bake 30 minutes.

---

6. Serve plain, with Sauce Caramel (page 292), whipped cream, or a combination of both for a taste treat.

TO PREPARE IN ADVANCE: Through step 5. Reheat just before tart is served.

TO FREEZE: Through step 4. Shell may be filled directly from freezer. Through step 5: Defrost, wrapped, at room temperature and then continue with recipe.

NOTE: If pears are sliced and you do not use immediately, squeeze a little lemon juice over them and cover with cold water.

VARIATION: Substitute apples for pears and use Calvados or applejack brandy instead of pear brandy.

LEMON MOUSSE
Serves 6

4 medium lemons
⅔ cup sugar
4 whole eggs plus 4 egg yolks

6 tablespoons unsalted butter, at room temperature, in small pieces
1 cup heavy cream
Sliced fruit

1. Using vegetable peeler, peel lemons. Using STEEL BLADE, combine with sugar and process until finely grated.

2. Cut lemons in half and squeeze enough juice to make 1 cup. Reserve.

3. Add whole eggs, egg yolks, and lemon juice to work bowl and process just until incorporated, scraping down sides of work bowl once.

4. Transfer to stainless steel mixing bowl over bain-marie on moderate flame. Using wire whisk and whipping constantly, cook until mixture thickens and becomes mousselike, about 5 minutes.

5. Whisk in butter, a small amount at a time. Let cool.

6. Cover with buttered waxed paper, with buttered side directly on top of mousse (to prevent formation of film). Chill until needed.

TO PREPARE IN ADVANCE: Through step 5.
TO FREEZE: Do not freeze.

VARIATION: Whip 1 cup heavy cream. Fold into lemon mousse when it has cooled. Chill and serve topped with fruit and/or whipped cream. Spoon into individual serving dishes or serve from a glass bowl.

STRAWBERRY AMARETTO MOUSSE

Serves 6

3 or 4 Amaretto Madeleines (page 262), cut in 1-inch pieces
2 boxes frozen strawberries, thawed

2 cups heavy cream
2 egg whites
4 tablespoons sugar

1. Using STEEL BLADE, crumb Madeleines with on/off turns to desired texture. Crumbs should not be too fine. Reserve. Clean work bowl.

2. Using STEEL BLADE, purée strawberries, scraping down sides of work bowl as necessary. Strain through fine sieve and reserve in large mixing bowl. Clean work bowl.

3. Using STEEL BLADE, whip cream (it will whip to Chantilly stage). Fold cream into strawberries.

4. Using wire whisk or rotary beater, beat egg whites until firm. Slowly add sugar and continue to beat until stiff, but not dry. Fold into strawberry mixture.

5. Pour half the strawberry mixture into 8-cup glass bowl, sprinkle with half the crumbs, and top with remaining mixture. Sprinkle with remaining crumbs and freeze 6 to 8 hours. (The mousse can be served in individual dishes as well.)

TO PREPARE IN ADVANCE: Through step 5.
TO FREEZE: Through step 5. Defrost in refrigerator.

VARIATION: Frozen raspberries or peaches can be substituted for strawberries.

A refreshing way to end a meal . . . so simple and so delicious.

STRAWBERRY SORBET

Serves 8

1 cup water
2 cups sugar
1 quart ripe, fresh raspberries

Juice of 2 lemons
Juice of 1 orange

1. In small saucepan, bring water and sugar to boil. Boil for 10 minutes, then remove from heat and cool.

2. Meanwhile, lightly wash berries and hull, reserving 6 or 7 berries. Using STEEL BLADE, purée berries and remove to large bowl.

3. Add lemon and orange juices and cooled sugar syrup to puréed berries. Freeze in commercial ice cream machine according to standard freezing directions. (Or freeze in ice trays until slightly firm. Remove to food processor and process with STEEL BLADE. Return to trays and freeze until ready to serve.*)

4. Using MEDIUM SLICING BLADE, and with light pressure, slice reserved berries.

5. Serve scoops of strawberry sorbet topped with sliced berries.

TO PREPARE IN ADVANCE: Through step 4.
TO FREEZE: Must be frozen. Taste and texture is best when prepared no longer than 24 hours in advance.

*This will not be as smooth as when frozen in a commercial machine.

Melon Sorbet

3 medium honeydew melons,   Juice of 2 medium lemons
    peeled, seeded, and cut in 1-inch ½ cup sugar (approximately)
    pieces   Sliced strawberries for garnish

1. Using STEEL BLADE, purée melon until smooth. Add lemon juice and sugar to taste. (If melons are sweet, less sugar is needed.)

2. Strain mixture through fine sieve.

3. Freeze in commercial ice cream machine according to standard freezing directions. (Or freeze in ice trays until slightly firm. Remove to food processor and process with STEEL BLADE. Return to trays and freeze until ready to serve.*)

4. Serve in small scoops surrounded by sliced strawberries.

TO PREPARE IN ADVANCE: Through step 3.
TO FREEZE: Through step 3. (Must be frozen. Taste and texture are best when prepared no longer than 24 hours in advance.)

*This will not be as smooth as when frozen in a commercial machine.

This makes a thick applesauce; more water can be added for a thinner texture.

Applesauce

Serves 6

6 medium apples, quartered,   ½ cup water
    peeled, and seeded   Ground cinnamon and/or nutmeg
½ cup sugar

1. In medium saucepan, over moderate flame, cook apples with sugar and water until apples are very soft, about 20 minutes, stirring occasionally. Season with cinnamon, nutmeg, or a combination of both, to taste.

2. Remove to work bowl and purée, using STEEL BLADE until smooth.

3. Refrigerate in covered container until needed.

TO PREPARE IN ADVANCE: Through step 3.
TO FREEZE: Through step 3. Defrost in refrigerator.

VARIATIONS: 1. *Mustard Applesauce:* Eliminate cinnamon and nutmeg and add ¼ cup prepared mustard to work bowl when puréeing. Add more mustard to taste.
2. *Horseradish Applesauce:* Eliminate cinnamon and nutmeg and add 2 teaspoons freshly grated horseradish when puréeing. Correct flavor to taste.

Apple Omelet

Serves 2 to 3

*1 medium apple, peeled and
   quartered*
3 tablespoons unsalted butter
Pinch of salt

Pinch of freshly ground pepper
6 eggs
½ teaspoon powdered sugar
1 tablespoon brandy

1. Using WIDE SLICING BLADE, slice apple, 1 or 2 quarters at a time.

2. In medium omelet pan, melt butter and sauté apple, over moderate flame, until lightly browned on both sides. Season with salt and pepper.

3. Using PLASTIC BLADE, lightly beat eggs, then pour over apples. Turn flame to high and, using a fork, push eggs from sides of pan toward the center, lifting eggs so that all the liquid runs under and omelet will have an even thickness. Keep shaking pan with your other hand so that omelet does not stick to bottom. Cook about 3 minutes; center should still be soft.

4. Turn out on heated serving platter, sprinkle with sugar, and pour brandy over. Ignite brandy and baste omelet until flame goes out. Serve immediately.

TO PREPARE IN ADVANCE: Do not prepare in advance.
TO FREEZE: Do not freeze.

DESSERT
FILLINGS;
SAUCES,
AND
TOPPINGS

This is so simple to prepare and so good, you will never again buy almond paste.

Almond Paste

1½ cups blanched, sliced almonds
1⅔ cups powdered sugar, sifted
  after measured

1 large or extra-large egg white
1¼ to 1½ teaspoons almond
  extract

1. Using STEEL BLADE, chop almonds fine.

2. Add powdered sugar and continue to process until combined, scraping down sides of work bowl as necessary.

3. Add egg white and almond extract to taste and process until ball begins to form on blade.

4. Turn out of bowl and wrap securely. Refrigerate and use as needed.

TO PREPARE IN ADVANCE: Through step 4. Almond paste will keep up to 1 week.
TO FREEZE: Do not freeze.

Chestnut Cream

Makes about 1¾ cups

½ cup chestnut spread
½ cup Crème Fraîche (page 205)
2 tablespoons Grand Marnier

½ cup heavy cream, whipped
8 to 10 strawberries

1. Using STEEL BLADE, combine chestnut spread and *Crème Fraîche* and process until smooth. Transfer to medium mixing bowl.

2. Add Grand Marnier to mixture and fold in whipped cream quickly.

3. Using MEDIUM SLICING BLADE, with light pressure, slice berries. Fold into chestnut cream and serve.

TO PREPARE IN ADVANCE: Through step 3.
TO FREEZE: Do not freeze.

VARIATIONS: 1. Pour chestnut cream into baked Tartlet Shells (page 252) and top with sliced berries.
2. Use as filling for Basic Crêpes (page 233) and serve with Raspberry Sauce (page 293).

CREME CHANTILLY

Makes 2½ cups

2 cups heavy cream, chilled
¼ cup powdered sugar
1 teaspoon vanilla extract

Grand Marnier or Cointreau to
taste (optional)

1. Using STEEL BLADE, process cream just until it begins to thicken slightly.

2. Add sugar and process just to blend.

3. Stir in vanilla and liqueur to taste.

TO PREPARE IN ADVANCE: Through step 3.
TO FREEZE: Do not freeze.

MOCHA CHANTILLY

Makes about 3 cups

6 ounces semisweet chocolate, cut
   in 1-inch pieces
½ cup hot, strong coffee

2 cups heavy cream, chilled
¼ cup powdered sugar

1. Using STEEL BLADE, chop chocolate fine.

2. With motor running, pour coffee through feed tube and process until smooth. Transfer to spouted vessel and let cool to room temperature. Clean work bowl.

3. Using STEEL BLADE, whip cream. As cream thickens, add sugar and process until smooth.

4. With motor running, pour cooled chocolate through feed tube and process until combined. Chill.

5. Use as a filling for Basic Crêpes (page 233) or to fill prebaked 8- or 9-inch Pâte Sucrée shell (page 251), or as is.

TO PREPARE IN ADVANCE: Through step 4.
TO FREEZE: Through step 4. Defrost in refrigerator.

VARIATIONS: 1. Substitute ¼ cup boiling water and ¼ cup rum for coffee.
2. Use 2 tablespoons coffee liqueur and 6 tablespoons hot, strong coffee for a more pronounced coffee flavor.

LEMON CURD

Makes 1½ cups

Peel of 2 large lemons
½ cup sugar
Juice of 2 large lemons

4 tablespoons (½ stick) unsalted
*   butter, cut in 6 pieces*
5 egg yolks or 3 whole eggs, at
*   room temperature*

1. Using STEEL BLADE, combine lemon peel and sugar and process until peel is chopped fine. Remove to small, heavy saucepan.

2. Add lemon juice and butter to saucepan and cook, over low flame, until butter melts and sauce begins to bubble.

3. Using STEEL BLADE, process eggs (yolks or whole eggs) about 10 seconds. With motor running, in very thin stream, pour *hot* butter mixture through feed tube. If butter is hot enough, eggs will thicken immediately. (If not, pour mixture into heavy saucepan over low flame. With wire whip, whisk until thickened.) Cool.

4. Refrigerate and use as needed, as a filling for Tartlet Shells (page 252), as a spread for toast and breakfast rolls, or topped with berries.

TO PREPARE IN ADVANCE: Through step 3. This will keep, refrigerated, 3 months.
TO FREEZE: Through step 4. Defrost in refrigerator.

VARIATIONS: 1. To prepare Lemon Curd and Cream, combine equal portions lemon curd and whipped cream. Spoon into tall glasses and garnish with fresh fruit slices and mint leaves.
2. Lighten curd with whipped cream or *Crème Fraîche* (page 205), and use as filling for cakes or cream puffs (*Pâte à Choux*, page 249). Serve with a berry sauce such as Raspberry Sauce (page 293).
3. Thin with heavy cream as a sauce for gingerbread.

CUSTARD FILLING FOR CREAM PUFFS

Makes enough for 12 large puffs or eclairs

½ cup sugar
⅓ cup cornstarch
2 eggs

2 cups milk
1 tablespoon vanilla extract

1. In small saucepan, combine sugar and cornstarch. Stir in eggs and milk and cook, over low flame, stirring until custard thickens.

2. Remove from heat and stir in vanilla extract. Cover with buttered wax paper, buttered side on top of custard to prevent a film from forming. Chill over bowl of ice cubes.

3. Refrigerate, and use as needed.

TO PREPARE IN ADVANCE: Through step 3.
TO FREEZE: Do not freeze.

This is a very versatile sauce. It can be spooned over apple or pear tart or ice cream.

SAUCE CARAMEL

1 cup sugar
½ cup water
1½ cups heavy cream

3 tablespoons unsalted butter, at
room temperature, cut in small
pieces

1. In small saucepan, combine sugar and water. Cook until mixture caramelizes, 15 to 20 minutes.

2. Remove saucepan from heat and immediately add cream, stirring until smooth. Sprinkle butter over top. When it dissolves, stir through. Serve hot.

3. Reheat as needed.

TO PREPARE IN ADVANCE: Through step 2. This may be refrigerated for weeks.
TO FREEZE: Do not freeze.

CREME ANGLAISE

1 cup milk
1 cup heavy cream
1 vanilla bean or ½ teaspoon
vanilla extract

6 egg yolks
½ cup sugar

1. In medium saucepan, over moderate flame, bring milk, heavy cream, and vanilla bean to boil. Let boil 1 minute.

2. Using STEEL BLADE, combine egg yolks and sugar. Remove vanilla bean from saucepan and, with motor running, pour contents through feed tube.

3. Return to saucepan with vanilla bean and, over moderate flame, stirring with wooden spoon, cook just until sauce thickens and coats back of spoon, about 1 minute. Do not allow to boil.

4. Strain and chill immediately over ice.

5. Use as needed, as sauce, or freeze for ice cream. (Use commercial ice-cream freezer, according to manufacturer's directions.)

TO PREPARE IN ADVANCE: Through step 4.
TO FREEZE: Through step 4. For sauce, defrost in refrigerator.

VARIATION: Add liqueur of your choice to cooled sauce.

RASPBERRY SAUCE
Makes about 2 cups

4 cups fresh raspberries　　　　*2 tablespoons framboise*
1 cup superfine sugar

1. Using STEEL BLADE, combine all ingredients and process until puréed. Strain to remove seeds. Correct seasoning to taste.

2. Refrigerate and use as needed on ice cream, pudding, etc.

TO PREPARE IN ADVANCE: Through step 1.
TO FREEZE: Through step 1. Defrost in refrigerator.

VARIATION: Substitute strawberries, hull, and continue as above. Cognac may be substituted for framboise. Strain only if desired.

CREAM CHEESE ICING

8 ounces cream cheese, at room
    temperature, cut in 6 pieces
¼ pound (1 stick) unsalted butter,
    at room temperature, cut in 6
    pieces

1 teaspoon vanilla extract
2 teaspoons lemon juice
1 pound powdered sugar

1. Using STEEL BLADE, cream together cream cheese, butter, vanilla, and lemon juice.

2. Add sugar and process until smooth, scraping down sides of work bowl as needed.

TO PREPARE IN ADVANCE: Through step 2.
TO FREEZE: Do not freeze.

This is absolutely foolproof and worthy of all you chocolate lovers.

GANACHE
(Chocolate Glaze)

Makes about 2 cups

8 ounces semisweet chocolate*
    broken into ½-inch pieces

1 cup heavy cream
1 vanilla bean

1. Using STEEL BLADE, chop chocolate fine.

2. In small saucepan, over moderate heat, bring cream and vanilla bean to boil. Let simmer 1 minute. Remove vanilla bean (see note below).

3. With motor running, pour hot cream through feed tube over chocolate. Chocolate will be melted by the time all the cream has been poured. Do not process any more than necessary.

4. Remove to covered jar, using spatula to scrape out all the chocolate. Cool and refrigerate.

5. Use as sauce or frosting.

TO PREPARE IN ADVANCE: Through step 4. This will keep for weeks.
TO FREEZE: Do not freeze.

NOTE: Vanilla bean can be rinsed, thoroughly dried, and used again. Store, wrapped in paper towel, and split before using a second time.

VARIATIONS: 1. For mocha flavor, add 1 teaspoon instant coffee to chocolate in work bowl and continue as above, adjusting amount of coffee to taste.
2. Add liqueur of your choice to taste before chilling *ganache*.

*Any semisweet or bittersweet chocolate may be used; just make sure that you use real chocolate. *Ganache* will thicken as it stands; to thin, heat slowly over low flame.

PRALINE

Makes about 1 cup

¼ *cup hazelnuts*
¾ *cup sugar*
¼ *cup water*

¼ *teaspoon cream of tartar*
¼ *cup blanched almonds*

1. Spread hazelnuts on a baking tray and lightly toast in a hot oven. Place nuts in a towel and rub to remove as much skin as possible.

2. In medium saucepan, combine all ingredients. Cook, over moderate flame, without stirring, until caramel-colored.

3. Pour contents of saucepan onto buttered baking sheet and let cool as it hardens to a nut brittle.

4. Break brittle into pieces and transfer to work bowl fitted with STEEL BLADE. Process until finely ground.

5. Refrigerate in tightly covered container and use as needed. (This is delicious sprinkled over ice cream.)

TO PREPARE IN ADVANCE: Through step 5. The powder will keep for weeks.
TO FREEZE: Do not freeze.

Suggested Menus

1. LATIN DINNER
AVOCADO DIP (page 32)
QUESADILLAS (page 44)
SPANISH SALAD ANA
  (page 176)
TAMALE PIE (page 132)
LEMON MOUSSE (page
  281)

2. FORMAL
LUNCHEON
ASPARAGUS SOUP (page
  89)
CUTLET POJARSKY (page
  119)
GÂTEAU de CARROTTES
  (page 155)
TOMATO SALAD (page
  174)
TANGY LEMON TARTE
  (page 277)

3. ELEGANT DINNER
PARTY
TERRINE de SAUMON
  (page 53)
CHICKEN WRAPPED IN
  LETTUCE (page 118)
SCALLOPED TOMATOES
  (page 165)
YORKSHIRE PUDDING
  (page 235)
MARJOLAINE (page 270)

4. INFORMAL
DINNER
MEAT LOAF (page 130)
SCALLOPED POTATOES
  (page 164)
MIDDLE EASTERN
  CABBAGE SALAD (page
  168)
CHOCOLATE CAKE (page
  269)

5. HEARTY DINNER
CREAM of MUSHROOM
  SOUP (page 92)
STUFFED BREAST OF
  VEAL (page 138)
AUNT RUTH'S
  CABBAGE-NOODLE
  CASSEROLE (page 155)
APPLESAUCE (page 284)
VANILLA BEAN COOKIES
  (page 265)

6. INFORMAL
SUPPER
BORSCHT (page 94)
RUSSIAN MEAT PIE (page
  124)
CUCUMBER SALAD (page
  179)
CREAMY CHEESE PIE
  (page 279)

7. LIGHT
  LUNCHEON
COLD AVOCADO SOUP
  with CAVIAR (page 97)
SALMON MOUSSE with
  DILL SAUCE (page 105)
TARTLET SHELLS (page
  252) filled with LEMON
  CURD (page 290)

8. FORMAL DINNER
CONSOMMÉ JULIENNE
  (page 88)
PARSLIED RACK of LAMB
  (page 135)
PURÉE of PEAS (page 160)
  in POTATO BASKETS
  (page 160)
PEAR TARTE (page 280)

9. BUFFET-BRUNCH
TOMATO à l'ANTIBOISE
  (page 173)
HAM AND SPINACH
  TORTE (page 62)
BAKED SPAGHETTI (page
  143)

SPICED VEAL SAUSAGES
  (page 139)
RAW VEGETABLE SALAD
  (page 177)
MUSHROOM
  RATATOUILLE (page
  159)
ALMOND TEA CAKE (page
  275)
SOUR CREAM COFFEE
  CAKE (page 272)

10. COCKTAIL PARTY
COUNTRY PÂTÉ (page 52)
SMOKED FISH MOUSSE
  (page 55)
CRÊPE QUICHE (page 59)
EMPANADAS CHILENAS
  (page 74)
GOUGÈRE (page 48)
MUSHROOMS à la
  GRECQUE (page 171)
VEGETABLE KNISHES
  (page 45)

INDEX